STRONG COMPETITIVE BIDDING

BY MARSHALL MILES

Introduction by EDDIE KANTAR

A Master of Contract Bridge explains the successful weapons needed for winning a competitive bidding battle.

LAWRENCE & LEONG PUBLISHING

Printed in the United States of America

Lawrence & Leong Publishing
10430 Greenview Drive
Oakland, California 94605

Library of Congress Catalog Card Number: 92-070047

ISBN 1-877908-03-7

CONTENTS

INTRODUCTION

I HAVE JUST READ THE "BRIDGE BOOK OF THE YEAR"—the book you are holding in your hand.

Marshall has tackled a subject few authors have dared to deal with—competitive bidding. In most bidding books the opponents listen in awe as you and your partner blissfully describe your hands and arrive at the perfect contract. They hardly dream of interfering.

In this book as in real life the opponents are in there on every hand. Their entry into the auction gives you new weapons. Marshall tells you how best to use these weapons. The chapter on "Doubles" is worth the price of the book and then some.

If I were you I wouldn't dream of picking up this book without pencil in hand. Seldom have I read a book where I was making margin notes about sequences I MUST discuss with my partners and ideas that have eluded me.

I believe any partnership that goes over this book together will improve their game at LEAST 50%. My only fear is that too many other people are going to read this book and use some of the ideas suggested against me.

Marshall, my hat is off to you. You have outdone yourself with one marvelous book.

Eddie Kantar
February, 1992

Chapter One

WHEN TO COMPETE

STRONGER, MORE EFFECTIVE COMPETITIVE METHODS are available—both when the opponents have already bid and when they are likely to bid unless you make it difficult for them. In chess the better player almost always wins. Only a mental lapse or failure to play up to form can result in defeat since there is no element of luck. In bridge anything can happen on a single hand, but the better players win in the long run because they make the percentage bids and plays.

It is impossible to take double dummy action on every hand. Take this example. You are Vulnerable against Not Vulnerable opponents and your opponents compete to 5♣. The question is whether you should bid 5♠ or double when your North–South cards are:

NORTH
♠ K1085
♡ AJ7
♢ 7654
♣ 82

SOUTH
♠ A9642
♡ KQ8
♢ AJ103
♣ 7

The winning action depends upon how the opponents' cards are distributed. If the hands are:

	NORTH	
	♠ K1085 ♡ AJ7 ◇ 7654 ♣ 82	
WEST ♠ Q7 ♡ 965 ◇ Q8 ♣ AKJ542		EAST ♠ J3 ♡ 10432 ◇ K92 ♣ Q1063
	SOUTH ♠ A9642 ♡ KQ8 ◇ AJ103 ♣ 7	

you should double at IMPS, matchpoints or rubber bridge and accept the four trick set. With these hands, however, the opponents probably would not have bid so high.

Suppose the hands are instead:

[SEE THE NEXT PAGE]

The bidding might have gone

WEST	NORTH	EAST	SOUTH
—	—	—	1♠
3♣	3♠	5♣	?

Now 5♠ is the winning bid scoring +650 instead of +300. However, 5♠ is not the percentage action. In addition to the sure loser in each minor there is a 50% chance of losing a trump trick and almost a 50% chance of losing an extra trick in diamonds after the first diamond trick is lost to West. The odds are nearly 3 to 1 against your making 5♠.

	NORTH	
	♠ K1085	
	♡ AJ7	
	◇ 7654	
	♣ 82	
WEST		EAST
♠ Q7		♠ J3
♡ 5		♡ 1096432
◇ K82		◇ Q9
♣ KJ109543		♣ AQ6
	SOUTH	
	♠ A9642	
	♡ KQ8	
	◇ AJ103	
	♣ 7	

At IMPS, if your opponent facing the same decision doubles, you gain 8 IMPS by bidding 5♠ when it makes and lose 9 IMPS (–100 vs +300) when it doesn't. If your teammates should sell out to 4♠ the odds would be different. Now you lose 8 IMPS by doubling and only 4 IMPS more by going down one at 5♠, but double would work out best in the long run. This analysis assumes 5♣ would be set two. If West's distribution were either 1–3–3–6 or 1–3–2–7, the odds would even more strongly favor doubling.

At matchpoints the percentage decision depends on the quality of the field. If few East–West pairs would bid 5♣, you might risk 5♠ rather than accept a poor result. In a good field you should double.

This previous example assumed the partners knew each others holdings. Bidding at the table you won't see partner's hand—not to mention the opponents' hands. Consequently you must be guided by general principles. These should be your objectives, IN ORDER OF PRIORITY.

Competitive Bidding Objectives

1. **Don't let the opponents make a contract when you can outbid them and make one of your own.**
2. **Don't settle for a small penalty when a better score can be obtained by bidding on.**
3. **Don't sacrifice against an unmakeable contract; don't exchange a plus for a minus.**
4. **Double to increase the penalty if the opponents are going down and a better score cannot be obtained by bidding on.**

The most costly decision results from allowing the opponents to make a game when your side can outbid them and make one of your own. Suppose the opponents bid and make 4♡ while you can make 4♠. By selling out, you lose (or fail to gain) 840–1240 points, or 13–16 IMPS. By bidding on, you profit when EITHER side can make game or when the opponents bid one more and are set. That is why competing when both sides might make game has top priority.

Even in a partscore battle, there is still a lot to lose by letting the opponents make 3♡ when you can make 3♠ yourself. The difference is 7 IMPS, or quite likely 7 or 8 matchpoints out of 12. If only one contract can make the adverse swing is somewhat smaller but still costly.

Avoiding an adverse game swing affects many of your competitive bidding decisions and, in particular, your treatment of so–called penalty doubles. Suppose the bidding with, None Vulnerable, goes

WEST	NORTH	EAST	SOUTH
4♠	Pass	Pass	?

With which hand would you prefer to double?

1. ♠ QJ108 ♡ 64 ♢ AK73 ♣ A82 or
2. ♠ 6 ♡ A1096 ♢ AQ87 ♣ AJ85?

Most books play a double of 4♠ for penalty because you are seldom strong enough to force partner to bid at the five level. With the first hand a two trick set is likely, so a double would increase your profit from +100 to +300. With the second hand a one trick set is more likely, and the opponents might conceivably make their contract. But I advise passing with the first hand and doubling with the second. Why? Because at this level it isn't practical to make your doubles strictly for penalty or strictly for takeout. With the first hand game is very unlikely, and a double, if left in, would only result in a 200 point profit. With the second hand, game is more likely, and it might be a hand where both sides could make game. In that case your double would result in at least an 800 point profit. The whole deal might be:

	NORTH	
	♠ xx ♡ KJxxxx ♢ J10xx ♣ x	
WEST		EAST
♠ AQJ10xxxx ♡ None ♢ Kxx ♣ 10x		♠ Kx ♡ Qxx ♢ xx ♣ KQxxxx
	SOUTH	
	♠ x ♡ A109x ♢ AQxx ♣ AJxx	

or

	NORTH	
	♠ x	
	♡ KJxx	
	◇ J109xxx	
	♣ Qx	
WEST		EAST
♠ KQJ10xxxx		♠ Axx
♡ x		♡ Qxxx
◇ None		◇ Kxx
♣ Kxxx		♣ 10xx
	SOUTH	
	♠ x	
	♡ A109x	
	◇ AQxx	
	♣ AJxx	

At this level, partner will usually pass your double. When he does, 4♠ will be set more often than not. But with a distributional hand, especially with high cards in his long suit, partner will bid. At least he should bid if your double shows both offensive and defensive values. If you double with the first hand there is too great a chance that partner will bid at the five level and be set, probably doubled, instead of being plus by passing.

The doubler can't wait for the perfect hand to double. He may hold

1. ♠ xx ♡ AQx ◇ AKxx ♣ K10xx or
2. ♠ Ax ♡ Axxx ◇ KQ ♣ KQxxx

but never

3. ♠ KQ10x ♡ x ◇ KJxxxx ♣ Ax or
4. ♠ AQJ9 ♡ Qx ◇ KQxx ♣ xxx.

The same considerations should apply when you contemplate a double in balancing position.

Doubles of preemptive bids should show cards that will be useful for either offense or defense, or "transferable" values. Given a choice, it is more important to have a method to avoid a large double adverse swing (first priority) than a method to increase the penalty (fourth priority).

You hold ♠ AKJxxxx ♡ x ◇ K10x ♣ xx.

WEST	NORTH	EAST	SOUTH
1♡	Pass	4♡	?

The opponents can probably make 4♡. You might make 4♠. Perhaps both games will make. With such a high ratio of offensive to defensive values, you must bid 4♠. You will profit if either game makes, and have everything to gain and nothing to lose if the opponents bid on to 5♡.

You hold ♠ K10xx ♡ x ◇ AJ10xxxx ♣ x.

WEST	NORTH	EAST	SOUTH
4♡	Pass	Pass	?

Both South players in a team game bid 5◇. 4♡ would have been set two tricks, and 5◇ was doubled, down two. While 5◇ could have been the winning action—either making or a cheap sacrifice, the odds were against it. Opener probably has about 10 points, most of which are in hearts. That leaves 22 HCP to be divided between partner and RHO. Give partner

♠ QJx ♡ xxx ◇ KQx ♣ Axxx,

and you will be a hero. But notice partner was given perfect cards. Change his hand to either:

1. ♠ xxxx ♡ Qxx ◇ K ♣ KQ10xx or
2. ♠ Axxx ♡ Kxx ◇ xx ♣ KJxx

and your bid won't work out so well. You have two probable defensive tricks and, if partner has his share of the missing high cards, you will set 4♡. He could easily have enough strength to set 4♡ but not enough for you to make 5◇, and it is extremely unlikely that both contracts will make.

Change your diamonds to ◇KQJxxxx and a 5◇ bid is barely justified. Your hand is worse defensively but is better offensively since you are unlikely to lose two trump tricks.

With which hand would you rather open 4♡?

1. ♠ x ♡ KQJ10xxx ◇ Jxxx ♣ x or
2. ♠ Qx ♡ AKJxxxx ◇ Jx ♣ xx

Surely you would rather open with the first hand. If partner has nothing, the opponents will be cold for a slam. If he has an average hand the opponents should be able to make game. In either case if you do go for a minus your loss should be minimal. But when you hold the latter hand, it is very unlikely the opponents belong in a slam, and partner doesn't need much to set a game. So when you go down there is no compensation. More important than the Rule of Two and Three is that your preempts contain a high ratio of offensive to defensive values. Otherwise, even when the opponents choose the wrong action, partner may rescue them by taking a phantom sacrifice.

Offensive and defensive values have been referred to without explanation. Suppose the opponents are bidding spades and diamonds while you and partner are bidding hearts and clubs. Presumably either you or partner is short in each of the opponents' suits. Opposite your ♠ QJx, partner may have a singleton, perhaps a doubleton. Your spade holding will usually win a trick on defense, but it won't be worth anything when your side plays the hand.

When you and partner have all your high cards in two suits, with singletons or voids in the opponents' suits, you have "pure" hands.

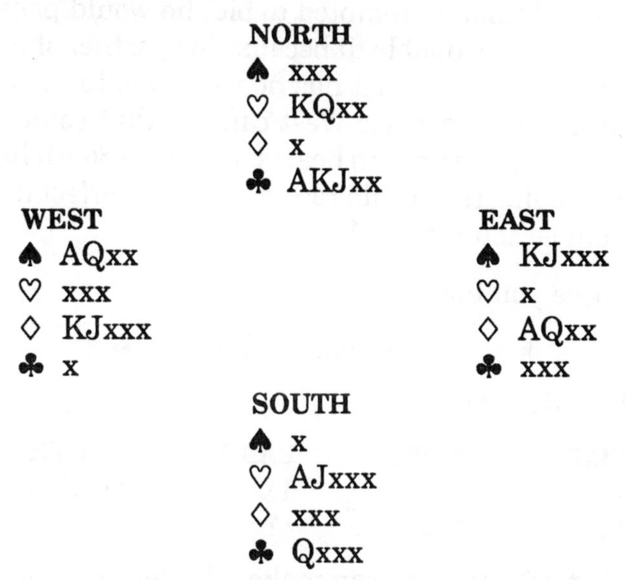

In this example both sides have very pure hands, and each side can make five of a suit despite the high card strength being evenly divided. Change the singletons to voids, and each side might make a slam. It is not often that both sides have such pure hands. Nevertheless, when all your high cards are in your suits and you have a singleton or void, you should suspect that each side can make more tricks than normal, which means that you should tend to keep bidding and refrain from doubling if the opponents outbid you.

Quite likely all four suits will not get bid. In the hand above the bidding might go:

WEST	NORTH	EAST	SOUTH
—	1♣	1♠	Double
4♠	Pass	Pass	5♣
Pass	Pass	5♠	Pass
Pass	Pass		

South bids 5♣, expecting it to be a cheap sacrifice. He can't tell that the hands fit so well. West suspects a double fit because his high cards are in his partner's suit and the unbid suit. Although tempted to bid, he would pass, and East suspects the double fit because his partner should be short in clubs where East has no wasted values. On this bidding neither East nor West can tell that some of his partner's values are not in hearts. If North–South had bid both their suits, they could recognize their perfect fit more easily, but so could East–West!

Suppose you hold

♠ x ♡ AKJxxx ◇ KJxxx ♣ x

and the bidding goes

WEST	NORTH	EAST	SOUTH
—	—	1♡	Double
2♡	3♠	?	

If you bid 4◇, partner can make a better decision when the opponents compete to 4♠. Partner would definitely compete to the five level with either

1. ♠ xxx ♡ Qxx ◇ AQxx ♣ xxx or
2. ♠ xx ♡ 10xxx ◇ Axxxx ♣ Qx

On the other hand, the 4◇ bid will help the opponents to evaluate their holdings. I still recommend bidding 4◇ in the hope that we can evaluate our hands better than the opponents can evaluate theirs.

Have you heard of the LAW OF TOTAL TRICKS? According to this law, when the strength is fairly evenly divided, and both sides are competing, you should bid to take the same number of tricks as your combined trump holding. With an eight card fit bid to the two level; with a nine card fit bid to the three level; with a ten card fit bid to the four level. Suppose your partnership hands are:

WEST	EAST
♠ KJxxx	♠ A10xxx
♡ Kx	♡ xx
◇ AQx	◇ xx
♣ xxx	♣ Axxx

The Law of Total Tricks says that when the opponents are competing in hearts, you should compete to the four level, if necessary, in spades. When the honors in the red suits are located favorably, you can make it. When both finesses are off, the opponents can surely make 4♡. If one finesse is on and one is off, each side might be down one, but this is too close for comfort—and one of the opponents might have a spade void.

The Law of Total Tricks is only a rough guide, and it doesn't take into consideration how pure your hands are. I seldom use the law but may resort to it with a close decision.

You hold ♠ J65 ♡ Q85 ◇ K74 ♣ K852.

WEST	NORTH	EAST	SOUTH
—	1♠	Pass	2♠
Double	Pass	3◇	?

In high cards you have close to a maximum for your raise so many players would bid 3♠. But bidding is wrong! Your values are just as good for defense as for offense. Give partner a balanced hand such as

♠ AKxxx ♡ Kxx ◇ Jx ♣ Q10x

and bidding 3♠ would change a plus to a minus. With any sort of distributional twist partner probably would bid 3♠ immediately. When partner has a balanced hand, you should be defending. At matchpoints you might double. At IMPS you should pass.

WEST	NORTH	EAST	SOUTH
—	2♣	2♠	?

Partner's 2♣ bid is strong and artificial. Most people play a double for penalty. A Negative Double is not needed to make partner bid. He has already committed himself to taking some action if you pass. I prefer that a double shows a positive response without a decent suit, typically 7 HCP including an ace or 8 HCP including a king, because one gets a proper penalty double so seldom. However, if the double is penalty, it must deny offensive values. You would double with

♠ QJ10xx ♡ xxx ◇ xx ♣ Jxx

hoping for a big set or with

♠ J10xx ♡ xx ◇ xxxx ♣ xxx

to discourage partner from bidding. To make game, he will have to do it all by himself, and defending against 2♠ doubled may be your only way to go plus. But you can't double with either

1. ♠ QJ10x ♡ Qx ◇ Jxxx ♣ Kxx or
2. ♠ A10xx ♡ xxxx ◇ xx ♣ Kxx.

Unless you deny offensive values, how can partner afford to pass your double? Suppose he holds

♠ x ♡ AKJxx ◇ AK ♣ AQJxx

If he passes when you hold either of the latter hands, you will miss a cold slam.

Vulnerable vs Not Vulnerable
You hold ♠ xxx ♡ Kxx ◇ AJ10x ♣ xxx.

WEST	NORTH	EAST	SOUTH
—	—	1♣	Pass
1♠	3♡	4♠	?

Regardless of vulnerability you should be willing to compete to the five level. Your values are offensive when they are in partner's suit and the unbid suit. South decided to pass because of the vulnerability. But at unfavorable vulnerability partner needs more for his bid. Partner held

♠ x ♡ AQJxxxx ◇ Qxxx ♣ x,

and his side was cold for 5♡. East had the ◇ K. If West had the ◇ K, unlikely on the bidding, 5♡ would be down one, but 5♠ would have made. With

♠ Q10x ♡ Kxx ◇ Jxxx ♣ Kxx,

you should pass regardless of vulnerability. This time your values are primarily defensive rather than offensive.

Perhaps too much space has been devoted to a basic concept: that for every competitive decision tend to bid when the ratio of offensive to defensive values is high; pass or double for penalty when the ratio is low. But since this concept is so important, the emphasis is worthwhile.

Another basic competitive principle is the earlier a competitive bid is made, the more effective it is. Also, the earlier you stick your neck out, the safer it is!

Suppose, as dealer at favorable vulnerability, you hold:

♠ Kx ♡ AJ109xxx ◇ Qxx ♣ x

Four actions are possible. Each would attract a faction of support. Thirty years ago the popular choice would have been 3♡ since you don't have enough playing tricks to open 4♡. But if you are a modern player who opens 3♡ with

♠ xx ♡ Q109xxxx ◇ xxx ♣ x

at favorable vulnerabilty you may be afraid of missing a game if you open 3♡ with this much stronger hand.

Therefore you might choose 4♡. For a one bid the hand is rather weak in high cards. Since every bid has flaws, some players would Pass. However, a 1♡ bid would be my choice, and a pass appeals to me the least. Somehow, before the auction is over, you want to bid hearts. If the bidding goes

WEST	NORTH	EAST	SOUTH
—	—	—	Pass
1♠	Pass	3♠	?

are you going to be content to pass? To be consistent, you should. Suppose East raised instead to 2♠. Now you would surely bid 3♡, but the bid is more dangerous and less effective than opening. The opponents have had a chance to describe and limit their hands. If they can't make game, it will be much easier for them to double for penalty or for East to double to show a maximum balanced raise and for West to pass for penalty.

Likewise you should avoid sequences like:

WEST	NORTH	EAST	SOUTH
1◇	1♠	Double	2♠
3◇/3♡	Pass	Pass	3♠?

When strong enough (or brave enough) to bid 3♠ now, you should have bid it immediately. The opponents have the problem of being forced to choose between showing their distributional pattern at an uncomfortably high level or doubling. They are much happier when they can do both.

Twenty years ago a popular treatment was to play that a simple overcall showed opening bid values. With less, one would either make a preemptive jump overcall or pass, planning to bid later if the auction developed favorably. When the bidding went

WEST	NORTH	EAST	SOUTH
—	—	1♡	Pass
2♡	Pass	Pass	2♠

South might have a decent spade suit, but less than an opening bid

1. ♠ QJ10xx ♡ xx ◇ Axx ♣ Kxx
2. ♠ KJxxx ♡ x ◇ Kxx ♣ Q10xx

or he might have a four card spade suit with opening bid values, but a hand unsuitable for a takeout double

3. ♠ KQ10x ♡ AQ ◇ x ♣ Jxxxxx
4. ♠ AQxx ♡ Ax ◇ Qx ♣ xxxxx

The modern tendency is to overcall 1♠ immediately with all four hands. If you find a fit you can often outbid the opponents, especially when you have the ranking suit. If you don't find a fit, the opponents will bid whatever they were going to anyway, and no harm has been done. The probability of their doubling for penalty at the one level or doubling for takeout and passing for penalty is too remote to worry about. To reenter the bidding after the opponents have exchanged information concerning their distribution and strength is more dangerous. Sometimes if you pass, hoping to bid later, you are afraid to bid later because the level is too high. Consequently you miss a good game or sacrifice.

The safest time to compete is by opening the bidding immediately. Not only is it safer. Making the first bid gives you a great competitive advantage. When the strength is evenly divided, the side that opens the bidding is much more likely to find its fit and judge how high to go. Later I'll discuss the 10–12 HCP opening 1NT, with its pros and cons, but it is not crucial to open light with balanced hands. Partner can usually tell from the opponents' bidding when you have some high cards. When you open light balanced hands, unless your bid shows specifically 10–12 HCP, it is hard for partner to make allowances and bid less than game with an opening bid of his own. With distributional hands, especially with broken suits, it is safer and better to open the bidding than to pass and hope that you can describe your hand later. Obviously there must be a cut–off point somewhere, but all of the following hands should be opened:

1. ♠ AQ10x ♡ x ◇ xxx ♣ KJ109x
2. ♠ AJ9xxx ♡ K10xxx ◇ x ♣ x
3. ♠ x ♡ AQ10xxxx ◇ Kxx ♣ xx
4. ♠ A109xxxx ♡ xx ◇ A109 ♣ x
5. ♠ xx ♡ xx ◇ AKQJxxx ♣ xx
6. ♠ Ax ♡ xx ◇ xx ♣ AQxxxxx

All of these hands have good offensive values. Hand One has no rebid problems. Hand Two has both majors. Hand Three is too good for 3♡ unless vulnerable against not. Hand Four has the ranking suit and two defensive tricks. Hand Five has seven tricks for playing in notrump. An opening preempt in a suit at the three level should DENY a solid suit. Concerning the last hand, when partner has 12–13 scattered points, you probably belong in 3NT. If you don't open, how will you describe this hand, especially if you are playing Drury?

When I advise you to open these hands, the primary reason is to get your bid in before the opponents bid. This is not necessarily the most accurate way to bid in a bidding contest in which the opponents keep quiet and allow you to bid unmolested. These are practical tactics. You want to do unto your opponents before they do unto you.

A third general principle is "Changing Priorities." When the opponents compete your objectives change. So your bidding methods should also change.

For example, in the following sequences

WEST	NORTH	EAST	SOUTH
1♢	Pass	2♠	

WEST	NORTH	EAST	SOUTH
1♠	Pass	3♢	

should responder's bid be weak or strong? Some experts play it weak since weak hands occur more frequently than strong hands. A majority of experts play the jump shift as strong on the theory that there is more to gain. To improve your slam bidding, you can afford to lose a little accuracy at the partscore level. My preference is to save the jump shift for strong hands.

But if the opponents overcall in the following sequence

WEST	NORTH	EAST	SOUTH
—	—	1♢	1♠
3♡			

there are several reasons why 3♡ here should be weak although not terribly weak. While a one level overcall doesn't guarantee a strong hand, the probability of making a slam decreases some when the opponents interfere. The overcall could be made with as few as 6 or 7 HCP, but the average overcall contains at least 11 HCP, leaving only 29 HCP for the other three players. With less chance of slam there is less reason to save the jump shift for a slam try.

Because you can no longer bid hearts at the one level, a pretty good hand is needed to bid 2♡—something like:

1. ♠ xx ♡ KQxxx ♢ Kx ♣ Kxxx or
2. ♠ Kxx ♡ QJxxxx ♢ x ♣ K10x

as a minimum. So what do you bid with

1. ♠ xx ♡ KQ10xxxx ♢ Qx ♣ xx or
2. ♠ x ♡ KJ10xxx ♢ xx ♣ Q109x?

Thirty years ago the orthodox call was to pass. But passing risks an adverse game swing. Suppose partner holds either

1. ♠ x ♡ Axx ◇ AKJxxx ♣ Kxx or
2. ♠ xx ♡ Axxx ◇ AKQxxx ♣ x

If you are allowed to bid hearts, you will either buy the bid or force the opponents too high. If you pass and the opponents bid 3♠ or 4♠ it is too risky to bid. Because it is so important to be able to bid with offensive hands like these, 3♡ should show an offensive hand too weak in high cards to bid 2♡.

You really need to play weak jump shifts when your bid is at the three level. When the bidding goes

WEST	NORTH	EAST	SOUTH
—	—	1◇	1♡
2♠			

should 2♠ be weak or strong? There is more room for a difference of opinion. No bidding room has been taken from you. Nothing prevents you from making the bid you would have made. However, slam is less likely and a 2♠ bid could be used to show a very weak defensive hand, for example

1. ♠ J10xxxxx ♡ x ◇ Qxx ♣ xx or
2. ♠ QJ10xxx ♡ xx ◇ xx ♣ xxx

Most experts choose to play all competitive jump shifts as weak.

When partner opens 1NT and there is no interference my favorite method of responding is the Walsh system. It includes ordinary Stayman, Minor Suit Stayman, Jacoby Transfer bids, and other transfer bids so that you can make slam tries in all four suits and show singletons. There are double relays and other gadgets designed to find perfect fitting distributional slams. All that is given up is the ability to play two of a minor.

But suppose there is a penalty double of partner's strong notrump opening. My priorities change.

WEST	NORTH	EAST	SOUTH
—	1NT	Double	?

If the double has its orthodox meaning, East will be at least as strong as partner, and you and LHO will have, at most, about 8 HCP between you. Slam is impossible and game is extremely unlikely without a very distributional hand. Your best chance for a good score is to play 1NT redoubled or to double the opponents if they run. The bad thing is that the opponents might penalize you.

When you have a weak hand with a long suit half the time your longest suit will be a minor. Not being able to bid 2♣ or 2♢ AS A RESCUE BID is a very serious drawback. You should give up your fancy conventions, ideal for finding the best game or slam, and utilize all four suits as natural, showing a weak hand. You need save only one call, redouble, for all "good" hands—like 6–8 HCP, which is the most you should hold.

Now suppose partner overcalls 1NT.

WEST	NORTH	EAST	SOUTH
1♠	1NT	Pass	?

Should you play the same system as though partner had opened 1NT? Theoretically, the answer must be "no." Slam is virtually impossible, game unlikely. Also it is less important than in uncontested auctions for the notrump bidder to be declarer. Since East won't have many high cards, you need not worry much about the opening lead going through North's tenaces if he is dummy. Likewise after

WEST	NORTH	EAST	SOUTH
1♠	Pass	Pass	1NT

a 1NT bid in the balancing position has a much lower range than an opening 1NT. But after

WEST	NORTH	EAST	SOUTH
—	—	2♠	2NT

a 2NT overcall shows roughly the strength for a strong opening 1NT bid. The lower the range, the more likely you belong in a partscore.

Until recently, over all 1NT overcalls or reopening balances, I played non–forcing Stayman without transfer bids. After 2NT overcalls or balances, I played the cue bid the opponents' suit in place of "Stayman" when the 2NT bid showed the strength of an opening 1NT bid (like a 2NT overcall of a weak two bid). I also played a convention called Gladiator in which 3♣ was a transfer to diamonds, initiating a sign–off sequence. The gain was in being able to sign off in diamonds after a notrump overcall. The loss was in confusion and misunderstandings when either partner forgot or when a hybrid sequence came up. My practical recommendation is to use the same conventions over all 1NT or 2NT overcalls and balances as over openings.

What should the double mean in this auction?

WEST	NORTH	EAST	SOUTH
1NT	Pass	2♣/2♢	Double

Presumably 2♣ is Stayman and 2♢ is a transfer to hearts. If the opponents are playing a strong notrump opening, you are unlikely to outbid them. The double should merely suggest a lead, perhaps with

1. ♠ Ax ♡ xxx ♢ xxx ♣ KQ10xx or
2. ♠ xx ♡ xx ♢ AQJ10 ♣Jxxxx.

The risk that the opponents will redouble and make an overtrick or two will be small compared to the gain by indicating the best lead on the other hands. Against a weak notrump there is a substantial chance that you can outbid them or penalize them. The double should not necessarily show the suit bid by responder but a hand good enough to have doubled 1NT if responder had passed. Otherwise, responder can bid with a yarborough and you will have no way to make him pay or let partner know when you had a strong hand.

You will see many more applications of the principles discussed in this chapter, but commencing with the next chapter we shall discuss specific sequences. It is important for you to take the quizzes at the end of each chapter. Besides testing you on the material already covered they will sometimes introduce new concepts or applications of the principles covered.

Quiz One

1. As South, Both Vulnerable, Matchpoints
   You hold ♠ AK74 ♡ J83 ◇ 9 ♣ AK652.
   Your RHO opens 4♠. What do you bid?

2. As East, Vulnerable vs. Not Vulnerable, IMPS
   You hold ♠ K10 ♡ KJ74 ◇ K1042 ♣ A63.

WEST	NORTH	EAST	SOUTH
—	1◇	Pass	Pass
Double	Pass	?	

   What do you bid?

3. As South, Both Vulnerable, IMPS
   Your hold ♠ 6 ♡ J98754 ◇ 62 ♣ 9865.

WEST	NORTH	EAST	SOUTH
1♠	2♡	Double	?

   What do you bid?

4. As East, None Vulnerable, Matchpoints
   Your hold ♠ KJ75 ♡ 98 ◇ A975 ♣ KQJ.

WEST	NORTH	EAST	SOUTH
1◇	2NT*	Double	3♡
Pass	Pass	?	

   *Shows Hearts and Clubs
   What do you bid?

5. As South, Vulnerable vs. Not Vulnerable, Matchpoints
   Your hand is ♠ KQ10 ♡ AJ5 ◇ AQ84 ♣ A108

WEST	NORTH	EAST	SOUTH
—	—	1♠	Double
4♠	Pass	Pass	?

   What do you bid?

6. As South, Vulnerable vs. Not Vulnerable, IMPS
Your hand is ♠ A109 ♡ 74 ◇ K ♣ AKQ10742.

WEST	NORTH	EAST	SOUTH
—	—	—	1♣
Pass	1♡	3◇	?

What do you bid?

7. As North, Not Vulnerable vs. Vulnerable, Matchpoints
Your hand is ♠ AJ874 ♡ None ◇ AJ10765 ♣ 83.

WEST	NORTH	EAST	SOUTH
—	—	3♡	Pass
4♡	?		

What do you bid?

8. As West, Vulnerable vs. Not Vulnerable, IMPS
Your hand is ♠ QJ985 ♡ 7 ◇ 84 ♣ J10742.

WEST	NORTH	EAST	SOUTH
—	—	1♣	Pass
1♠	3♡	4♡	5♡
?			

What do you bid?

9. Not Vulnerable vs. Vulnerable, IMPS.

WEST	EAST
♠ A763	♠ 854
♡ AJ10962	♡ KQ753
◇ 6	◇ Q7543
♣ A4	♣ None

WEST	NORTH	EAST	SOUTH
—	—	—	3♣
3♡	4♣	4♡	5♣
Double	Pass	Pass	Pass

South had a void in hearts and made 5♣ doubled while East–West are cold for 5♡. Assess the blame.

Answers

1. **PASS!** Surprisingly two expert Souths in a bidding contest doubled. North, believing he had strength to spare, bid 5♢ holding two aces and a six card diamond suit. Doubling persuaded North to bid, changing a plus score to a minus.

2. **TWO HEARTS, TWO DIAMONDS, OR TWO NOTRUMP** are reasonable bids. 2♡ allows for partner having shaded his double in fourth position. 2NT also allows partner some leeway for a light fourth hand double, and the hand may belong in notrump even when there is a 4–4 heart fit. A cue bid gives you a chance to find a heart fit on the way to 3NT. I don't like a penalty pass. The level is too low, and if partner has a singleton diamond, your offensive prospects are better than your defensive prospects. As it so happens, game can be made in either hearts and notrump, but 1♢ can't be set.

3. **FIVE HEARTS.** It is inconceivable that the opponents won't bid a game or that you won't bid 5♡ as a sacrifice. An immediate 5♡ bid makes it more difficult for the opponents to describe their hands and guess what to do. If the opponents bid a slam anyway, partner will know when to sacrifice since he can't count on any heart tricks.

4. **THREE SPADES.** Normally a suit introduced at the three level would be at least five cards long. But partner should realize that you don't have many alternatives and with a heart stopper partner should tend to bid notrump. In the unlikely event that partner lacks a heart stopper you hope that he has four spades or that game will be playable on a 4–3 fit. A bidding panel chose 3♠ almost unanimously.

5. **PASS**. Things look too good to be true. What do you think partner has? Probably something like:

♠ None ♡ xxxxx ◇ xx ♣ Jxxxxx.

Perhaps he will pass a double, but if he pulls you will exchange a plus for a minus. With such a high ratio of defensive to offensive values you should pass.

6. **THREE SPADES**. This answer is similar to problemfour in that you are bidding a shorter suit than expected by partner, hoping he will bid 3NT. However, if he raises to 4♠, bid 5♣ despite the fact that 4♠ could be the only game that makes when partner has

♠ KQJx ♡ QJxxx ◇ xxx ♣ x.

7. **FOUR SPADES**. It is possible that you can set 4♡. Partner could even have a couple of trump tricks. A set is possible but not probable. Your hand is too offensive to sell out, and a double would not describe this hand. Partner wouldn't know to pull with

♠ Qxx ♡ xxx ◇ Kxxx ♣ Qxx

for example. Bid 4♠, but run to 5◇ if 4♠ is doubled. If you can't trust your opponents, whom can you trust? They don't know you have a second, longer suit and wouldn't be doubling just to bluff you out of your best contract.

8. **CHOOSE YOUR LEAST ENCOURAGING SEQUENCE** whether it is to bid 5♠ right away or to pull partner's double, but don't let the opponents play 5♡. It is unusual to bid beyond game as a probable sacrifice in front of partner. Partner COULD have enough to set 5♡. But the vulnerable opponents must have something to justify their bidding, and your hand has negative defensive values. Besides, 5♠ might make.

9. **WEST IS MOSTLY AT FAULT**. East can't be sure that West doesn't have three defensive tricks in his own hand. East hadn't misled his partner since his heart raise did not promise defensive values. West failed to realize how great his hand was offensively and that the preempter by bidding again, showed a heart void. West should have passed, leaving the decision to partner who would bid 5♡. Perhaps, West should have bid it anyway. This might be a case of carrying partnership confidence too far.

Chapter Two

COMPETITIVE BIDS

CHARLES GOREN, THE RECOGNIZED BRIDGE AUTHORITY in 1957, said a "free bid," even at the one level, should show a fairly good hand with at least 9 or 10 points. A "free bid" was a bid you didn't have to make to keep the bidding open because the opponents had already done partner that favor. The specific sequence discussed was

WEST	NORTH	EAST	SOUTH
1♣	1♡	?	

and how strong you would need to be to bid 1♠. A free raise after

WEST	NORTH	EAST	SOUTH
1♠	2♣	2♠	

showed 9–12 points. Roth–Stone, in their latest book (prior to 1957) recommended a pass after

WEST	NORTH	EAST	SOUTH
1♢	1♡	?	

with ♠ KJ10xx ♡ x ♢ Jxx ♣ Kxxx

and after

WEST	NORTH	EAST	SOUTH
—	1♢	Pass	1♠
2♣	?		

with ♠ Axxx ♡ Kx ♢ AKxx ♣ xxx.

My book, HOW TO WIN AT DUPLICATE BRIDGE, also published in 1957, contained some radical ideas.

WEST	NORTH	EAST	SOUTH
1♢	1♡	?	

I recommended passing with

1. ♠ Kxxx ♡ Qxx ♢ Jxx ♣ xxx

but bidding 1♠ with either

2. ♠ KQxx ♡ xxx ♢ xxx ♣ Q10x or
3. ♠ Kxxx ♡ xxx ♢ xx ♣ Axxx.

This was before Negative Doubles were introduced, so that alternative was unavailable. If the choice were between bidding and passing, I would make the same recommendations today.

I suggested another radical treatment. Raise with a normal raise and make a limit raise with 11–12 "support points." The latest fashion is to play limit jump raises in an uncontested auction and preemptive jump raises in competition. A cue bid of the opponents' suit shows a limit raise or better. I'm not sure that this solution is best, but anything is better than requiring 9–12 points for a single free raise.

Gradually the inflated requirements for free bids and free raises were dropped. Today NO ONE would refuse to raise to 2♠ with the Roth–Stone hand

♠ Axxx ♡ Kx ♢ AKxx ♣ xxx.

In fact, this hand has strength to spare. Even should there be more bidding, a pass would create problems later. The modern tendency is to raise automatically with any opening bid which includes either three card or four card support or, better still, make a support double with three card support. Raising immediately makes competitive bidding much easier and safer.

In the 1950's there was more emphasis on constructive bidding and less tendency to preempt. If you held either

1. ♠ Q10xx ♡ Kxx ◇ xx ♣ xxxx or
2. ♠ Kxx ♡ Kx ◇ xxx ♣ xxxxx

and the bidding went

WEST	NORTH	EAST	SOUTH
—	1♠	2◇	Pass
Pass	Double	Pass	?

you would bid 3♠ to show a good hand for your previous pass or 4♠ to show an even better hand. Today, if you fail to raise, the bidding is much more likely to go

WEST	NORTH	EAST	SOUTH
—	1♠	2◇	Pass
3◇/4◇	Pass	Pass	?

Wouldn't you wish you had raised immediately rather than guess what to do now?

Suppose you hold the following South hands:

HAND ONE

NORTH
♠ Axxx
♡ xx
◇ AKJx
♣ Jxx

WEST
♠ J10x
♡ AJx
◇ 10xx
♣ Kxxx

EAST
♠ xx
♡ KQ10xx
◇ Qxx
♣ Axx

SOUTH
♠ KQxx
♡ xxx
◇ xxx
♣ Q10x

HAND TWO

	NORTH	
	♠ Ax	
	♡ xx	
	◇ AQxxx	
	♣ QJxx	
WEST		EAST
♠ J10xx		♠ Qxx
♡ AJx		♡ KQ10xx
◇ xxx		◇ KJx
♣ Kxx		♣ xx
	SOUTH	
	♠ Kxxx	
	♡ xxx	
	◇ xx	
	♣ Axxx	

HAND THREE

	NORTH	
	♠ Ax	
	♡ Kxx	
	◇ AJxxx	
	♣ Jxx	
WEST		EAST
♠ J10xxx		♠ xx
♡ Jx		♡ AQ10xx
◇ 10x		◇ KQx
♣ AKxx		♣ xxx
	SOUTH	
	♠ KQxx	
	♡ xxx	
	◇ xxx	
	♣ Q10x	

With the first two hands North will open 1◇; East will overcall and, whatever you do, West will bid 2♡. If your first call as South was a pass, neither you nor partner can safely take further action, and the opponents will score +110. I would bid 1♠ with the first hand although some players would prefer a Negative Double. But taking SOME ACTION will allow you to buy the contract for 2♠, scoring +110 your way. With the second hand you should make a Negative Double, suggesting play in either spades or clubs. After a Negative Double you will buy the contract (at 3♣) instead of the opponents. In the third hand, if you pass, everyone else will pass, and the opponents will score 110 or 140. If you Double or bid 1♠, partner will rebid 1NT, probably going down one. (Why should you expect double dummy defense?) Immediate bidding on skimpy values scored two clear–cut victories, when a fit was discovered, and one inconclusive result when there was no fit. Notice that when the opponents had a fit, you had a fit.

You should bid a suit at the one level or make a Negative Double with all 8 HCP hands or more. With 5–7 HCP, bid only with a good distributional feature like a five card suit or singleton in the opponents' suit, or with well placed high cards. In a nutshell, with greater offensive values than defensive values you should bid.

Suppose the bidding has gone

WEST	NORTH	EAST	SOUTH
—	1♢	1♡	?

What would you bid holding each of the following hands?

1.	♠ KQxxx	♡ xxx	♢ xx	♣ xxx
2.	♠ Qxxxx	♡ xx	♢ Kxx	♣ xxx
3.	♠ Kxxx	♡ xx	♢ xx	♣ Kxxxx
4.	♠ Qxxx	♡ x	♢ Qxxx	♣ Qxxx
5.	♠ Qxxx	♡ xx	♢ Kxxxx	♣ Jx
6.	♠ KQ10x	♡ xxxx	♢ xx	♣ J10x
7.	♠ Jxxx	♡ Q10x	♢ Qx	♣ Qxxx
8.	♠ Qxxx	♡ KQ98	♢ xx	♣ xxx

The first two hands are clear 1♠ bids. A five card suit is a positive feature, and if a spade fit can be found, none of your points will be wasted. Give partner

♠ AJxx ♡ x ◇ AQJxx ♣ Axx

and both sides might make game. Hand Three is best shown by a Negative Double. If partner has a four card fit with either black suit, you may be able to outbid your opponents. Hand Four is also worth a Negative Double. Although your hand is defensively weak , your ratio of offensive–defensive values is quite high. You must have a fit somewhere. Hand Five is another hand worth a Negative Double. Again your offensive–defensive ratio is high since your length in partner's suit cuts down on your defensive strength. Obviously if partner bids clubs, you will return him to diamonds. Bid 1♠ with Hand Six. You reject a Negative Double because you don't want to encourage partner to compete in either minor. If partner raises with three card support opposite your strong four card suit, the contract should be playable. Pass with Hand Seven. If you bid 1♠ with a weak suit on this mostly defensive hand, and partner stretches to 3♠ after the bidding continues 3♡ by LHO, you won't be happy. Partner may raise with only three card spade support rather than be shut out. Pass with the last hand also. You have too much defense and too little offense. Very often, when the bidding goes

WEST	NORTH	EAST	SOUTH
—	1◇	1♡	1♠
4♡	?		

partner will compete to 4♠ with a singleton or void in hearts because from his point of view either you might make it or it might be a good sacrifice. You know 4♠ is unlikely to make, and it definitely will not be a good sacrifice. Although I recommend a pass, a Negative Double with Hand 7 and Hand 8 is better than a 1♠ bid. At least it will avoid a high level spade contract on a 4–3 fit, but partner may still be induced into bidding when it would be better to defend.

Suppose you hold ♠ xxx ♡ Axx ◇ Jxx ♣ Jxxx, and partner opens 1♡. If the next hand passes, bid 1NT (forcing) and hope to take a preference back to hearts. A 2♡ raise is too encouraging with this featureless hand. But if RHO overcalls, it is slightly better to bid 2♡ than to pass. Making a competitive heart raise is clear with:

♠ xxx ♡ Axx ◇ xx ♣ J10xxx

After the auction

WEST	NORTH	EAST	SOUTH
—	1♡	1♠	2♡
4♠	?		

partner with

♠ x ♡ KJxxxxx ◇ AQx ♣ Ax

will bid 5♡ as a two–way bid. If you had passed, what could he do?

What is the difference between a free bid and a competitive bid? The theoretical difference is that a free bid is made immediately over an opponent's bid while a competive bid is made in fourth position. Supposedly a free bid shows extra values. Since the opponents have kept the bidding open for partner, you only bid because you want to. A competitive bid can, and usually does, show less than normal values. You bid again, not to try for game, but to prevent the opponents from buying the contract. That is the theory. As a practical matter, it is often safer for second hand to bid, perhaps because he has distribution while his partner is balanced. So I recommend that you treat free bids and competitive bids the same. Bidding a minimum number of your agreed suit in competition is generally considered competitive, while a new suit would be a game try.

WEST	NORTH	EAST	SOUTH
1♠	2♢	2♠	3♢
3♠?			

WEST	NORTH	EAST	SOUTH
1♣	1♢	1♠	2♢
2♠	3♢	3♠?	

Both the 3♠ bids are competitive while a 3♡ bid would be invitational.

Suppose the bidding starts:

WEST	NORTH	EAST	SOUTH
—	—	—	1♠
Pass	2♠	3♢	?

WEST	NORTH	EAST	SOUTH
—	—	—	1♠
Pass	2♠	Double	Pass
3♢	?		

When should North–South compete to 3♠, and which hand should take the push? Let's look at some hands.

HAND 1	HAND 2	HAND 3	HAND 4	HAND 5
NORTH	NORTH	NORTH	NORTH	NORTH
♠ Qxx	♠ Jxxx	♠ Qxxx	♠ Qxx	♠ Qxx
♡ Kxx	♡ Kxx	♡ Kx	♡ Kxx	♡ Kxx
♢ xxx	♢ xxx	♢ xxx	♢ xxx	♢ xxx
♣ Kxxx	♣ Kxx	♣ Kxxx	♣ Qxxx	♣ Qxxx
SOUTH	SOUTH	SOUTH	SOUTH	SOUTH
♠ AKxxx	♠ AKxxx	♠ AKxxx	♠ AKxxx	♠ AKxxx
♡ Qxx	♡ xxx	♡ Axx	♡ Axxx	♡ A109x
♢ xx	♢ Qx	♢ xx	♢ x	♢ xx
♣ Axx	♣ Axx	♣ Qxx	♣ J10x	♣ Kx

With the first hand North–South should defend. If the spades split 3–2 North–South probably have the five defensive tricks needed to set 3♢ but have five losers in a 3♠ contract. If the spades split 4–1 there will be six losers.

Defend also with the second hand. The ♢Q is worthless on offense, and there is no chance to make 3♠, even in the the unlikely event the ♡A is favorably placed. With bad breaks, down three is very possible. The opponents can probably make 3♢, but East might have no entry to dummy to take the heart finesse. Also, with enough entries, declarer might take a losing trump finesse. The ♢Q has a far better chance of scoring a trick on defense than on offense.

Bid 3♠ with the third hand. Nine tricks are almost a cinch unless trumps are 4–0, in which case the opponents could make a lot of diamonds. With the fourth and fifth hands, there is a good chance of making 3♠ unless the spades split 4–1 but then East–West can surely make their contract.

When both hands are completely balanced, it pays to defend. Even if either hand were slightly stronger this would be true. If North–South can make 3♠, perhaps because all of their finesses are working, East–West won't make 3♢. Frequently, neither contract will make.

The fourth trump in responder's hand decreases the chance of a bad break so that even when the hand is going down, the opponents can seldom double. The fourth trump sometimes is worth a trick because you can ruff two losers or pull the trumps and ruff the fourth round of declarer's side suit. The fourth trump also decreases your defensive prospects. So with four card support tend to compete. Take the conservative view only with 4–3–3–3 distribution as in Hand 2. Also take the push with three card support including prime values and some ruffing feature like:

1. ♠ K10x ♡ xx ◊ xx ♣ A10xxxx
2. ♠ Qxx ♡ Axxx ◊ x ♣ 10xxxx

Opener should tend to compete with a singleton in the opponents' suit or any sort of distributional twist. Since

WEST	NORTH	EAST	SOUTH
—	—	—	1♠
Pass	2♠	3◊	3♠?

denies game interest, South must either jump to game or bid a new suit to make a game try. Thus, 3♡ would simply be an artificial game invitation. Opener's heart holding could even be a singleton.

If East's overcall had been 3♡, there would be no new suit left to bid. Some experts play a double as a game try. Others are unwilling to give up a penalty double. It would be different if West had overcalled 2♡ and East had raised to 3♡. Now a double would be a maximal double, inviting game, since a penalty double is unlikely to be needed when a suit has been bid on your left and raised on your right.

Since the auction

WEST	NORTH	EAST	SOUTH
—	—	—	1♠
2◊	2♠	3◊	3♠

denies game interest, can responder ever bid 4♠? I think so if it looks as though the hands fit perfectly. For example, responder might hold either

1. ♠ Qxxx ♡ xx ◊ xxxx ♣ AQx or
2. ♠ Q10x ♡ xx ◊ xxx ♣ AQ10xx

Opener must have diamond shortness, and responder has no wasted values. However, responder should be conservative if the decision is close. Incidentally, with the first responding hand 3♠ should have been bid immediately.

In competition it pays to stretch with prime values and good trump support. There are several reasons:

1. In an uncontested auction a single major raise is slightly constructive since you can bid a forcing notrump and support partner later with a weaker hand. Since your minimum raise in competition is lower, your maximum should also be lower.
2. In an uncontested auction, partner can invite game over your single raise. In a contested auction partner may have no room to invite. The bidding may go 1♠–2♡–2♠–3♡ or 1♠–2◇–2♠–4◇.
3. When the opponents have a fit your side has a fit, sometimes in two suits. Game can often be made with only a slight preponderance of high cards.
4. In a competitive auction it pays to overbid early. If you can't make your contract the opponents can often make theirs.
5. It especially pays to overbid when you have a high ratio of offensive to defensive values. After 1♠–2◇–? you should bid 3♠ (or possibly 4♠) with either

   ♠ Q10xxx ♡ xx ◇ xx ♣ KJ10x or
   ♠ Kxxx ♡ xxx ◇ x ♣ QJxxx

   Even if you get too high, it should be a good sacrifice.

That reminds me. Suppose you are playing Drury and you hold ♠ xxx ♡ Q10xxx ◇ KQxx ♣ x.

WEST	NORTH	EAST	SOUTH
Pass	Pass	1♡	Pass
?			

It would be a mistake to bid 2♣, which your RHO might double, leading to a good sacrifice or being outbid by the opponents. Just bid 3♡. Make the same 3♡ bid with

♠ xx ♡ Kxxxx ◊ KJxx ♣ xx

The fact that both opponents have passed does not eliminate the danger of successful competition if you make it too easy for them. With more high cards and a more balanced hand, Drury is great.

If the bidding goes

WEST	NORTH	EAST	SOUTH
—	—	—	1♣
Pass	1♠	Pass	?

you would bid 2♠ with either

1. ♠ Kxxx ♡ xx ◊ Axx ♣ AKxx or
2. ♠ AQx ♡ xx ◊ xxx ♣ AKQxx.

Suppose the bidding goes

WEST	NORTH	EAST	SOUTH
—	—	—	1♣
Pass	1♠	3♡	?

You are forced to bid 3♠. If you pass, partner would have to pass with

♠ Jxxxx ♡ Ax ◊ KQxx ♣ xx.

Any time opener has a good 2♠ raise, he must bid 3♠ rather than pass. When opener has a 3♠ bid, he has to bid 4♠ like with either

1. ♠ Kxxx ♡ Kxx ◊ Kx ♣ AKQx or
2. ♠ Kxxx ♡ xx ◊ Ax ♣ AKQxx.

Occasionally, you will get too high, but overall, this method of raising works pretty well PROVIDED partner has a decent suit. Some players would respond 1♠ to an opening 1♣ holding

♠ xxxx ♡ Jx ◇ AQxxx ♣ xx

which has never made sense to me. Why skip over a perfect descriptive bid to show what you don't have? This is not the way to bid, even if you were promised the opponents would not interfere. But it is particularly unwise when the opponents may preempt or even make a simple overcall. Partner is then forced to raise with three card support and overbid with four card support. Would you like to play 3♠ with the following hands?

YOU	PARTNER
♠ xxxx	♠ AQx
♡ Jx	♡ xx
◇ AQxxx	◇ xxx
♣ xx	♣ AKQxx

Or 4♠ with the following hands?

YOU	PARTNER
♠ xxxx	♠ Kxxx
♡ Jx	♡ Kxx
◇ AQxxx	◇ Kx
♣ xx	♣ AKQx

Suppose partner opens 1♣, RHO passes and you hold

♠ AQxx ♡ xxxx ◇ xxx ♣ Jx.

A 1♡ bid here isn't a deliberate perversion like the 1♠ bid made with four small spades and five or more good diamonds. You are afraid of missing your 4–4 heart fit. But bidding 1♡ is against the odds. Even when partner has four hearts, the hand may play just as well in notrump, and you will find your fit if partner is strong enough to reverse. Suppose you disregard my advice and respond 1♡, and LHO overcalls 2◇. Partner could be given four spades and three hearts to create a disaster and make my point, but suppose he has

♠ Kxx ♡ Kxx ◇ xx ♣ AK10xx

He will raise whichever suit you bid. Wouldn't you rather be in spades? I would also raise partner's major suit with the latter hand in an uncontested auction. When partner has a long suit it makes the bidding much easier because he knows the hands fit. You also have a chance to get to a good 4–3 fit when the four card suit is strong and ruffs can be taken in the hand with three trumps. However, you may belong to the school that rebids 1NT with this hand and hopes to recover later. Maybe you will in an uncontested auction. But when the opponents compete, partner can bid with much more confidence if he can assume that you have a "biddable" suit such as Qxxx, J10xx, or better. Sometimes responding with four small is the least of evils, but if you avoid it whenever you can, it will help you in your competitive bidding since partner will make more "right" decisions. Even when your suit is "biddable" don't go out of your way to bid it. With

♠ Q432 ♡ Q8 ♢ QJ874 ♣ 52

how will it gain to respond 1♠ rather than 1♢ when partner opens 1♣? It might prevent you from missing your 4–4 spade fit if LHO is planning to preempt in hearts, but partner needs a fairly good hand for us to outbid the opponents, and if he has a strong hand he can bid spades himself. For that matter, if the bidding should go

WEST	**NORTH**	**EAST**	**SOUTH**
—	—	—	1♣
Pass	1♠	4♡	4♠

would you feel confident? Give partner

♠ Axxx ♡ xx ♢ x ♣ AKQJxx

and you will be set for sure, perhaps several tricks, doubled. Whenever partner doesn't have four spades and frequently when he does, you will have gotten off to a better start by responding 1♢.

Logically, extra values are required to raise the bidding level opposite what could be a weak hand. If the bidding goes

WEST	NORTH	EAST	SOUTH
—	—	—	1♢
Pass	1♡	2♣	?

you need extra values to bid 2♠. But if the bidding goes

WEST	NORTH	EAST	SOUTH
—	—	—	1♣
Pass	1♢	1♡	?

no extra values are needed to bid 1♠. Bid 1♠ whenever you would have made that bid in an uncontested auction.

WEST	NORTH	EAST	SOUTH
—	—	—	1♠
Pass	2♣	2♢	?

Bid 2♡ in this situation any time you would have rebid 2♡ in an uncontested auction. The possibility of finding an eight card major suit fit is too valuable to give up for any reason. Whether you should rebid 2♠ is a different matter. You would have rebid 2♠ for lack of anything better to do with

♠ AK10xx ♡ Axx ♢ xxx ♣ Jx.

Now you should pass. You have nothing you want to say, and a 2♠ bid takes away one of partner's options—a penalty double which you would be glad to leave in. Nor would a pass necessarily show a minimum. You would also pass with

♠ AKxxx ♡ AKx ♢ xxx ♣ Jx

since partner is obligated to take some action. With

♠ KQJxxx ♡ Q10x ♢ xx ♣ Kx

despite your minimum opening it would be a mistake not to take advantage of the opportunity to rebid your spade suit. A good spade suit is the main feature of your hand.

You hold ♠ Qx ♡ Kxxx ◊ Axx ♣ Axxx.

WEST	NORTH	EAST	SOUTH
—	—	—	1♣
1♠	Double*	2◊	?

*Negative

You started with a minimum hand, and it looks worse when West bids 1♠ since your ♠Q is probably worthless. However, partner asked you to bid 2♡ if you had a heart suit. Since you can bid 2♡, you should do so. If East had bid 2♠ you would pass. To bid 3♡ you would need extra values or something like

1. ♠ xx ♡ Kxxx ◊ Ax ♣ AJ10xx
2. ♠ xxx ♡ KQxx ◊ xx ♣ AKJx

The first hand has good distribution, no wasted cards and the second hand is a "pure" hand, good hearts.

WEST	NORTH	EAST	SOUTH
—	—	—	1♣
1♡	Double*	2♡	?

*Negative

No extra values are needed to bid 2♠. Whether partner has a minimum double or not, you don't want to allow the opponents play at the two level when your side has half the high cards and an eight card fit in a higher ranking suit.

WEST	NORTH	EAST	SOUTH
1♣	Double	1♡	?

Very little is needed besides a four card spade suit to bid 1♠. Partner asked you to bid and you should oblige him before the bidding gets too high.

♠ Q10xx ♡ xxx ◇ Qxxx ♣ xx

is enough. Remove one of your queens and a pass is a good idea to warn partner against competing too vigorously.

WEST	NORTH	EAST	SOUTH
1♣	Double	2♣	?

A little more is needed to bid at this level. Perhaps

1. ♠ Q10xx ♡ xxx ◇ Kxxx ♣ xx or
2. ♠ Jxxxx ♡ xx ◇ K10x ♣ xxx

Partner still has room to invite game by raising to 3♠ or STRONGLY inviting game by bidding 3♣. Needless to say, you will reject all invitations.

WEST	NORTH	EAST	SOUTH
1♣	Double	3♣	?

If you bid 3♠, partner will have no room to invite and must guess whether to bid game. So you need something like

♠ Jxxxx ♡ Q10x ◇ Kxx ♣ xx

or better to bid 3♠ and with a good 3♠ bid you should stretch and bid 4♠. Sometimes when you can make exactly 3♠ there is no practical way to play it there. If either partner bids, the other will insist upon game. That is why people preempt. It causes problems.

You hold:

1. ♠ AKxx ♡ Qxxx ◇ Kxx ♣ xx
2. ♠ A10x ♡ AKQx ◇ xxxx ♣ xx

WEST	NORTH	EAST	SOUTH
—	—	1♣	Double
2♣	2♡	3♣	?

Withthe first hand the only good feature about your hand is your four trumps rather than

♠ AKxx ♡ Qxx ◇ Kxxx ♣ xx.

You should pass because 3♡ might be too high, and partner might possibly bid 4♡ if you raise. With the second hand bid 3♡. Having such good trump support means it will be hard for partner to bid again and hard for the opponents to double if you are too high. If partner has

♠ KJx ♡ 10xxxx ◇ xx ♣ xxx,

your hand is worth much more to him than if your values were elsewhere as in the following hands:

1. ♠ A10x ♡ xxxx ◇ AKQx ♣ xx or
2. ♠ AQ10x ♡ Jxx ◇ Axxx ♣ Kx

In other words, partner should not be expected to bid again with 4–5 HCP after having made a "free bid" at the two level. In all such sequences each player should assume that his partner's bid is competitive rather than a game invitation. A "free bid" merely denies a misfit or a rock bottom minimum.

WEST	NORTH	EAST	SOUTH
—	—	1♣	Double
1♡	1♠	2♣	?

Suppose you hold either

1. ♠ Q10xx ♡ Kxxx ◇ Axx ♣ Kx or
2. ♠ Kxxx ♡ AJx ◇ Kxxxx ♣ x.

Kit Woolsey recommends a raise to 2♠ on the ground that the Law of Total Tricks calls for it. In fact, Kit would raise even if West had passed and partner's bid was forced. I agree with most of Kit's theories, but not this one. If you raise with these hands, what would you bid with

♠ AQxx ♡ Axx ◇ AQxx ♣ xx?

Partner won't know what to do if your raise covers such a wide range of strength. At least 15 support points are needed to raise, even in competition, compared to 16–18 when there is no competition. Consequently my absolute minimum raise would be either

1. ♠ KJxx ♡ Kxxx ◇ Axx ♣ Kx or
2. ♠ Kxxx ♡ AQx ◇ Kxxxx ♣ x

Partner should compete to the two level without any more encouragement from you with

♠ Axxxx ♡ xx ◇ J10x ♣ xxx,

and partner should bid 4♠ over a raise to 2♠ with

♠ Axxx ♡ Qx ◇ Q10xx ♣ xxx.

When partner holds ♠ Axxx ♡ Qxx ◇ J10x ♣ xxx he can't very well rebid spades when you might have only three, but he can double 2♣ to say he has enough to bid again with a four card spade suit, and you should find some spot to play in, perhaps 2♣ doubled.

Quiz Two

In the following problems disregard the vulnerability and the form of scoring.

1. You hold ♠ xx ♡ KQxxx ◊ Jxx ♣ AQ10.

WEST	NORTH	EAST	SOUTH
—	—	1◊	1♡
Pass	2♡	3◊	?

What do you bid?

2. You hold ♠ Axxx ♡ KQxx ◊ Jxxx ♣ x.

WEST	NORTH	EAST	SOUTH
—	—	1♣	Double
2♣	2♡	3♣	?

What do you bid?

3. You hold ♠ Qxxx ♡ Kxx ◊ x ♣ AJ109x.

WEST	NORTH	EAST	SOUTH
—	Pass	Pass	1♣
Pass	1♡	2◊	?

What do you bid?

4. You hold ♠ Jxxx ♡ KQJ9 ◊ Qxx ♣ xx.

WEST	NORTH	EAST	SOUTH
—	1♣	1♡	?

What do you bid?

5. You hold ♠ 10xx ♡ AJx ◇ xxxx ♣ Axx.

WEST	NORTH	EAST	SOUTH
1◇	1♠	Pass	2♠
3♣	Pass	Pass	?

What do you bid?

6. You hold ♠ Jxxx ♡ Qxxx ◇ Q10xx ♣ x.

WEST	NORTH	EAST	SOUTH
—	1◇	Pass	1♡
Double	Pass	2♣	?

What do you bid?

Answers

1. **PASS.** Your hand is too balanced to justify further bidding. You have a safe lead and good cards for defense. Even the ♢ J could be worth something on defense.

2. **PASS.** You have good distribution, but you took that into account when you doubled. The hand is slightly better than if your major holdings were reversed, but you are very close to a minimum. Partner will probably find another bid such as doubling with

♠ Q10x ♡ Axxx ♢ Qxx ♣ xxx,

and you can correct to 3♡. Bidding a direct 3♡ might encourage partner to bid game.

3. **PASS.** Again you have a very weak hand for your bidding but unlike the last hand, you have neither shown nor implied a fit for partner's suit. I would be inclined to make a Support Double, if playing that convention; otherwise I would pass on the theory that there is a greater danger of getting too high if you bid than of being stolen from if you pass.

4. **PASS.** Usually some action should be taken with 8 HCP or more. Because this hand is so weak offensively and so good defensively, you should make an exception (and I'll bet that Al Roth agrees with me). If partner reopens with a double, you should pass and never show the spades! Naturally on opening lead, you will lead a trump. A 1NT bid is also acceptable against not vulnerable opponents.

5. **PASS**. You should almost never bid 2♠ and then 3♠ in a situation like this. In this sequence a raise is more dangerous than usual with your weak trump holding because LHO has bid two suits, and RHO should have most of the missing spades. Besides, you have excellent cards for defense.

6. **PASS**. A 2♢ bid looks harmless, but it is not. Partner needs a very good hand for your side to outbid the opponents. With a distributional hand partner would not have passed, so his hand should be balanced. With 18–19 HCP he will jump to 3NT over 2♢, not suspecting that your hand is so weak. You should pass and if you don't get a chance to show distributional diamond support later, it is definitely not your hand. If you pass and partner now bids 2NT, bidding 3♢ would show weakness.

Chapter Three

DEFENSIVE BIDDING

THIS CHAPTER DEALS WITH THE PROBLEMS faced by the side that does not open the bidding. For convenience we will call that side "the defenders"—even though they may buy the bid. Suppose RHO opens one of a suit. There are numerous actions you can take:

1. Pass.
2. Make a simple overcall.
3. Make a preemptive jump overcall (but a game bid is not necessarily preemptive; you may bid to make, figuring your slam possibilities are remote after an opening bid by an opponent).
4. Make an intermediate jump overcall or a strong jump overcall. (Obviously your jump overcall can't be weak, intermediate, and strong—you have to choose. I recommend playing intermediate jump overcalls when vulnerable or in fourth position after two passes. In other situations, I play weak jump overcalls.)
5. Make a takeout double.
6. Overcall 1NT.
7. Overcall 3NT.
8. Make some conventional bid to show a two–suiter.

Pass is the most frequent call. At one time "trap passes" were more popular than they are now. If RHO opened one of a suit and you held KJ9x of his suit and a good hand, the tendency was to pass and hope the opponents would bid too much or LHO would pass and partner could reopen with a double, which you would convert for penalties. Now most experts overcall 1NT if the hand falls within range, or double and bid 2NT the following round with a stronger hand. Too many things can go wrong when you lurk in the bushes. When the opponents have a better spot they will usually find it, and you will seldom have a chance for a big penalty. Why should partner have most of the remaining high cards so that LHO will have to pass, while partner is strong enough to reopen with a double? If we train partner to double with 6–7 HCP in case we were trapping with 18 HCP and a stack in trumps, what happens when we pass his double with 11 HCP and a stack in trumps? They make it! So a pass these days simply means that no other action is appealing.

A simple overcall is the next most frequent action. It is difficult to state hard and fast rules for when to overcall since many factors come into play. These factors, in order of importance, are:

1. To buy the bid for a plus score.
2. To find a good sacrifice.
3. To interfere with the opponents' bidding.
4. To suggest a lead.

Seldom will an overcall be followed by three passes. Usually when we outbid the opponents it is after partner raises.

The last objective is the least important. Frequently you will be on lead when the opponents play the hand. Sometimes you have to overcall with a bad suit with a good hand, so partner can't count on your overcall to indicate a good lead. Besides, partner can often make the right lead without your help, just by listening to the bidding.

The third factor depends upon the suits you shut out. When the opponents open a minor and you overcall at the two level or bid 1♠, you create problems for them. Despite the availability of a Negative Double their bidding has been interfered with. If partner raises your overcall, especially when he makes a double or triple raise, the opponents have to decide whether to pass to show a minimum or bid to show a fit.

With favorable vulnerability you might bid with a bad hand, hoping to find a good sacrifice, but generally that is not your main objective. You simply overcall because you like your offensive–defensive ratio and let the chips fall where they may. Suppose you overcall 1♠ with

♠ AQ10xx ♡ x ◇ Kxxx ♣ xxx.

When you overcall, you don't know whose hand it is. Partner with ♠ KJxxx ♡ xxxx ◇ Axx ♣ x. will bid 4♠, figuring that you might make it or that it will be a good sacrifice. He also likes his ratio of offensive to defensive values. Note, the hands fit beautifully and 4♠ is cold. If the overcaller's ◇ K were the ♣ K, 4♠ would be down one, but since the opponents could make 4♣ or 5♣ you would still get a good result.

You hold ♠ AQ10x ♡ x ◇ Kxxxx ♣ xxx. If RHO opens 1♣ the most cowardly call is pass, but 1◇ is a very close second. What does it accomplish? It doesn't create any problems for the opponents. LHO can still bid 1♡. If partner is on lead against the final contract, you don't particularly want a diamond lead. You are not likely to outbid the opponents in diamonds. At any form of scoring a 1♠ overcall is better. It jams the opponents' bidding. If partner has a good spade fit, we might buy the contract. Suppose he has the hand he had before:

♠ KJxxx ♡ xxxx ◇ Axx ♣ x.

We can still make 4♠. If we do not interfere, the opponents might bid and make game their way.

The easiest game to bid and make is four of a major. That is the main reason we use Stayman over notrump. That is why some misguided souls respond 1♠ rather than 1♢ with

♠ xxxx ♡ xx ♢ AQxxx ♣ Jx.

Because we have to take eleven tricks in five of a minor, we usually need more strength. Even when we belong in five of a minor, it is harder to predict, consequently harder to bid. Suppose RHO opens 1♡ and we overcall 2♣ with

♠ KJ9x ♡ x ♢ Ax ♣ KJxxxx.

If partner has

♠ Ax ♡ xxx ♢ Jxxx ♣ Axxx,

we belong in 5♣. If he has

♠ Qxx ♡ xxxx ♢ J10 ♣ AQxx,

we don't belong in any game. Is our bidding accurate enough to get to game with the right hand and stop short with the other? I doubt it! Instead of overcalling 2♣, suppose we overcall 1♠. There are many more hands that will make game in spades, and these games are biddable. Any time partner has a good spade holding, we are well along toward reaching and making game. Give him ♠ AQxxx with nothing else, and I'd be willing to take my chances in 4♠, or ♠ Qxxx plus the ♣ A.

Admittedly a 2♣ overcall might get you there. If partner raises, you can introduce the spade suit, and he will know you have a good offensive hand with only four spades. Perfect! But what if the bidding goes

WEST	NORTH	EAST	SOUTH
—	—	1♡	2♣
2♡	Pass	3♡	?

or

WEST	NORTH	EAST	SOUTH
—	—	1♡	2♣
4♡	Pass	Pass	?

In the first sequence you know partner doesn't have a club raise, but he could still hold either

1. ♠ Axxxx ♡ xxx ◇ Kxx ♣ xx or
2. ♠ Qxxxx ♡ xxxx ◇ Kxx ♣ Q.

Do you dare bid 3♠ or Double?

When it is so unlikely that you will bid and make 5♣, you should give up on clubs and try to find a spade fit. If partner is acquainted with your style, you still have a chance to play a club partscore after

WEST	NORTH	EAST	SOUTH
—	—	1♡	1♠
2♡	Pass	Pass	3♣

Having failed to support spades, partner shouldn't take a preference with equal length in your two suits. Another safety factor which prevents partner from even being tempted to return you to spades is that the opponents have stopped at the two level despite finding a fit. That marks partner with a few high cards. Why didn't he raise spades? Because he is short. When short in spades and probably longer in your second suit, partner won't return you to spades.

The best time to overcall a minor and hope to show your major later is with a mediocre hand and a weak four card major. You don't want to play in spades with Axxx opposite Jxx. If you lose control, you may have to discard your six card minor on the opponents' winners. One thing in favor of overcalling the major is our system of responding to overcalls. As you will soon discover, partner usually lets you know whether he has three or four card support, and that can be crucial with hands of this type.

With 11 or 12 HCP you can frequently show your major after overcalling a minor. SOMEBODY will bid, giving you another chance (if you are brave enough to take it). With 16 or 17 HCP, there is a strong likelihood that your overcall at the two level will be followed by three passes. If opener has 13 or 14 HCP with some length in your suit, he won't feel like reopening the bidding. Neither LHO nor partner, with 5 HCP each, will find a bid. If RHO opens 1♢, a 1♠ bid is the best choice holding

♠ AK10x ♡ xx ♢ Ax ♣ KQJxx.

Give partner either

1. ♠ Qxxx ♡ xxx ♢ KJxx ♣ xx or
2. ♠ Jxxxx ♡ Qxxx ♢ xx ♣ Ax.

He would raise spades but pass 2♣. If you were to make a takeout double instead, you wouldn't know what to do if partner were to bid 2♡ or 3♡ in competition.

Here is another situation where you should bid a four card major in competition

You hold ♠ KQ10x ♡ x ♢ xx ♣ AKQ10xx.

WEST	NORTH	EAST	SOUTH
1♢	Pass	2♢*	?

*Not an inverted raise

To make 5♣ you must find partner with two aces. There is a much better chance of finding partner with one ace plus spade support. RHO won't have four spades. If either opponent has four spades, it will be LHO. That's not too likely; if he has a side four card suit, it is more likely to be hearts. But if LHO doubles you at any level, I'd tend to believe him and run out to clubs.

At how high a level should you risk an overcall with a four card suit? It depends upon several factors including whether the opponents can force you to ruff early and lose control. The following hand was dealt in a home team game and used later in a bidding panel.

Vulnerable vs Not Vulnerable
You hold ♠ AKQ8 ♡ K ◊ 7642 ♣ KJ75.

WEST	NORTH	EAST	SOUTH
3◊	Pass	Pass	?

Every panelist agreed a 3♠ bid was the least of evils. The hand is too strong to pass. If you belong in notrump, partner is the logical person to bid it. Partner will be short in diamonds. East may overruff the dummy, perhaps with a natural trump trick, but at least you won't be forced to ruff in your hand. It would be dangerous to double with a singleton heart, while if partner bids 4♡ over 3♠ he should have a good suit, and you won't be afraid to pass.

With a balanced hand, close to an opening bid is needed to overcall, even at the one level, unless your strength is concentrated. If you overcall with

♠ xx ♡ KQJxx ◊ Kxx ♣ xxx,

it will be hard for the opponents to get to 3NT with only a single heart stopper. You could conceivably buy the contract, and if partner is on lead, you will probably get the best lead.

An overcall is not worth the risk, especially when vulnerable with

♠ xx ♡ KJxxx ◊ KQx ♣ xxx.

You are not likely to be severely punished at the one level, but if partner competes, you could easily take a two trick set. Change the suit to spades, and the risk of taking a set is just as great, but since you shut out the heart suit, you have a little more to gain. Change your hand to

♠ xx ♡ KJxxx ◇ KQxx ♣ xx,

and the additional playing strength makes the overcall worth while.

I like to overcall with a four card major, but always with some sort of hidden potential—not with 4–3–3–3 or 4–4–3–2 distribution. Well, maybe with 4–4–3–2 and concentrated strength. Overcall 1♠ with

♠ AK109 ♡ xx ◇ xxx ♣ AJ10x.

Exchange the red suit holdings, and over 1◇ I prefer a takeout double. The ideal distributions are 4–1–4–4 (with the singleton in an unbid major), 4–1–5–3 and 4–1–2–6. Then if partner raises to game preemptively with length in your suit, you have a chance to make it. I don't mean to imply that the main reason for overcalling is to get to game, but when your bid has several ways to gain, it is the percentage bid. Overcall an opening 1◇ bid with your four card major when holding any of the following hands:

1. ♠ x ♡ AQJx ◇ xx ♣ Kxxxxx
2. ♠ AJ109 ♡ x ◇ Axxx ♣ Kxxx
3. ♠ xx ♡ KQ10x ◇ AJ9xx ♣ Ax
4. ♠ AKQx ♡ xx ◇ x ♣ AKxxxx.

Pass with ♠ AQ10x ♡ xxx ◇ Kxx ♣ Qxx;
Double with ♠ Axx ♡ AQJx ◇ xxx ♣ Kxx.

Overcalls at the one level have a very wide range of strength, roughly 7–17 HCP. The overcaller's partner should give a single raise almost as though the overcall were an opening bid. The raise gives overcaller a chance to bid or try for game if he is at the top of his range, but the primary purpose is preemptive. When responder has a good three card raise he should cue bid the opponents' suit. (This does NOT guarantee a rebid; most cue bids by the defenders' side do not).

You hold ♠ Axxx ♡ Kxx ◇ Kxxx ♣ xx.

WEST	NORTH	EAST	SOUTH
1♣	1♡	Pass	?

Bid 2♣ intending to pass if partner can merely rebid 2♡. Partner will assume that the cue bid shows a three card limit raise and will bid accordingly. After a cue bid new suits are forcing for one round. With a limit raise and four card support, overcaller's partner should make a jump cue bid. A jump raise is preemptive. However, with only so many bids available, you may have a close choice between an invitational raise and a preemptive raise. It is more important to make some sort of jump with four card or longer support and an unbalanced hand than to show exactly how many points you have. With 4–3–3–3 distribution, even with four of partner's suit, you MAY treat it like a three card raise.

WEST	EAST
♠ xx	♠ Kxxx
♡ KQxxx	♡ Axx
◇ xx	◇ xxx
♣ KQxx	♣ Axx

WEST	NORTH	EAST	SOUTH
—	—	—	1◇
1♡	Pass	2◇	Pass
2♡	Pass	Pass	Pass

WEST	EAST
♠ Ax	♠ Kxxx
♡ KJ10xx	♡ Axx
◇ xx	◇ xxx
♣ KQxx	♣ Axx

WEST	NORTH	EAST	SOUTH
—	—	—	1♢
1♡	Pass	2♢	Pass
3♣	Pass	4♡	Pass
Pass	Pass		

WEST	EAST
♠ xx	♠ Axx
♡ KQxxx	♡ AJx
♢ xx	♢ xxxx
♣ KQxx	♣ AJx

WEST	NORTH	EAST	SOUTH
—	—	—	1♢
1♡	Pass	2♢	Pass
2♡	Pass	3♡	Pass
4♡	Pass	Pass	Pass

WEST	EAST
♠ x	♠ Jxxx
♡ KQ10x	♡ Axxxx
♢ Ax	♢ Qx
♣ KQxxxx	♣ xx

WEST	NORTH	EAST	SOUTH
—	—	—	1♢
1♡	Pass	3♡	Pass
4♡	Pass	Pass	Pass

A jump to 2NT by the partner of the overcaller shows about 13–14 HCP and is non–forcing. If the overcaller rebids his suit, it is not forcing. A new suit rebid over 2NT is forcing. A 1NT response to the overcall shows about 9–12 HCP. The requirements for all notrump bids are higher than opposite an opening bid since both the minimum and maximum limits for an overcall are lower.

In choosing whether to raise partner's overcall or bid 1NT no single factor (such as degree of support, distribution, holding in the opponents' suit) is controlling. All factors must be weighed.

WEST	NORTH	EAST	SOUTH
—	—	—	1♣
1♡	Pass	?	

Both of these hands:

1. ♠ xxxx ♡ Q10 ◊ Axxx ♣ Axx and
2. ♠ xx ♡ Qx ◊ Kxxxx ♣ Axxx

look better for suit play than notrump, so I recommend a 2♡ raise. You COULD be on a 4–2 fit, but it doesn't pay to worry about it. The odds are that partner has a five card or longer heart suit since, to overcall with a four card suit, several factors have to be right. For one thing, he would usually have five or more diamonds, so as to give him some playing strength, and that doesn't seem likely opposite your diamond holding.

Prefer a 1NT response with

♠ Q10x ♡ AQx ◊ xxx ♣ QJxx,

despite the excellent heart support. Your club values will be wasted in a heart contract, and 3NT is your most likely game. If partner has an unbalanced hand and you belong in hearts, the notrump bid shouldn't prevent you from getting there.

A new suit bid is constructive but not forcing. It implies that you lack support for partner's major since, if you had support you would raise or cue bid rather than look for a better spot. After

WEST	NORTH	EAST	SOUTH
1♣	1♡	Pass	?

Bid 1♠ with either

1. ♠ AQ10xxx ♡ x ◊ Kxx ♣ Qxx or
2. ♠ KQ10xx ♡ xx ◊ Kxx ♣ xxx.

Bid 2♢ with

♠ Axx ♡ x ♢ KQJxxx ♣ xxx.

With a bad suit or a bad hand such as:

1. ♠ Jxxxx ♡ x ♢ AKx ♣ xxxx
2. ♠ xx ♡ x ♢ KJ109xxx ♣ xxx.

simply pass instead of risking worse trouble.

This is the standard method of responding to overcalls. Jeff Rubens, Kit Woolsey, and I have written articles advocating some transfer responses to overcalls. As of this writing the ACBL won't permit them except in national events when the "superchart" is in effect. I don't believe this restriction will continue. Hopefully, by the time you read this, transfer responses will be permitted in all ACBL tournaments. The idea is after the auction,

WEST	NORTH	EAST	SOUTH
1♣	1♠	Pass/Dble	?

it would be more efficient to play 2♣ as a transfer to diamonds, 2♢ as a transfer to hearts and 2♡ as a "cue bid" showing a good raise in spades, than to play 2♣ as a cue bid with 2♢ and 2♡ as natural. Over

WEST	NORTH	EAST	SOUTH
1♢	2♣	Pass	2♢

would be a transfer to hearts, 2♡ a transfer to spades, and 2♠ is the "cue bid." The advantage of switching the suits around is that you can transfer with a weak hand and a good suit, intending to pass; transfer and bid again with an intermediate hand; and transfer and cue bid or jump to game with a good hand. After the auction:

WEST	NORTH	EAST	SOUTH
1♣	1♠	Pass	?

and with the following hands:

1. ♠ x ♡ KQJxxx ◇ xxx ♣ xxx
2. ♠ x ♡ KQJxxx ◇ AJx ♣ xxx
3. ♠ Qx ♡ KQJxxx ◇ AKx ♣ xx

Bid 2◇ with Hand One planning to pass partner's 2♡ bid. Transfer to 2♡ and raise to 3♡ with Hand Two. Transfer to hearts and cue bid with Hand Three.

The overcaller doesn't have to accept the transfer.

1. ♠ AKQJxx ♡ x ◇ Jxxx ♣ xx
2. ♠ AKxxx ♡ Qxx ◇ Axx ♣ xx

With Hand One he should rebid 2♠ instead of 2♡. With Hand Two he should bid 3♡ instead of 2♡.

The transferer doesn't need a strong suit to transfer if he is planning to bid something else next round. After

WEST	NORTH	EAST	SOUTH
1◇	2♣	Pass	?

with the following hands:

1. ♠ Axx ♡ KQxxx ◇ xx ♣ Jxx
2. ♠ AQxxx ♡ Jx ◇ KJx ♣Kxx

Bid 2◇ followed by 3♣ with the first hand. Bid 2♡, transfering to spades, followed by 3NT with the second hand. If partner has ♠ Kxx ♡ xx ◇ Qx ♣ AQ10xxx he should bid 4♠.

The formula from these examples is: All bids to, but not including, opener's suit are natural. The opponent's suit is a transfer to the cheapest remaining unbid suit; if there is room, the next suit is a transfer to the other remaining suit.

Thus, after the auction:

WEST	NORTH	EAST	SOUTH
1◇	1♠	Pass	?

1NT is natural; 2♣ is natural; 2♢ is a transfer to hearts; 2♡ is the "cue bid"; 2♠ is just a raise. The more room the overcall has taken, the more room you have for transfer bids. When the overcall is in the next highest suit there are no transfer bids.

The ideal distribution for a takeout double is 4–4–4–1 with a singleton in the opponents' suit. With that distribution you may double with as few as 10 HCP such as

♠ Jxxx ♡ x ♢ AKxx ♣ Q10xx

With less ideal distribution you need more high card strength. In 1957, I recommended that a takeout double of one major should "guarantee" four card support for the other. The only exceptions occurred when you had a singleton in the opponents' suit and good three card support or considerable extra values. I now think my recommendations were too conservative. It is safer to double 1♡ with

♠ Kxx ♡ xx ♢ KJxx ♣ AJxx

than to pass and perhaps reopen later. Even with 13 or 14 points, all outside the opponents' suit, and 4–3–3–3 distribution I tend to double with

♠ KJx ♡ xxx ♢ KQxx ♣ A10x.

When partner holds either

1. ♠ Qxx ♡ xx ♢ A10xxx ♣ Qxx or
2. ♠ Q10xx ♡ xx ♢ Axx ♣ Q9xx

you get better results from competing than from selling out to 2♡, and the safest time to compete is now.

One way bidding styles have changed drastically is in choosing between an overcall and a takeout double. People used to play that an overcall denied the values for a good opening bid. The top limit was about 14 HCP. With more than that you would double and hope to show your suit next round. Nowadays the next round is likely to be at the three or four level.

Suppose RHO bids 1♠ and you hold

♠ x ♡ AQJxx ◊ KQx ♣ A10xx.

You think, "This hand is too strong to overcall 2♡. We might miss a game that way. So I'll double and plan to bid 2♡ over partner's minor suit response." That is a good idea, and the best way to describe your hand if allowed to do so.

In real life what usually happens is that you double, LHO bids 2♠ or 3♠, and the bidding comes back to you. Now you have three choices: to bid hearts at an uncomfortably high level, double again or pass. Any action you choose could be wrong, and you didn't get to do what you planned: to double and bid 2♡ next round. However, if you bid 2♡ immediately and LHO bids some number of spades, partner will tend to support hearts whenever he has heart support as a two–way bid. With a good hand you may make it; with a mediocre hand, especially with his heart length killing your defensive values, the bid may be a good sacrifice. At least partner will be aware of the fit when you bid hearts.

The disadvantage of the overcall is that it puts all your eggs in one basket. If you belong in a minor suit, you may not find your fit. However, LHO is less likely to preempt over your 2♡ bid than over a takeout double, and if the bidding goes 2♠ by him, pass, pass, you can double, which shows this type of hand.

In fact, I would probably double if the opponents bid to 3♠ although double would then be more dangerous. (Does the fact that the opponents didn't bid game mean that partner has a few useful high cards? Or did the opponents tread carefully because their trump suit was weak, leaving partner with ♠ KJ10x and nothing else?) If you add a point or two (like exchanging the ♣10 for the ♣Q or ♣J), you have to double, although you may have to do some good guessing later. When your suit is spades, you can more easily afford to double since you can bid your suit later at a lower level.

You hold ♠ Kxx ♡ AQxxx ◇ Ax ♣ Qxx. Suppose RHO bids 1◇. If you overcall 1♡ you may miss a 5–3 spade fit. If you double you may get to the wrong contract when partner holds four spades and three hearts. Besides, if you double, you can't bid hearts yourself unless partner cue bids.

WEST	NORTH	EAST	SOUTH
—	—	—	1◇
Double	Pass	2♣	Pass
2♡			

would show a stronger hand. The present expert style is to overcall your five card major. If the bidding goes

WEST	NORTH	EAST	SOUTH
1◇	1♡	2◇	Pass
Pass	?		

or

WEST	NORTH	EAST	SOUTH
1◇	1♡	Pass	Pass
2◇	?		

you can double. From the opponents' failure to bid more strongly and partner's failure to raise hearts, you can assume that partner has a few points, heart shortage, and length in one of the unbid suits. It is remarkable how much we tend to trust the opponents' bidding these days! If either opponent bids 1NT we would have to pass. Why? Because when the hands are balanced, nobody will make much. When the opponents have a fit, you have a fit. When RHO is distributional, as indicated in the second sequence by his 2♢ rebid, partner is likely to be also distributional.

Suppose the bidding goes 1♡ by LHO followed by two passes to you. Everybody agrees that you can bid with less in reopening position than in direct position. RHO, by passing, has put his side at a competitive disadvantage. Whatever you bid, RHO will be unable to double. LHO doesn't know whether his partner has a yarborough or is just short of a response, so he can't double for penalty if you bid too much. The only real dangers are that

1. You will bid too much on your own, and possibly change a plus to a minus, or
2. LHO will rebid a new suit which RHO fits, and the opponents will get to a better contract than if you had passed the opening bid, or
3. If your reopening bid is a double, partner will pass for penalty (and if you have sub–normal values, the contract will make).

Some players make a reopening double whenever they are short in opener's suit, even with

♠ Qxxx ♡ x ♢ Kxxx ♣ Jxxx.

This is losing bridge. You may get a great result if partner has

♠ KJx ♡ KQJ9x ♢ Ax ♣ Qxx.

He is strong enough to lead trumps himself. But what is partner supposed to do with either

1. ♠ Kxx ♡ KJ98x ♢ xx ♣ Qxx or
2. ♠ Ax ♡ KJ10xx ♢ J10x ♣ Qxx?

If he can't afford to pass with hands like these, there is something wrong with your system. A double should show at least 9 HCP and cater to the hands partner is more likely to be dealt.

Since trapping is no longer popular, and immediate action is taken with more types of hands than formerly, there is less need to "protect" partner.

You hold

1. ♠ K10xxx ♡ xxx ◇ Kxx ♣ Qx
2. ♠ AQ10x ♡ xxx ◇ Kxxx ♣ Jx
3. ♠ Qxx ♡ xxx ◇ AKJxx ♣ xx
4. ♠ xx ♡ Jxx ◇ AKJxxx ♣ xx

WEST	NORTH	EAST	SOUTH
1♡	Pass	Pass	?

Bid 1♠ with either of the first two hands. Bid 2◇ withthe third hand. With anything weaker, Pass. I would also pass with the fourth hand. Why didn't partner take action? Where are the spades? There is a real danger that if you bid 2◇, LHO will bid 2♠ and RHO will raise to game with either

1. ♠ Axxx ♡ x ◇ xxx ♣ xxxxx or
2. ♠ Kxxxx ♡ xx ◇ x ♣ 10xxxx.

Many players treat any action by the reopening bidder, except a double, as weak. Thus, with

♠ x ♡ AKxxx ◇ Axx ♣ Kxxx,

after the auction

WEST	NORTH	EAST	SOUTH
1◇	Pass	Pass	?

they would double since a 1♡ bid would tend to deny an opening bid. This treatment seems illogical to me. You wouldn't consider a double with this hand in second position since partner would probably bid spades (maybe lots of spades), and you wouldn't want to bid your suit at a higher level and risk finding your partner with a singleton. Many of the same factors weigh against a double in fourth position. If you can handle a range of

7–17 HCP for overcalls in second position, why can't you handle a similarly wide range in fourth position? Perhaps both the top and bottom range should be a point or two lower for fourth hand bids, but the general structure should be the same. Any time partner bids a suit and you hold KQxx of his suit or the equivalent, you are going to raise on the theory that if partner can't make his bid, the opponents can surely score more their way. In other words,

WEST	NORTH	EAST	SOUTH
—	—	—	1♢
Pass	Pass	1♡	Pass
2♡			

is not a game try.

Because of the wide range for reopening bids, some bids have entirely different meanings in the pass out position than they would in direct position.

WEST	NORTH	EAST	SOUTH
1♢	Pass	Pass	?

With a bad hand you could pass 1♢. There is no need for a preemptive jump overcall. Consequently, 2♠ is an intermediate jump overcall showing a good suit and at least opening bid strength, such as either

1. ♠ KQ10xxx ♡ xx ♢ xx ♣ AKx or
2. ♠ KJ9xxxx ♡ x ♢ Ax ♣ Kxx.

This will simplify partner's problem when he has a good hand but poor spade support and no stopper in the opponents' suit. He can raise 2♠ to 4♠ with

♠ xx ♡ AKx ♢ xxx ♣ Axxxx

I don't know what he would bid over 1♠.

WEST	NORTH	EAST	SOUTH
1♡	Pass	Pass	2NT

is not unusual. Since many players bid 1NT in fourth position with as few as 10 HCP, there is a tremendous range to cover. If 1NT shows 10–14 HCP, and double, followed by 2NT over a minor shows 15–17 HCP, then an immediate 2NT bid should show 18–20 HCP.

Incidentally, I am stating what is commonly played. I recommend a reopening 1NT (over a major) should show 12–16 HCP; a double followed by 2NT should show 17–18 HCP, and an immediate 2NT bid show 19–21 HCP (or the equivalent with a long, running minor). With 22 HCP or more, force to game and gamble on picking up a few points in partner's hand. These ranges are still too wide for accuracy, but what alternative is there?

While a 2♠ bid is a Michaels bid in this auction.

WEST	NORTH	EAST	SOUTH
1♠	2♠		

2♠ in the balancing seat in this auction

WEST	NORTH	EAST	SOUTH
1♠	Pass	Pass	2♠

should be a "takeout double" with a spade void. This bid and the reasons for it will be explained in a later chapter.

Suppose the bidding goes

WEST	NORTH	EAST	SOUTH
1♡	Pass	2♡	Pass
Pass	?		

or

WEST	NORTH	EAST	SOUTH
1♡	Pass	1NT	Pass
2♡	Pass	Pass	?

Usually your side has half the high card strength when the opponents are willing to stop below game. That is especially true in the first sequence. Having found a fit, the opponents would bid game or try for game with a slim majority of high card strength. When your side has eight spades, you should compete to 2♠. But how will you know when you have a combined total of eight spades? The trouble is that you won't. In either example hand, if you have a five card spade suit, tend to bid it. With offensive distribution such as ideally 4–1–4–4 you should double. With a good five card minor or six card minor tend to bid your suit. When the opponents have a fit, you have a fit.

You may have a difficult problem with balanced distribution. Should you reopen with either

1. ♠ Axx ♡ Kxx ◊ Axx ♣ Qxx or
2. ♠ AQx ♡ xxx ◊ KQx ♣ xxxx?

In neither case do you want to play the hand since you have a low ratio of offensive to defensive values, but perhaps you are selling out too cheaply and could push the opponents to the three level. My advice is to pass. If partner overcalls and doubles as light as recommended, you know it is not your hand, and the risk of competing is too great. With ♠ AJx ♡ xx ◊ Kxxx ♣ Qxxx you should double. For one reason, you have a pure hand. Add a couple of ten spots and a double would be even safer.

Ironically ♠ AJx ♡ Qx ◊ Kxxx ♣ Qxxx is a less desirable hand for a double. The opponents should have 18–22 HCP, and if they are missing the ♡Q, they are more likely to have additional values in the unbid suits.

In the second sequence where East responded 1NT the opponents had not found a fit. Consequently, you should be more cautious about reopening. When the bidding goes

WEST	NORTH	EAST	SOUTH
1◊	Pass	1♠	Pass
2♣	Pass	Pass	?

you should be extremely careful. The opponents haven't found a fit. In fact, the hand may be a horrible misfit for the opponents, which means that it is probably a misfit for you, also. The opponents' misfit for offensive purposes means a great hand for them defensively. With a good suit, you may risk bidding. Bid 2♡ with

♠ AJx ♡ QJ109x ◇ xxxx ♣ x.

Partner has some high cards and you have a playable suit. But with most hands you should pass.

We have been discussing true reopening bids where the opponents' last bid has been followed by two passes. This situation is somewhat similar after a notrump response and a minimum rebid.

WEST	NORTH	EAST	SOUTH
1◇	Pass	1NT	Pass
2◇	?		

West's hand is limited and East showed no interest in game. Nine times out of ten West will pass, and your partner may not be able to reopen. You have a sounder reopening double with

♠ J10xx ♡ Kxxx ◇ x ♣ Axxx

than partner does with

♠ Axx ♡ QJxx ◇ Axx ♣ Q10x.

SOMEONE ought to compete, and it is safer for the player with distribution to take action than for the player with the balanced hand. Similarly South should bid 2♡ with

♠ xx ♡ J109xx ◇ Kx ♣ Axxx

because his hearts are strong enough to play opposite a doubleton. The danger in passing is that North might bid 2♠ with

1. ♠ Qxxxx ♡ Qx ◇ Axx ♣ Q10x or
2. ♠ AJxxx ♡ Kxx ◇ xx ♣ Q10x.

With a singleton spade you have an even stronger reason for bidding 2♡—to keep partner from bidding 2♠.

WEST	NORTH	EAST	SOUTH
1♡	Pass	1NT	Pass
2♡	?		

You would surely double with

♠ Kxxx ♡ x ◇ Kxxx ♣ Kxxx.

You would have a closer decision with either

1. ♠ Kxx ♡ xx ◇ Kxxx ♣ KJxx or
2. ♠ Axxx ♡ Kx ◇ Qxx ♣ Qxxx

If the 1NT response over a major was forcing, West might be planning to rebid 2NT or to show a three card limit raise in hearts. A "reopening" double is more dangerous than when One Notrump was bid in response to a minor, and therefore limited. Nevertheless, I would risk the double. Most of the time West is planning to pass. When he has a three card limit raise, it will seem more logical to him to try for game than to penalize you. The only time you are likely to lose by reopening is when he is planning to rebid 2NT. In that case he might redouble and catch you for a good penalty. However, even if West has the hand you fear, partner may have a long suit or the opponents may misjudge their best action.

WEST	NORTH	EAST	SOUTH
1◇	Pass	1♠	Pass
1NT	?		

WEST	NORTH	EAST	SOUTH
1◇	Pass	1♠	Pass
2◇	?		

In both sequences shown above the situation is entirely different. East hasn't limited his hand. His next bid, if you pass, could easily be 3NT. A "delayed" takeout double would be extremely dangerous so the double should be for penalty. North should hold

1. ♠ x ♡ Axx ◇ KJ108x ♣ AQxx or
2. ♠ x ♡ AJx ◇ AQ108 ♣ Qxxxx,

not

3. ♠ xx ♡ QJxx ◇ xx ♣ AQxxx or
4. ♠ x ♡ Jxxxx ◇ xx ♣ AKxxx.

If you double the 1NT rebid in the last auction and partner bids 2◇, you should pass! He couldn't be cue bidding to show a decent hand since, if he had a decent hand, he would pass.

WEST	NORTH	EAST	SOUTH
1♠	Pass	1NT	Pass
2♡	Double		

Because of the opponents' potential misfit this isn't a true "reopening" double. It shows a good hand with a singleton heart, such as

♠ AJxx ♡ x ◇ KJxx ♣ AQxx.

Preemptive bids create problems no matter how well prepared you are to combat them. As we have seen from the first chapter, your primary objective is to avoid letting the opponents make their bid when you could successfully outbid them. This is especially true when you are likely to have a game. Consequently, doubles below the four level are takeout (although partner will occasionally pass), and doubles at the four level should show a hand suitable for takeout when partner has an unbalanced hand with a good suit of his own.

When considering an overcall of a preempt the key test should be, "Are we likely to make game, even though partner's hand is weaker than mine?"(If partner has the stronger hand, he is the one who should take action). In deciding whether we are LIKELY to make game, assume that the strength is fairly evenly divided between your partner and the preempter's partner. This assumption will sometimes lead to surprising conclusions.

None Vulnerable
You hold ♠ Qx ♡ J ◇ Q98x ♣ AQJ10xx.

WEST	NORTH	EAST	SOUTH
3◇	Pass	Pass	?

Bid 3NT! A typical nonvulnerable 3◇ bid is

♠ Jx ♡ xx ◇ AJ10xxxx ♣ xx,

and West might be even weaker. A hand such as

♠ Jx ♡ xx ◇ AK10xxxx ♣ xx

would be a very good preempt. Let's give West his typical 6 HCP, which leaves 22 points for partner and RHO. Suppose partner holds

♠ Kxxx ♡ KQxxx ◇ K ♣ 9xx,

which would leave RHO with

♠ A10xx ♡ A10xxx ◇ x ♣ Kxx.

It is hard to predict how the play would go, and dummy's ♣9 might be crucial, but quite likely you will make your contract. West won't have the entries to establish and cash his long suit, but you can establish and cash your long suit. If you think I cheated by picking ideal cards for partner, try exchanging his hand with RHO's and you are still likely to make 3NT.

You hold ♠ Ax ♡ xx ◇ xx ♣ AKQJxxx. After the same bidding I would still bid 3NT again rather than pass up the most probable game. Since modern preempts deny a solid suit, and East didn't raise as a further preempt, partnerprobablyhasadiamondstopper. Partner is more likely to have one trick in diamonds than three tricks elsewhere.

You hold ♠ Ax ♡ AKQJxxx ◇ xxx ♣ x. If RHO opens 3♠ I like a 3NT bid since I only need to find partner with one of the two missing aces to make it, and I might make it when partner is aceless and RHO has no entries. Partner might hold ♠ xx ♡ xx ◇ QJxx ♣ KQxxx. But the main reason is that LHO is less likely to bid 4♠ over 3NT than over 4♡, and from my point of view, I would rather declare with this hand than defend. The whole hand might be

[SEE THE NEXT PAGE]

If the bidding goes

WEST	NORTH	EAST	SOUTH
—	—	3♠	4♡
?			

West might bid 4♠, figuring it could be a good sacrifice or a possible make. (It will make unless you get a club ruff.) He would be more inclined to defend against 3NT since, if you have a balanced hand, you might run out of tricks; also your 3NT bid sounds like a good defensive hand with, perhaps, two spade tricks.

Change your hand to

♠ Ax ♡ AKQJxxx ◇ QJx ♣ x,

and 4♡ is the better bid. With a stronger hand you have more defense. Also you have more chances of making your contract (partner needs only the ◇ K).

	NORTH	
	♠ xx ♡ 10x ◇ A10xx ♣ QJxxx	
WEST ♠ Jx ♡ xxx ◇ KJxx ♣ AK10x		EAST ♠ KQ10xxxx ♡ x ◇ Qx ♣ xxx
	SOUTH ♠ Ax ♡ AKQJxxx ◇ xxx ♣ x	

Change your hand to ♠ Axx ♡ AKQJxxx ◇ xx ♣ x, and 4♡ is again the percentage bid. Partner might have a ruffing trick in spades, and West is slightly less likely to compete since there are fewer spades outstanding.

Another factor which hasn't been mentioned is that when someone preempts and you have a balanced hand, the suits are less likely to split well for you. If no one bids, 4♡ will be a good contract with these two hands:

YOU	PARTNER
♠ xx	♠ KQx
♡ AKxx	♡ xxxx
◇ Axx	◇ KQx
♣ AQ109	♣ xxx

If an opponent preempts 3♠, the opponents' misfit gives them better than normal defense against a suit contract. Quite likely the opponents can get a spade ruff (which may or may not cost you a trick), and the hearts are no longer 68% to split 3–2.

The defenders' misfit, which helps them on defense against suit contracts, hurts them on defense against notrump. When the preempter's partner has a singleton in preempter's long suit, the long suit can seldom be established.

You hold ♠ Kxxx ♡ Qxx ◇ Jxx ♣ Qxx.

WEST	NORTH	EAST	SOUTH
3◇	Double	Pass	?

One way of looking at this situation is that you might have had a yarborough, but instead, you have 8 HCP. Shouldn't you make some sort of bid to show your values? The answer is "no" . The preempter typically has 6–8 HCP. Partner, for his double, typically has 14–18 HCP. (With the lower range he needs ideal distribution). On an average you and the preempter's partner hold 8–9 HCP each. So, at best, you have an average hand. I would call it below average because your distribution is balanced and the ◇J is worthless. Partner shouldn't play you for a yarborough, and if he has

♠ AQxx ♡ AKx ◇ x ♣ KJxxx,

he will raise your 3♠ bid to 4♠. He would pass if you bid 3♡. Of course partner is sticking his neck out when he raises spades. You COULD have a much weaker hand. In responding to the double jump when your points are offensive and you have a good suit. Jump to 4♠ with

1. ♠ KQxxx ♡ xx ◇ xxx ♣ Kxx or
2. ♠ KJxxxx ♡ x ◇ xx ♣ Q10xx.

Suppose you hold ♠ Kxxx ♡ Qxxx ◇ xxx ♣ Qx. Your values call for a non–jump response (and without the ♣Q you would bid 3♡). The decision is close, but it is better to cue bid and risk getting too high than to guess which major to bid and perhaps pick the wrong one. Suppose partner has the hand previously shown:

♠ AQxx ♡ AKx ◇ x ♣ KJxxx.

Wouldn't you rather be in 4♠ than in 3♡? Partner would assume that you were asking him to bid his better major when you bid 4◇.

You hold ♠ AQxxx ♡ AK10xx ◇ x ♣ xx. What do you bid when RHO bids 3◇? Even a bid at the three level is risky. You certainly don't have the values to force to game. If you overcall, which suit should you bid? Despite the risk most experts would cue bid 4◇. They would assume partner has his share of the high cards—about 10 HCP—and consider it less dangerous to force the hand to game than to risk playing in the wrong suit.

You hold ♠ Jxxxx ♡ Qx ◇ Axx ♣ AJx.

WEST	NORTH	EAST	SOUTH
3◇	4◇	Pass	?

You have a pretty good hand, but it would be dangerous to bid more than 4♠.

You hold ♠ Kxxx ♡ AK10x ◇ Ax ♣ Axx.

WEST	NORTH	EAST	SOUTH
3◇	Double	Pass	4◇
Pass	4♡	Pass	4♠
Pass	?		

Since partner didn't jump directly to 4♠ or pass 4♡, does that mean that he is inviting a slam? Could he hold

♠ AQxxx ♡ Qxx ◇ x ♣ KJxx?

Most pairs lack a firm agreement regarding sequences like this, but I wouldn't interpret partner's series of bids as a slam try. With the hand just shown partner should just jump to 4♠ directly even though, in this case, he would miss a good slam. For this sequence partner should hold something like

♠ AJxx ♡ Jx ◇ Qx ♣ KJ10xx.

He wanted to give you an alternative to 4♠ if you didn't have four card spade support. He was hoping you would bid 5♣ over 4♠ if your hand were either

1. ♠ Qxx ♡ AKQx ◇ x ♣ Axxxx or
2. ♠ Kxx ♡ AKxx ◇ xx ♣ AQxx.

The moral from these last examples is that you should give partner a lot of leeway and assume that his cue bids are attempts to find the best trump suit, not slam suggestions. When the opponents open a one bid, assume that you are trying for a part–score, not a game. When the opponents preempt, assume that you are looking for the best game, not slam. With an unusually strong hand, you may change your mind, but these assumptions should apply to all borderline decisions.

If you have been playing any length of time, you already know how to respond to a takeout double. I have just a few observations. First, when the bidding goes

WEST	NORTH	EAST	SOUTH
1◇	Double	1♠	?

you don't need a spade stopper to bid notrump. You need a diamond stopper, but you can assume that partner has length and at least a stopper in spades for his takeout double. Bid 1NT with ♠ 10x ♡ KQx ◇ Q98x ♣ Jxxx. Second, the modern tendency is to jump or cue bid when a simple response would be better.

You hold ♠ Qxxx ♡ Kxx ◇ Ax ♣ xxxx.

WEST	NORTH	EAST	SOUTH
1♣	Double	Pass	?

This is a nice hand, but a 1♠ bid is enough. If partner has four card spade support, he will usually be able to raise when you belong in game. If he doesn't have four spades, even 2♠ might be too high. With one more spade you would easily have a 2♠ bid. Now add a couple of jacks:

♠ Qxxx ♡ KJx ◇ xxxx ♣ AJ.

and you are too strong to bid 1♠. 2♠ would be my choice. Some players prefer a cue bid, but you are not strong enough to force to game. Suppose you bid 2◇, partner bids 2♡, and you bid 2♠. When and how will the bidding stop below game? As we said a few pages back, partner will tend to overcall, rather than double, with three spades and five hearts, unless he has a very strong hand. So if partner doesn't have four spades, there will be no eight card trump fit and conservatism will be rewarded.

The most popular conventions for showing two–suited overcalls are the unusual notrump and Michaels cue bids. Both conventions are great in concept but often abused in practice. The whole key to their proper use is the ratio of offensive to defensive values.

You hold ♠ A ♡ Kx ◇ QJxxx ♣ Q10xxx.

WEST	NORTH	EAST	SOUTH
1♡	?		

If you bid 2NT, partner will jump to 5♣ with

♠ xxxx ♡ xx ◇ Kx ♣ KJxxx

as a premature sacrifice. He has the ideal hand—cards in your suits, length in one of them, and not much defense. If you held

1. ♠ x ♡ x ◇ AQ10xxx ♣ Q10xxx or even
2. ♠ x ♡ xx ◇ QJ10xx ♣ AQ10xx,

his bid would work out well. (The latter hand is not worth a 2NT bid except at favorable vulnerability). But if partner jumps to 5♣ and you hold the first hand shown above, it will be a disaster—a phantom sacrifice against nothing, because the 2NT bidder has his high cards in his short suits. It would also be a mistake, in my opinion, to overcall 2NT with

♠ x ♡ xx ◇ Axxxx ♣ QJxxx.

The minor suits are too weak. Give partner a typical balanced hand:

♠ K10xx ♡ Qxxx ◇ Kxx ♣ xx

and the opponents may defend against 3◇ doubled (with 24 HCP they should find a double) while they probably would have played 3NT or 4♠, down one, if you had left them alone. Bidding the Unusual Notrump should be somewhat constructive bid, varying from

1. ♠ x ♡ x ◇ AQ10xxx ♣ Q10xxx

to either

2. ♠ xx ♡ x ◇ KJ10xx ♣ AQJxx or
3. ♠ xx ♡ x ◇ AKJ10x ♣ AQJ9x.

With concentrated strength you have a good chance to outbid the opponents. Since you could have a fairly strong hand, partner should bid the limit of his hand. he should bid 4♣ with

♠ Axxx ♡ xx ◇ J10x ♣ Axxx ;

He should bid 5♣ with either:

1. ♠ xxxxx ♡ x ◇ xx ♣ KJxxx or
2. ♠ Ax ♡ xxxx ◇ Kx ♣ Kxxxx

In the first case it should be a good sacrifice. In the second case, he should expect to make it.

Michaels over a major shows the other major plus a minor. With a good five card major I believe that overcalling the major works out better, and the best use of Michaels is to show a four card or weak five card major plus a six card minor. Over 1♠ bid 2♠ with

1. ♠ x ♡ AQxx ◇ xx ♣ AK10xxx or
2. ♠ x ♡ Kxxxx ◇ AQ10xxx ♣ x.

The first hand is very hard to describe if you don't bid Michaels. Partner may pass a 2♣ overcall with

♠ xxxx ♡ Jxxxx ◇ AKx ♣ x,

but he would jump to 4♡ over Michaels. Over 1♡ bid 2♡ with

1. ♠ Jxxxx ♡ A ◇ AQJ10xx ♣ x or
2. ♠ K10xx ♡ xx ◇ x ♣ AKJ10xx.

All of the example hands are strong enough to risk playing your minor at the three level when you don't find a major fit, and overcalling the major isn't practical. But if the opponents open 1♡ and you hold

♠ KQ10x ♡ x ◇ A10xxxx ♣ xx,

it is much safer to overcall 1♠. When the hands are misfits, 3◇ could be in serious danger.

When you have both majors there is a good chance of outbidding the opponents in one of them, perhaps even making game. Over 1◇, I would bid 2◇ with

♠ AK10x ♡ AQ10x ◇ xxxx ♣ x.

The danger is that partner will think you have five card support, but what are the alternatives? Pass, when all partner needs is ♠ xx ♡ Kxxxxx ◇ xx ♣ xxx for game? Bid 1♠ when you might belong in hearts? Neither opponent will help by keeping the bidding open because he will have spade length and heart shortness. Double, and contend with partner's 2♣ response? No, I'd rather say, "I have the majors."

Some players say that Michaels over a minor should show either a good hand

♠ AKJ10x ♡ KQxxx ◇ AQ ♣ x

or a bad hand

♠ AJ10xx ♡ Q10xxx ◇ xx ♣ x,

but not an in–between hand such as

1. ♠ AK10xx ♡ AQ10xx ◇ x ♣ xx or
2. ♠ KQ10xx ♡ AQxxx ◇ Kx ♣ x.

With a good hand they force partner to take a preference and raise to game. With a bad hand they make their bid and leave the rest to partner.

I prefer a continuous range. It is now considered almost unsportsmanlike for the opponents not to keep the bidding open for you when you overcall. Many players plan how they can best describe their hand in two or three bids. But I hate to depend upon the opponents. It seems like an unnecessary risk to overcall 1♠ with either

1. ♠ AK10xx ♡ AQ10xx ◇ x ♣ xx or
2. ♠ KQ10xx ♡ AQxxx ◇ Kx ♣ x

when partner could hold

♠ xx ♡ Kxxxx ◇ xxx ♣ Axx.

Why not bid Michaels and raise partner's response? Or cue bid again as a strong raise with

♠ AK10xx ♡ AQ10xx ◇ x ♣ Kx?

If it is all right to bid Michaels with 4–4 in the majors (with very strong four card suits and a singleton in the unbid minor), it must be all right to bid Michaels with

5–4 in the majors provided you use good judgment. Over a 1♢ opening I would overcall 1♠ with

♠ AQ10xx ♡ Kxxx ♢ xxx ♣ x

since, unless something startling happens, that will be my last bid. Partner needs a good hand for us to belong in 4♡, and with a good hand he will bid without more encouragement from me. I would overcall 1♡ with

♠ Qxxx ♡ AKJxx ♢ xx ♣ Qx.

There is too much discrepancy between the weak four card suit and the strong five card suit; if partner has

♠ Jxx ♡ Qx ♢ xxx ♣ KJxxx,

we should be playing in hearts, not spades. However, with

1. ♠ AK10x ♡ Qxxxx ♢ Axx ♣ x or
2. ♠ Kxxxx ♡ AQJx ♢ Axxx ♣ None,

why not bid Michaels over an opening 1♢ bid? You could easily miss a game by overcalling when partner is short in your suit and has length in the other major.

Quiz Three

1. You hold ♠ 106 ♡ A105 ◇ AQ986 ♣ A62.

WEST	NORTH	EAST	SOUTH
—	—	3♡	?

What do you bid?

2. You hold ♠ K72 ♡ 2 ◇ AQJ10753 ♣ 106.

WEST	NORTH	EAST	SOUTH
3♠	4♡	Pass	?

What do you bid?

3. You hold ♠ AKQ7 ♡ 105 ◇ A6 ♣ QJ875.

WEST	NORTH	EAST	SOUTH
—	—	2◇*	?

*Weak

What do you bid?

4. You hold ♠ AJ95 ♡ Q7 ◇ K106432 ♣ 9.

WEST	NORTH	EAST	SOUTH
Pass	1◇	1♡	Pass
?			

What do you bid?

5. As North, you hold ♠ QJ ♡ A109xx ◇ AKxx ♣ xx.

WEST	NORTH	EAST	SOUTH
1♣	1♡	Pass	1♠
Pass	?		

What do you bid?

6. You hold ♠ 8654 ♡ QJ8 ◇ 54 ♣ A985.

WEST	NORTH	EAST	SOUTH
1♣	2NT	Pass	?

What do you bid?

7. You hold ♠ 8 ♡ AJ95 ◇ KJ85 ♣ K742.

WEST	NORTH	EAST	SOUTH
—	—	1♠	Double
Redouble	Pass	Pass	?

What do you bid?

8. Who's at fault for missing a good game?

WEST	EAST
♠ K8642	♠ AQ7
♡ K85	♡ 1073
◇ AJ1083	◇ Q94
♣ None	♣ QJ87

WEST	NORTH	EAST	SOUTH
—	—	—	1♣
1♠	Pass	1NT	Pass
2◇	Pass	3♠	Pass
Pass	Pass		

9. Who is at fault for missing game?

WEST	EAST
♠ AKJ7	♠ 6
♡ K104	♡ J
◇ 5	◇ AQJ743
♣ KQJ43	♣ 109862

WEST	NORTH	EAST	SOUTH
—	Pass	Pass	1♡
1♠	Pass	2◇	Pass
2NT	Pass	3◇	Pass
Pass	Pass		

Answers

1. **THREE NOTRUMP!** I thought it would be very close between Pass or 3NT, but a computer run of random hands showed a 3NT bid prevailing by almost a 2 to 1 margin. Any heart honor in partner's hand will give you a double stopper. East can often be shut out by ducking a round or two of hearts, which will give you the time needed to establish more tricks. Partner's fair share of the outstanding cards is about 10 HCP, and 8 HCP will be enough if they include the ♢ Kxx and the ♣ KQ.

2. **FIVE DIAMONDS.** There are few certainties in life. Perhaps partner can make 4♡ and any bid by you will result in a minus. But probably you can do better in diamonds. Partner doesn't have to have a solid heart suit for his bid. Could you blame him for bidding 4♡ with either

1. ♠ x	♡ AKJxxx	♢ Kx	♣ AJxx	or
2. ♠ None	♡ AJxxxxx	♢ xx	♣ KQJx?	

Your hand is worth many tricks at diamonds and very few tricks at hearts unless partner has a solid trump suit and can draw the opponents' trumps before running your diamonds. Don't confuse partner's 4♡ overcall with an opening 4♡ bid. The latter shows a good suit with few high cards on the side—a hand that will not play well in another suit. The overcall could be made with all sorts of hands.

WEST	NORTH	EAST	SOUTH
—	4♡	Pass	5♢

should be some sort of slam try in hearts, preferably an asking bid. You wouldn't try to find a better suit when partner preempts. When he overcalls and his alternative is to pass, he may have a strong suit, lots of high cards, or a combination of the two. Suppose partner has

♠ x ♡ AK10xxx ◇ Kxx ♣ AKx.

Your 5◇ bid would get you to a diamond slam when 4♡ might be defeated by a 5–1 heart break.

3. **TWO SPADES**. Not everyone will agree with me. If partner has good spades you will get to 4♠. If you belong in notrump, partner, with ♡ Kx(x) or ♡ Qxx, may bid it, and it will play better from his side. Bidding 2NT does not appeal to me because once your ◇ A is forced out, where will you get your tricks? Ax of the opponents' suit is a very undesirable holding for notrump. Axx isn't quite as bad since you can hold up until LHO is out of the suit. If you lead a good, clean life, whenever you overcall with a four card suit, partner will have at least four card support.

4. **TWO HEARTS**. What else? You are too strong to pass, and a 1♠ bid would show at least a good five card suit. Although partner could have only four hearts, it doesn't pay to worry about it; you should bid on the assumption he has five.

5. **TWO SPADES**. Partner shows a good enough suit so your doubleton queen–jack is adequate trump support. If partner has

1. ♠ K10xxxx ♡ xx ◇ Qxx ♣ Ax or
2. ♠ AKxxx ♡ x ◇ QJxx ♣ xxx,

you belong in game, and you can't get there if you pass. A 2◇ rebid implies a more distributional hand less suitable for spades.

6. **FOUR HEARTS.** You have to choose between 3♡ and 4♡. Your high cards will all be useful, and so may your doubleton diamond. It is not too much to hope that partner will hold

♠ x ♡ K10xxx ◇ AKxxxx ♣ x.

7. **ONE NOTRUMP.** If you bid 2♣ and are doubled, you won't know whether to look for a better spot and partner won't know when to rescue you with 4–3–4–2 or 5–3–3–2 distribution. If you bid 1NT first, partner will realize your subsequent run–out is to a four card suit, and he can cooperate in finding the best trump fit.

8. **WEST IS AT FAULT.** Many players would cue bid with East's hand instead, but I don't think it is strong enough since, IN SPADES the ♣ QJ won't be worth much. When West showed distribution including a diamond suit, East's hand improved. He had unusually good spade support for a 1NT bid, but the jump to Three Spades should mean SOMETHING. Most of a panel of experts disagreed with me. How can everybody be out of step but me?

9. **EAST IS AT FAULT.** Why didn't he show his second suit? Obviously a 2♣ overcall by West would have made things much easier this time, but it is not the percentage bid. West is too strong to be able to count on someone to keep the bidding open. If East had held either

1. ♠ Qxxx ♡ xx ◇ Axxxx ♣ xx or
2. ♠ xxxxx ♡ xxx ◇ AKxx ♣ x,

2♣ would be followed by three quick passes. Opener wouldn't reopen because he has club length.

Chapter Four

DOUBLES AND REDOUBLES

TAKEOUT DOUBLES AND PENALTY DOUBLES were the only two types of doubles around when I first played Bridge. The rules were simple and there was little room for misunderstanding. Doubles were for takeout at the three level or lower when partner had not bid. All other doubles were for penalty. Now there are many other kinds of doubles such as Negative Doubles, Responsive Doubles, Maximal Doubles, Support Doubles and various other conventional doubles (such as doubles of 1NT to relay to 2♣ and doubles of overcalls after partner's strong club bid to show a minimum number of points). More of these conventional doubles will be seen in this chapter. In fact, the pure penalty double is almost extinct.

With only a limited number of calls to describe your hand, reserving a call for a situation that rarely arises puts too much of a load on the other calls. It pays to assign meanings for bids (or doubles) that will occur frequently rather than adopt beautifully descriptive bids that you will seldom have a chance to use.

You hold ♠ x ♡ Axx ◇ Jxxx ♣ KQJ108.

WEST	NORTH	EAST	SOUTH
—	1♠	2♣	?

You would like to double for penalty and have partner pass almost regardless of his hand.

You hold ♠ xx ♡ KQJ9 ◇ AK ♣ Jxxxx.

WEST	NORTH	EAST	SOUTH
—	4♡	?	

You would like to make a penalty double and bar partner from bidding.

For every time you get a clear–cut penalty double you will get several general strength hands, with which you would like to show your strength and pattern; then let partner participate in the final decision. Even if your only concern were to penalize the opponents and you didn't care about reaching your own best contract, you would get more penalty doubles if you could say, "This looks like a good penalty double from my point of view; leave it in unless your hand is unsuitable," than if your double would mean, "I've finally got them; leave my double in no matter what."

You hold ♠ xx ♡ QJxx ◇ Kxx ♣ KQxx.

WEST	NORTH	EAST	SOUTH
—	1♠	Double	Redouble
Pass	Pass	2♡	?

If your double would require partner to pass, no matter what, you couldn't risk doubling. If your double suggests defending unless partner has a singleton heart or a freak, you can double and, perhaps 75% of the time, partner will leave it in. If you don't double, partner won't be able to double with either

1. ♠ AKxxx ♡ xxx ◇ Axx ♣ Jx or
2. ♠ AKxxx ♡ Kx ◇ Qxx ♣ xxx,

and a golden opportunity will be missed.

NEGATIVE DOUBLES

Many years ago Al Roth and Tobias Stone recommended Negative Doubles. Today, we wonder how we ever got along without them. When partner opens and RHO overcalls, low level doubles are for takeout rather than penalty. What is a "low level"? Some play Negative Doubles through 1♠. Others through 7♡. Only a small minority play Negative Doubles through 1♠. Those who play Negative Doubles through 7♡ are also a small minority. What they really mean is that all their doubles show transferable values; the higher the level, the more likely partner is to pass the double. The real difference of expert opinion is whether doubles of bids at the three level "guarantee" four card length in an unbid major. When the bidding goes

WEST	NORTH	EAST	SOUTH
1♢	1♠	Double	

or

WEST	NORTH	EAST	SOUTH
1♢	2♠	Double	

responder should have four hearts. Opener may jump to 4♡ with

♠ Ax ♡ KQxx ♢ AJxxxx ♣ x

over 2♠ (either bid immediately by the overcaller or after the overcall is raised). When the bidding goes

WEST	NORTH	EAST	SOUTH
—	—	—	1♢
3♡/3♠	?		

must North hold four of the unbid major to double? If so, he would have to pass with

1. ♠ Qxx ♡ Kxx ♢ xx ♣ AJxxx or
2. ♠ xxx ♡ AQx ♢ Kxx ♣ Qxxx.

In fact, with three small of the opponents' suit (so that he couldn't bid notrump), he would have to pass with 14 or 15 balanced points! It pays to double with these hands since when opener has a balanced hand, he can pass, and the double will increase the penalty; when opener has an unbalanced hand, he will bid and reach a makeable contract, perhaps after a preference by responder. These hands occur more frequently than

1. ♠ Kxxx ♡ x ◇ Qxxx ♣ Qxxx or
2. ♠ x ♡ KQxx ◇ KJxxx ♣ J10x,

with which you would like to compete and look for a major fit (after 1◇–3♡–? or 1◇–3♠–?) but don't want partner to pass unless he has a stack in the opponents' suit. My suggestion is that opener pass a three level double with a balanced hand and pull the double with an unbalanced hand. That makes responder's decisions easier. When the bidding goes

WEST	NORTH	EAST	SOUTH
—	1♣	3◇	Double
Pass	3♠	Pass	?

responder can raise to 4♠ with

♠ Qxxx ♡ Axx ◇ Kx ♣ J10xx.

Fortunately opener has bid spades, rather than hearts, and opener would have passed the double with

♠ Jxxx ♡ Kxx ◇ Qx ♣ AKxx.

To pull the double he should have something like

1. ♠ AKxx ♡ xx ◇ xx ♣ AQxxx or
2. ♠ KJxx ♡ KQx ◇ x ♣ Axxxx.

In the previous paragraph I said after a spade overcall, a Negative Double should show four hearts. Also, the auction

WEST	NORTH	EAST	SOUTH
—	1♣	1♢	Double

should show four or more cards in each major. Holding

1. ♠ Jxxxx ♡ AKxx ♢ xx ♣ xx or
2. ♠ AQxx ♡ Kxxxx ♢ x ♣ xxx

it is better to double than to bid your longer major. If West raises to 3♢ preemptively, you will be glad that you showed both suits in one bid rather than only one suit, and partner, with

♠ x ♡ Qxxx ♢ Ax ♣ AK10xxx,

will not be shut out because you bid his singleton. Some players adopt simple rules and follow them quite rigidly. According to them,

WEST	NORTH	EAST	SOUTH
—	1♣	1♡	?

a double would show four spades and a 1♠ bid would show five (or more).

WEST	NORTH	EAST	SOUTH
—	1♣	1♠	Double

would positively guarantee at least four hearts. The best solution is to imply these holdings rather than guarantee them, and partner should bid assuming that you have them.

You hold either

1. ♠ KQx ♡ QJx ♢ xxxx ♣ Q10x or
2. ♠ KQx ♡ xxxx ♢ xxx ♣ Axx.

WEST	NORTH	EAST	SOUTH
—	1♣	1♢	?

A double is supposed to show four or more of both majors while, with the first hand, you hold neither major. Still a double is the least of evils. When your hand is balanced, it is unlikely that the other players' hands will be wildly unbalanced. If the bidding should go

WEST	NORTH	EAST	SOUTH
—	1♣	1♢	Double
4♢			

partner would be justified in bidding four of his major with either

1. ♠ AJxx ♡ Kx ♢ x ♣ AKxxxx or
2. ♠ xx ♡ AKxx ♢ None ♣ AJxxxxx,

but partner's assumption (that you have four of each major) won't lead to disaster. It is extremely unlikely the bidding will go that way when you are balanced; even if it does, you could take a preference over 4♠ to 5♣, which partner should make. The most likely development is that West will pass or bid 2♢ over your double; partner will bid his major at a minimum level, and you will make two of a major on a 4–3 fit.

You hold ♠ xx ♡ KQx ♢ Kxxxx ♣ J10x

WEST	NORTH	EAST	SOUTH
—	1♣	1♠	?

It is better to double than to pass or bid 2♣, the only other choices. Partner should not worry about this possibility. He simply bids his hand assuming you have what you imply. Also, with 6–8 HCP and the wrong distribution you would pass. You need extra values to compensate for not having the distribution partner will expect.

As mentioned in Chapter Two, when you think you have an eight card fit you should show it, if necessary, at the two level, rather than pass to show a minimum. To bid at higher levels after a raise by RHO you need a little extra in high cards or distribution—but not much extra when you have a fit.

You hold ♠ KQxx ♡ xxx ◇ AKxxx ♣ x.

WEST	NORTH	EAST	SOUTH
—	—	—	1◇
1♡	Double	3♡	?

Bid 3♠. This might easily be a hand where both sides can make a three level contract. Over 4♡ I would bid 4♠ rather than allow myself to be shut out. Give partner

♠ AJxx ♡ x ◇ Qxxx ♣ Jxxx,

and both sides could make game.

A jump by opener, after a Negative Double, shows extra strength or distribution, but is not forcing. Only a cue bid is forcing.

You hold either

1. ♠ xxx ♡ x ◇ AKxxx ♣ AKJx or
2. ♠ Axx ♡ None ◇ A10xxx ♣ AJ10xx

After the sequences

WEST	NORTH	EAST	SOUTH
—	—	—	1◇
1♠	Double	Pass	?

WEST	NORTH	EAST	SOUTH
—	—	—	1◇
1♠	Double	2♠	?

With either hand jump to 3♣ in the first sequence and jump to 4♣ in the second. If you bid a minimum number of clubs, partner will pass, figuring he has already done his duty with 9–10 HCP.

On this controversial hand only Billy Eisenberg, out of seven panelists, agreed with me.

You hold ♠ J9xxxx ♡ AKxx ◊ Qxx ♣ None.

WEST	NORTH	EAST	SOUTH
—	—	—	1♠
2♣	Double	Pass	?

Some people wouldn't have opened the bidding. Most of those who opened would now bid 2♡, thinking they had as little as they could for their opening bid. But you have a good offensive hand. Partner probably has at least three clubs since East didn't raise preemptively; thus partner is probably short in spades; your void in clubs is a good offensive feature; your high cards, what few you have, are well placed; you have good trumps. With this hand I bid 3♡ and partner raised to 4♡ with

♠ x ♡ Qxxx ◊ KJ10xx ♣ Kxx.

Our opponents didn't get to game. Some players would raise a 2♡ rebid to 3♡ with the responder's hand. Others would not raise because of the potential misfit and the fact that opener might have bid 2♡ with a three card suit

♠ Kxxxx ♡ AKx ◊ xx ♣ Qxx.

or a weak four card suit

♠ AKJxx ♡ Kxxx ◊ xx ♣ Qx.

You hold ♠ Kx ♡ Jxxx ◊ Qxxx ♣ xxx.

WEST	NORTH	EAST	SOUTH
—	1◊	1♠	?

A 2♢ bid should deny four hearts. If you are strong enough to raise diamonds, you are strong enough to make a Negative Double provided you have hearts.

It is different when there are two unbid majors.

You hold ♠ Ax ♡ Qxxx ♢ Jxxx ♣ xxx.

WEST	NORTH	EAST	SOUTH
—	1♢	2♣	?

If you make a Negative Double and partner bids 2♠, a return to 3♢ would overstate your values. Raise to 2♢ and hope that partner, if strong enough to bid again, will look for a major fit.

A double, followed by a suit bid, is non–forcing.

WEST	NORTH	EAST	SOUTH
—	1♢	1♠	Double
Pass	2♣	Pass	2♡

South might have

1. ♠ xxx ♡ AQ109x ♢ Qx ♣ Jxx or
2. ♠ xx ♡ A109xxx ♢ Kx ♣ Qxx.

Both hands are too weak for an immediate 2♡ bid, which would be forcing.

Instead of playing a Negative Double followed by a suit bid as non–forcing, some players prefer to play an immediate suit bid at the two level as non–forcing and double followed by a suit bid as forcing. This treatment is called "Negative Free Bids." I have played this way with a couple of partners at their insistence, but I don't like it. Along with many other conventions and treatments, it works well when the right hand comes along, but creates problems in other cases.

You hold ♠ AQxxx ♡ KJ10xx ◊ Qx ♣ x.

WEST	NORTH	EAST	SOUTH
—	1◊	2♣	?

In standard bidding you would bid 2♠, planning to bid hearts next round. You are too strong for a non–forcing 2♠bid (if you are playing Negative Free Bids), so you have to double. Whether West raises or not, you probably won't be able to show both suits at a reasonable level. Nor does a double, followed by a cue bid in clubs, show 5–5 in the majors. While two–suiters cause the most serious problems, even a one–suiter may create a problem.

You hold ♠ AQJ10xxx ♡ AJx ◊ Jxx ♣ None.

WEST	NORTH	EAST	SOUTH
—	1◊	2♣	?

Wouldn't you be a little nervous about doubling? I would be. Those who play negative free bids say that they no longer need preemptive jump shift responses, so they might bid 3♠ with this hand. Since many top experts play Negative Free Bids, they must have some merit, but I prefer avoiding complications with good hands and to save Negative Doubles for hands where a penalty pass by partner will not automatically result in disaster.

A Negative Double at the one level should almost never be left in. The only exception happens when you are so solid in the opponents' suit that you want partner to lead a trump. Pass a Negative Double of a 1♠ overcall with

♠ KQJ10 ♡ x ◊ AKxx ♣ KJxx.

At the two level, passing the double means that the opponents have bid your second suit. If partner makes a Negative Double of 2♣, pass with

♠ Jx ♡ xx ◇ AKxxx ♣ KJxx.

You may not set the contract, but you probably will, and your alternatives are all worse. If partner has

♠ Q10xxx ♡ QJxxx ◇ xx ♣ x,

he should not double. Just as so–called penalty doubles of preempts should show offensive (transferable) values, Negative Doubles should show some defense. The higher the level, the more the hand should be suitable for defense in case partner passes. When partner opens 1◇ and RHO overcalls 2♣ you need to find partner with a very good hand, plus a fit, to make game opposite

♠ Q10xxx ♡ QJxxx ◇ xx ♣ x.

In the long run, it pays to pass and stay out of the bidding unless partner takes further action.

The worst problems arise when partner makes a Negative Double and you have no unbid four card suit or rebiddable suit of your own.

WEST	NORTH	EAST	SOUTH
—	—	—	1◇
2♣	Double	Pass	?

You hold either

1. ♠ AQx ♡ Kxx ◇ Kxxx ♣ Jxx or
2. ♠ AKx ♡ Axx ◇ Qxxx ♣ xxx.

Marty Bergen recommends bidding your cheapest three card unbid suit—in this case, hearts. Obviously having no good bid you must choose the least of evils. My inclination is to pass! Balanced hands often take more tricks defensively than you would expect, and partner may score a trick with the doubleton queen or jack of clubs. At IMPS, over

WEST	NORTH	EAST	SOUTH
—	—	—	1♢
2♡	Double	Pass	?

I would adopt Marty's solution and bid 2♠ with

♠ Axx ♡ xxx ♢ AJxx ♣ Axx

since letting the opponents score a game would be very costly. At matchpoints I would still gamble on a pass (as my best chance for a plus score). Perhaps my greater willingness to pass a Negative Double accounts for my reluctance to double with weak, distributional hands.

You hold either

1. ♠ AQ109x ♡ Axx ♢ xxx ♣ Q10 or
2. ♠ AJxxx ♡ AKx ♢ xxx ♣ xx.

WEST	NORTH	EAST	SOUTH
—	—	—	1♠
2♢	Double	Pass	?

Bid 2♠ with the first hand, but bid 2♡ with the second.

You hold either

1. ♠ xxx ♡ AK10 ♢ AQxxx ♣ xx or
2. ♠ xxx ♡ AJx ♢ KJxx ♣ Axx.

WEST	NORTH	EAST	SOUTH
—	—	—	1♢
1♠	Double	Pass	?

Bid 2♡ with the first hand and 1NT with the second. In none of these cases do I like my bid, but consider it less misleading than the alternatives.

Once partner makes a Negative Double, a later double will not change his hand pattern.

WEST	NORTH	EAST	SOUTH
—	1♢	1♠	Double
2♠	Pass	Pass	Double

South didn't double for takeout the first time and for penalty the second time. He might hold

1. ♠ x ♡ KJxx ♢ Axx ♣ Q10xxx or
2. ♠ xx ♡ Kxxx ♢ Kxx ♣ KQxx.

South probably has at most three diamonds since, with four, he would bid 3♢, having already shown hearts.

WEST	NORTH	EAST	SOUTH
—	1♢	1♡	Double
2♡	Pass	Pass	2♠?

South should have four GOOD spades and is suggesting play in a 4–3 fit. With fewer than three spades, North should rebid a minor since the Negative Double denies a five card spade suit.

Jeff Rubens and Roger Stern suggest an alternate treatment. With 5–4–2–2 or 5–3–3–2 distribution, including five spades, you would bid 1♠ with a minimum response such as

♠ KJxxx ♡ xx ♢ Kxxx ♣ xx

since you are too weak to do something else now and hope to bid spades later. With a game–forcing hand you would also bid 1♠. With

1. ♠ AQxxx ♡ Kx ♢ xxx ♣ Qxx or
2. ♠ KJxxx ♡ Ax ♢ Qxxx ♣ xx

you would make a Negative Double, expecting to have to bid spades at the two level next time. For example,

WEST	NORTH	EAST	SOUTH
—	1♢	1♡	Double
2♡	Pass	Pass	2♠

would be an invitational, but non–forcing, sequence. This treatment may be more useful than bidding 2♠ to show exactly four good spades. However, this treatment is not standard. In a Bridge World poll only three experts out of thirty apparently adopted this interpretation–and I say "apparently" because only Jeff explained what he thought the sequence should mean, and why. Also, this sequence is not needed if you play as I recommend. As explained later, 1♠ can be bid with first hand followed by a double of 2♡ to show a balanced hand with 9+ HCP. As explained in the next chapter, you could bid 1♠ followed by 3♢ over 2♡ as invitational with the second hand since you have another way to show a purely competitive hand.

What should these sequences mean?

WEST	NORTH	EAST	SOUTH
—	—	—	1♢
1♠	Double	2♠	Double

WEST	NORTH	EAST	SOUTH
—	—	—	1♢
2♠	Double	3♠	Double

In both sequences, rather than a penalty double, opener shows extra values and no other satisfactory call. In the first sequence opener probably doesn't have four hearts or a great suit such as

♠ x ♡ KQx ♢ AQxxx ♣ Kxxx.

This hand would be good in support of hearts if responder should hold five, while a 3♣ bid would make it difficult to get to a heart contract. However, if responder bids 3♣ or 3♢ over the double and opener now bids 3♡ this shows an invitational, rather than a competitive, 3♡ bid. With the weaker hand, he would bid hearts immediately rather than risk being shut out.

In the second sequence opener denies four hearts but could have various good hands. There is an implication since he didn't bid past the 3NT, that he hopes responder can bid 3NT. Opener might hold

1. ♠ Jx ♡ Ax ◇ AKQJxx ♣ xxx or
2. ♠ xx ♡ Kx ◇ AQJxx ♣ AQxx.

When you play Negative Doubles you are forced to pass with a penalty double, hoping partner can reopen with a double. Partner will strain to cooperate when short in the opponents' suit—just in case you have a penalty pass.

You hold ♠ x ♡ AQx ◇ Kxxxx ♣ AJxx.

WEST	NORTH	EAST	SOUTH
—	—	—	1◇
1♠	Pass	Pass	?

As opener you have an automatic reopening double. Perhaps responder can pass for penalty; if not, there may be some safe haven. Partner may hold

♠ xxxx ♡ Kx ◇ Qx ♣ Qxxxx,

which isn't the right distribution for a Negative Double. The fact that RHO didn't act suggests partner has spades plus other values. But reopening the bidding is often carried too far. Suppose your hand is

1. ♠ x ♡ Qxx ◇ KQJxx ♣ KJxx or
2. ♠ None ♡ Qxxx ◇ KQJxxx ♣ Kxx.

Quite likely partner has made a trap pass and is hoping you will double. But pass anyway! (Or bid 2◇ with the second hand.) Suppose partner has

♠ K107xx ♡ Kxx ◇ xx ♣ Qxx.

He will be delighted to pass your reopening double, but the opponents will make their contract, perhaps with an overtrick. Partner will be angry with you for not doubling when he has

♠ KQ109x ♡ Axx ◇ Ax ♣ Qxx,

but you should not play him for such a strong hand. Nor should partner pass, gambling that you will reopen, except at favorable vulnerability.

RESPONSIVE DOUBLES

Responsive doubles first applied when partner made a takeout double and RHO raised opener's suit to the two or three level. Seldom do you want to try a penalty double of a part–score when your strength is under the opening bidder, and his suit has been raised. So a Responsive Double is sort of a repeat takeout double, showing some high cards but probably no five card suit or good four card major suit.

You hold ♠ Kxx ♡ xxx ◇ Axx ♣ Qxxx.

WEST	NORTH	EAST	SOUTH
—	—	—	1♡
Double	2♡	?	

Double is more descriptive than putting all your eggs in one basket by bidding 3♣ since partner might hold

♠ AJxx ♡ x ◇ KQxxx ♣ Kxx.

A Responsive Double implies limited strength. More often than not, the Responsive Doubler will pass his partner's minimum bid. Consequently with extra values, the takeout doubler should cue bid or jump.

The Responsive Doubler can bid again. With

♠ 10xxx ♡ xx ◇ Axxx ♣ AJ10

a double enables you to raise if partner bids 2♠ and to arrive at a good contract if he does not. With

♠ Jxxx ♡ xx ◇ AJ10xx ♣ Qx,

a double is desirable despite the five card suit. A 4–4 spade fit might be found. Over partner's 3♣ bid 3◇. With the minors reversed you would simply bid 2♠. Over the Responsive Double West will usually bid a four card major at the same level. This is not misleading since a takeout double implies a four card major, not five. He will bid a minor ahead of a major if he has to bid at a higher level.

Because the Responsive Double principle works so well many players extend it to other sequences. How about this?

WEST	NORTH	EAST	SOUTH
—	—	—	1♡
1♠	2♡	Double	

A majority of experts use this double to show the other two suits. Ideally, it would show

♠ xx ♡ x ◇ KJxxx ♣ AQxxx,

but you don't get 5–5 in the unbid suits very often. Frequently the double is made with

♠ Qx ♡ xxx ◇ Axxx ♣ KJxx.

Double just shows high cards and a desire to compete. That is the standard treatment, but I suggest something different.

You will want to compete when you have a fit for partner more often than you will want to compete with a potential misfit. Responder's raise has deprived you of a cue bid to show a good raise to 2♠ with

♠ Qxx ♡ xx ◇ Axxx ♣ AJxx.

A 3♠ bid would be preemptive. A penalty double is not needed in this situation, but the best use of a double is to show a good spade raise. With a bad or ordinary raise you will simply bid 2♠. I call this a "cue bid double" since the double takes the place of a cue bid, which you can no longer make (at the appropriate level). A friend of mine calls it a "good raise" double. Similarly, after

WEST	NORTH	EAST	SOUTH
—	—	—	1♡
1♠	3♡	Double	

Double shows a good 3♠ bid, while bidding 3♠ shows a weaker hand.

WEST	NORTH	EAST	SOUTH
—	—	—	1♢
Double	1♠	Double	

When responder bids a new suit, double is penalty. Originally the purpose was to prevent the opponents from psyching and stealing your suit. Although it is not my style, some players would bid a "suit" with four small, even after a takeout double, which increases your need to be able to double for penalty. Undoubtedly one of the opponents will run, but you may find your fit and play a spade contract despite the opponents' having bid spades first.

MAXIMAL DOUBLES

WEST	NORTH	EAST	SOUTH
—	—	—	1♡
2♢	2♡	3♢	?

LHO has overcalled and RHO has raised. A Three Heart bid could be purely competitive. Is there any way to INVITE? Double should invite since you are unlikely to make a penalty double when the suit was bid on your left and supported on your right. Also, no other invitational bid is available. This is called a Maximal Double. What if there is room for a game invitation? After

WEST	NORTH	EAST	SOUTH
—	—	—	1♡
2♣	2♡	3♣	?

some players use 3♢ conventionally as a distributional game try and double as a more defensive oriented game try. Bid 3♢ with either

1. ♠ xxx ♡ AK10xx ♢ KQxxx ♣ None or
2. ♠ Axxx ♡ KJxxxx ♢ x ♣ Kx,

but double with

♠ Axx ♡ AK10xx ♢ K109x ♣ x,

not minding if partner elects to make a penalty pass. Discuss this with your regular partner. A majority of players play Maximal Doubles only when the suits are touching and no other invitational bid is available.

SUPPORT DOUBLES

WEST	NORTH	EAST	SOUTH
—	—	—	1♢
Pass	1♡	1♠	?

How often do you want to make a one level penalty double? Not very often!

WEST	NORTH	EAST	SOUTH
—	—	—	1♢
1♡	1♠	2♡	?

How often do you want to make a penalty double when the suit was first bid on your left and supported on your right? Not very often. It is much more useful to employ a double to describe some type of hand with spade support. Logically a raise should show four card support and a double should show three card support. On the rare occasions partner would like to pass for penalty

♠ Axxxx ♡ KQ10x ♢ x ♣ Jxx

your defensive prospects would be better when you have only three card support. Suppose the bidding goes

WEST	NORTH	EAST	SOUTH
—	—	—	1♢
1♡	1♠	2♡	2♠
3♡	?		

Partner, with ♠ KQxx ♡ xx ♢ KJxx ♣ xxx, would compete to 3♠ because of the double fit. If you had doubled, showing three card spade support, he would pass since your offensive prospects would be worse and your defensive prospects slightly better.

Where the overcall was at the one level or RHO supported the suit bid on your left, are the least likely situations in which you want to double for penalty. So you aren't giving up much not to be able to make a penalty double. When the bidding goes

WEST	NORTH	EAST	SOUTH
—	—	—	1♢
Pass	1♠	2♣/2♡	?

there is a much better chance that you want to double for penalty. Weighing what you gain by describing your spade support against what you lose by not being able to double for penalty, most experts think it pays to play Support Doubles in these sequences also. Ironically, you get to defend doubled contracts just about as frequently this way as you did the old way—provided you play the sort of doubles by responder which will be described later.

You hold ♠ x ♡ Kxx ♢ AKxxx ♣ KQ10x.

WEST	NORTH	EAST	SOUTH
—	—	—	1♢
Pass	1♠	2♣	?

You can no longer double but perhaps partner can to show a balanced hand with 9 HCP+, and you will pass the double for penalty. You actually gain when the strength is more evenly divided. When you have a good penalty double and partner is a weak, you will lose the opportunity to double for penalty. But suppose you hold

♠ xx ♡ Axx ◊ AKxx ♣ Q9xx

and partner holds

♠ AJxxx ♡ Kxx ◊ Jxx ♣ Jx.

You aren't strong enough to double for penalty, even if the double is for penalty (and that would be especially true if the opponents had bid hearts so an unsuccessful double would give them a game.) In standard bidding you would pass and partner would bid 2◊, which is a poor contract. Under the new way, partner would double and you would pass for penalty.

Failure to make a Support Double implies lack of three card support. However, when you wouldn't have raised partner's suit in an uncontested auction you are not required to double.

You hold ♠ 5 ♡ 873 ◊ AKQJ962 ♣ A10.

WEST	NORTH	EAST	SOUTH
Pass	1◊	Pass	1♡
1♠	?		

If West had passed, you would have bid 3◊ in an effort to get to 3NT. You should still bid 3◊.

You hold ♠ J54 ♡ KQ10 ◊ AQ74 ♣ J85.

WEST	NORTH	EAST	SOUTH
—	1◊	Pass	1♠
2♡	?		

With such a high ratio of defensive to offensive values you shpuld pass.

You hold ♠ K864 ♡ A75 ◊ AK5 ♣ 982.

WEST	NORTH	EAST	SOUTH
—	1♣	Pass	1♡
1♠	?		

A 1NT rebid best describes this balanced hand. Partner can still ask about your heart support if it is important. The decision is close. Change your spades to A864 and hearts to K75, and I prefer a double.

Suppose partner makes a Support Double and you have a weak four card suit with less than invitational values.

You hold ♠ A84 ♡ Q642 ◊ J763 ♣ 92.

WEST	NORTH	EAST	SOUTH
—	1◊	Pass	1♡
1♠	Double	Pass	?

This is an easy problem. Simply bid 2◊. You are lucky to be able to support partner's suit at the two level.

You hold ♠ Q642 ♡ A84 ◊ J763 ♣ 92.

WEST	NORTH	EAST	SOUTH
—	1◊	Pass	1♠
2♡	Double	Pass	?

2♠ may be as easy to make as 3◊. Besides, 3◊ should show at least invitational values. You have no reasonable alternative to bidding 2♠.

You hold ♠ J642 ♡ 8 ◊ K6 ♣ QJ10764.

WEST	NORTH	EAST	SOUTH
—	1◊	Pass	1♠
2♡	Double	Pass	?

If West had passed and partner had rebid 1NT you would have bid 3♣ to play. You should be able to bid 3♣, non–forcing and non–invitational in this sequence also.

If 3♣ is weak, what should responder do with a good hand? With five or more spades he should simply bid 4♠ or with 3♠ to invite game. With slam interest responder could cue bid or jump in a new suit. With

♠ A875 ♡ 984 ◇ A9 ♣ KJ74,

3♡ is a slight stretch, but the least of evils. The usual rule of new suits forcing does not apply because you are much more likely to have a weak than a strong hand. The opponents' two–level overcall shows a good hand, leaving fewer high cards for your side. With a strong, game–forcing hand with a four card major

♠ AJ75 ♡94 ◇ A9 ♣ KQ1083

you might have bid your minor suit, saving the major suit bid for the next round.

When opener is too strong for a single raise, a Support Double is not precluded.

You hold:

1. ♠ KJx ♡ Kxx ◇ AKQxx ♣ Qx
2. ♠ Qxx ♡ x ◇ AKJxxx ♣ AQx
3. ♠ KQx ♡ xx ◇ AQxxx ♣ AKx

WEST	NORTH	EAST	SOUTH
—	1◇	Pass	1♠
2♡	?		

With the first hand you should double. Partner will probably rebid 2♠, and now you can bid 2NT. As will be explained in a later chapter, an immediate 2NT bid is played as an artificial weakness bid (called a good–bad 2NT) by many experts. But even if 2NT were natural, the combination of a Support Double followed by 2NT is a better description of your hand. With the second hand you should double and bid diamonds next to show a good hand, long diamonds and three card spade support. With the last hand double and raise spades next. Partner will know you have only three card support.

DOUBLING PREEMPTIVE RESPONSES

What should a double mean in the following sequences?

WEST	NORTH	EAST	SOUTH
3♡	Pass	3♠	Double

WEST	NORTH	EAST	SOUTH
2♡	Pass	2♠	Double

In general, the double is for takeout since partner hasn't bid anything and the bid is below the four level. Should the general rule apply? Let's consider the first sequence. Why would East bid spades? If he had heart support he would raise hearts, even with a solid suit of his own. When the hands are as follows, the hand plays much better in the preempter's trump suit.

WEST	EAST
♠ x	♠ AKQJ10x
♡ KJ10xxxx	♡ Qx
◇ xx	◇ Ax
♣ J10x	♣ Kxx

4♡ is almost sure to make; 4♠ has little chance against good defense. With only a fair hand and a heart misfit, East would pass. East either has a very powerful hand an independent spade suit with no heart support such as with

♠ AKQJxxx ♡ None ◇ QJ10x ♣ Kx

or East is psyching with

♠ xx ♡ Jxxx ◇ Kxxxx ♣ xx.

Psychic bidding is not as popular as it once was, but it is most frequently used when partner has opened a preempt. When you know the opponents are cold for 5♠ or 6♠ and you have somewhere to run, if doubled, this is the safest time to psyche. I do not RECOMMENDING a psyche. If the opponents have their defenses worked out, raising hearts is best while the psyching gives the opponents additional options. I do recommend, to guard against any tricky business, that a double of a major suit response to a preempt be for penalty rather than for takeout. If the bid is serious and the opponents have overwhelming strength plus a misfit you don't belong in the bidding.

SLAM DOUBLES

The double of a competitively bid slam simply means, "Let's defend."

South has ♠ Jxxx ♡ KQ ◇ xxxx ♣ QJx.

WEST	NORTH	EAST	SOUTH
1♡	1♠	4♡	4♠
5♣	5♠	6♡	Double

There is a very good chance 6♡ will be set but South isn't positive, and he doesn't want his partner to sacrifice with

♠ KQ10xxx ♡ None ◇ QJ10xx ♣ xx

which he might easily do if South passes.

In a non–competitive auction doubling a slam asks for an unusual lead. Partner's first assumes you can ruff something. Only when a ruff seems improbable based on the bidding and his hand does he consider other leads—usually dummy's first bid suit. Incidentally, when you can ruff something, it pays to double, even when you can't see where the other trick will come from. If the opponents stop at six without knowing you can ruff the opening lead, they probably have another loser somewhere. Besides, you want partner to draw a negative inference: when you don't double you can't ruff the opening lead. Suppose the bidding goes

NORTH	SOUTH
1♢	1♠
3♠	6♠

and partner is on lead with

♠ xx ♡ QJ ♢ Jxxxxx ♣ xxx.

If you double, he will lead a diamond. If you don't double, he should lead a heart, rather than waste a tempo, trying futilely for a ruff.

You have read about hands where after a double to get a ruff someone ran, successfully, to 6NT. These hands are the exception, not the rule. Quite likely the opponents have bid a slam in a suit because they don't have twelve top tricks. They need to ruff some losers or they have a single stopper in one suit and a loser in their long suit. They can avoid your ruff by bidding 6NT, but they will be a trick or two short. Usually they are better off to stay where they are, let you ruff the opening lead, and hope you can't win another trick.

What about hands where you can't ruff the opening lead, and you think a specific lead would help your chances? Again you must consider the odds. If you think the slam will usually be bid (at matchpoints) your double has to work at least half the time to pay off. If you think the slam will be bid at the other table (at IMPS) your double has to work about 30% of the time to pay off. You lose about 6 IMPS when the doubled contract makes and gain 14–17 IMPS when the right lead sets the contract. When the slam won't be bid, the odds change considerably. You may lose nothing at matchpoints and only 1 IMP in a team game, compared to a 22–26 IMP gain when it works. Obviously you can't tell for sure what will happen at another table, but there are clues.

OPENER	RESPONDER
1♢	1♠
3♠	4NT
5♡	5NT
6♣	6♠

Apparently responder was hoping to get to a grand slam but stopped in a small slam. It sounds as though he has strength to spare, in which case all or most of the pairs will bid this slam. Also, if the opponents were interested in bidding seven, a favorable lead is unlikely to defeat six. You need a good reason to double in this sequence. Besides, you had a chance to double hearts and clubs. Partner will realize that you prefer a diamond lead or else you don't care what is led.

NORTH	SOUTH
Pass	1♢
1♠	2NT
3♠	4♠
6♠	

What kind of hand can North have to pass originally and leap to slam when his partner shows 18–19 balanced points? He must be very distributional and is gambling that his partner's values are favorably located. Quite likely other players would not be so optimistic. A lead directing double, if it improves your chances of setting the contract, has little to lose.

The bidding has gone:

WEST	NORTH	EAST	SOUTH
—	1♢	Pass	1♠
Pass	3♠	Pass	4♣
Pass	5♠	Pass	6♠
Pass	Pass	?	

With which of the following East hands should you double?

1.	♠ xx	♡ 10xxx	◇ AQx	♣ KJxx
2.	♠ xxx	♡ Qxx	◇ AQx	♣ 10xxx
3.	♠ x	♡ xxx	◇ KQ10x	♣ Jxxxx
4.	♠ xx	♡ Qx	◇ AK10xx	♣ xxxx.

Not with Hand One. Perhaps you could win the first two tricks with a diamond lead, but if so, you will probably win two diamond tricks eventually. There is no reason to think that South can get rid of one of his diamond losers. A double risks disaster if declarer is short in diamonds.

Not with Hand Two. As in the first example, if declarer has two or more diamonds, you will probably get your tricks eventually. There is no reason to discourage a heart lead, which is the normal lead on this bidding.

Yes, with Hand Three. A heart lead from partner's king could be disastrous since North doesn't have the ace of hearts on this bidding. A diamond lead will, at least, be safe. The fact that you hold a singleton spade increases your chances. Partner might have a natural trump trick, and only a heart lead would allow the slam to be made.

Not with Hand Four. Again, if your diamond tricks will cash, they should cash later as well as sooner. Nor do you mind a heart lead from partner.

As East, you hold ♠ xxx ♡ xx ◇ AQx ♣ xxxxx.

NORTH	SOUTH
1◇	1♠
2NT	3♡
4♡	6♡

You should double. Suppose declarer has

♠ AJxxx ♡ KQ10xx ◇ xx ♣ x.

Without a diamond lead he may get rid of a diamond on dummy's ♣AK. In fact, he might discard both diamonds on the ♣AKQ. Change your hand to

♠ x ♡ xxx ◇ AK10x ♣ xxxxx,

and you should pass. Your singleton spade is a danger signal. Partner probably has length in spades, and if you double, he will try to give you a ruff.

DOUBLING THREE NOTRUMP

Traditionally a double of 3NT said, "Lead my suit if I've bid. If I haven't bid, lead your suit. If our side hasn't bid, lead dummy's first bid suit." It should not surprise you to discover that my rules are more complicated than that. When you have bid a suit, doesn't partner usually lead it? Even when he has bid a suit of his own? The double should suggest a lead partner would not normally make. Yet, partner must apply logic to figure out what the double means.

WEST	NORTH	EAST	SOUTH
Pass	Pass	1♠	2◇
2♠	3◇	Pass	3NT
Pass	Pass	?	

What would West lead without a double? Almost surely a spade—for several reasons. Aside from the fact that spades have been bid and supported, East might have stretched to open 1♠ in third position just to suggest a lead. Suppose his hand is

♠ J10xxx ♡ AKQx ◇ Qx ♣ xx.

It is worth a speculative double to get partner to lead something else. When this hand was dealt West had

♠ Axx ♡ Jxxxx ◇ xx ♣ Jxx.

His best lead, if West doubles, is the ♠A to get a look at the dummy. A low spade could (and did) let the opponents steal a game.

WEST	NORTH	EAST	SOUTH
1♠	3♢	Pass	3NT
Pass	Pass	Double	

A double here can only have the old–fashioned meaning: "Lead a spade." East can't have a strong suit of his own. He just wants to be SURE partner doesn't try something else. East's hand:

♠ Q10x ♡ xx ♢ Kxxx ♣ xxxx.

Suppose North had overcalled 2♢ and East had passed. By not raising to 2♠ East has denied spade length (and enough strength to double 3NT). If he doubles 3NT, it means he has diamonds stacked, and West can use his judgment.

WEST	NORTH	EAST	SOUTH
—	1♢	1♡	1♠
2NT	Pass	3NT	Double

The double suggests opener lead his own suit instead of responder's suit.

"Surprise" doubles also ask for an unusual lead.

As West you hold ♠ Jx ♡ Kxx ♢ Qxxxxx ♣ Jx.

WEST	NORTH	EAST	SOUTH
—	—	—	1♠
Pass	2♠	Pass	4♠
Pass	Pass	Double	

What do you lead? Partner can't have a trump stack. What can he be doubling on? A void in diamonds! So lead your next to top diamond, as suit preference, to suggest a heart return. Partner holds

♠ xxx ♡ Axxx ♢ None ♣ Qxxxxx.

His bid is risky, but he has a lot to gain if it works.

East holds ♠ xx ♡ None ◇ AJ9xxxx ♣ Qxxx.

WEST	NORTH	EAST	SOUTH
—	—	3◇	3♠
Pass	4♠	Double	

When a player who has preempted doubles the final contract, it almost always indicates a void and a desire to ruff the opening lead. Again the bid is very risky, but the possibility of gaining two defensive tricks justifies the risk. Hopefully, partner will show, by the size of the heart lead, where his entry is (if he has an entry).

LEAD DIRECTING DOUBLES

You hold ♠ xx ♡ QJx ◇ AKJxx ♣ Qxx.

WEST	NORTH	EAST	SOUTH
—	—	—	1◇
1♠	Pass	3◇*	?

* Limit raise in spades.

Many players would double for a diamond lead. If they failed to double, it would indicate they didn't want a diamond lead. This could be the right way to bid, but I doubt it. The double should show a desire to compete, perhaps with

♠ x ♡ KJx ◇ AK109xxx ♣ Ax.

Another reason for passing with the example hand is that a double helps the opponents. The way I play with Ed Davis, 3♠ by the overcaller rejects the game invitation. Obviously 4♠ means he wants to play 4♠. But on close hands he can still show an game interest and let partner make the final decision. A redouble shows an game interest with three or more of the opponents' suit. If, by any chance, partner also has three of the suit, he will know that we are in danger of losing the first three tricks, perhaps by ace, king, and a ruff. If there is room, and in this case there is, a new suit shows game interest with a singleton in the opponents' suit while a pass shows game interest with a doubleton in the opponents' suit. If the overcaller passes or redoubles, his partner can sign off, bid game, or do something in between. This isn't the only way to handle the situation. There may be something better, but you can see that double gives the opponents extra options.

Similarly, double should serve a purpose after

WEST	NORTH	EAST	SOUTH
1♢	1♠	Pass	2♢
?			

After such a double, the overcaller should pass with a four card suit which he couldn't do without the double, redouble to show extra values when balanced; otherwise, make all the natural bids that were available without the double. Again the double should show more than just desire for a diamond lead since you were probably going to get that lead anyway.

WEST	NORTH	EAST	SOUTH
1♡	Pass	4♣*	?

* Splinter

If the 4♣ bid is a splinter bid, showing four card heart support, a club lead by partner is fairly safe. Even if he leads from his king into declarer's AQ(xx) one discard from the dummy won't help him. On the other hand, leading the splinter suit is not very aggressive; no tricks will be established. A double, instead of asking for a club lead, should suggest the lead of a diamond or spade, whichever you and partner agree upon (lower or higher unbid suit). Such a convention would be useful with AKx or KQ10x of the right side suit and nothing but small cards in the other.

Most doubles of artificial bids are lead directing. The four most common examples are doubles of Stayman, transfer responses, Blackwood responses, and cue bids. When you double a Blackwood response or cue bid, you should be pretty sure partner will be on lead. Otherwise, your double will help the opponents, not partner. If a king is missing, the opponents can tell which it is and whether their finesses are likely to win or lose. In the play declarer may adopt an unusual and successful line if you tell him what you have.

After a major suit opening, a minor suit overcall by partner, and a raise by responder of opener's suit the best use of a double is to show five of the unbid major and some sort of fit for partner.

You hold ♠ xxx ♡ KJxxx ◇ Qxx ♣ Qx.

WEST	NORTH	EAST	SOUTH
1♠	2♣	2♠	?

Doubling is safer than bidding 3♡, and partner can jump to 4♡ with ♠ x ♡ A10x ◇ Kxx ♣ AKxxxx.

When responder bids a new suit, especially at the two level such as in these auctions:

WEST	NORTH	EAST	SOUTH
1◇	1♠	2♡	?

WEST	NORTH	EAST	SOUTH
1♡	1♠	2♣	?

The defenders may have a good sacrifice, but they are very unlikely to have game. A double is not needed for constructive purposes. George Rosenkranz suggests that a double here shows a high honor in spades while a 2♠ bid would deny a high honor. This seems like a good idea. But when you have spade length and can afford to bid at the three level, preempting has a higher priority than making a lead directing call.

When you don't double a Blackwood response or a high level cue bid, partner will draw a negative inference.

WEST	NORTH	EAST	SOUTH
—	—	—	1♠
Pass	3♠	Pass	4NT
Pass	5♢	Pass	6♠
Pass	Pass	?	

If East passes, West will not lead a diamond unless his own hand calls for it. If East doubles, he is calling for a club or heart lead, probably because he has a void. Someone advanced the argument that the double asks for a diamond lead, and East didn't double for fear the opponents would stop short of slam. It doesn't pay to play that way; the opponents don't have that much confidence in your bidding, and it gets too complicated if partner can't draw the simple inference that you would have doubled 5♢ when you wanted a diamond lead. Suppose you had a diamond void or Kx. Would you be afraid to double for fear the opponents would redouble and make an overtrick? No, that is not a realistic fear. If the opponents are bidding a borderline slam, with a known nine card spade fit, would they elect to play a redoubled contract in a new suit? It is not often they would even be tempted, and they have no conventions to allow them to do so. A redouble would show a diamond control, not a desire to play 5♢ redoubled.

A good rule is that unless the vulnerability is favorable (and even then I have my doubts!), a double of a Blackwood response or a cue bid suggesting a slam is merely for lead directional purposes, and does not suggest a sacrifice.

This amusing hand occurred in a regional knockout:

None Vulnerable:

WEST	NORTH	EAST	SOUTH
—	—	—	2♡
Pass	4NT	5♢	5♠
Double	7♡	7♠	Pass
Pass	Double	Pass	Pass
Pass			

NORTH
♠ AKQJxx
♡ AJx
♢ x
♣ AKx

WEST
♠ None
♡ 10xxx
♢ Qxx
♣ QJ9xxx

EAST
♠ 109xxxx
♡ None
♢ KJ109xx
♣ x

SOUTH
♠ x
♡ KQxxxx
♢ Axx
♣ 10xx

West doubled, hoping to lead a diamond to his partner's ace and get a spade return. East figured that whatever his partner might have in spades (he failed to consider a void), 7♠ would be a cheap sacrifice against a grand slam. I sympathize with both East and West, but the result was down 11 for –2900 and a loss of 16 IMPS even though their teammates bid the grand slam!

Perhaps artificial preemptive bids (such as Namyats) gain in the long run, but they enable the opponents to compete with much less risk than over a natural bid. If RHO opens 4♡, a double by you runs the risk that partner will leave the double in, and the opponents will make it, or partner will bid, and his bid will be doubled and set. Consequently a double with

♠ Axxx ♡ x ◇ Axxx ♣ Kxxx

would be very risky. But suppose RHO opens 4♣, showing a good 4♡ bid. Now you can double safely, and when partner has

♠ KQxxx ♡ Qx ◇ xx ♣ QJxx,

he will bid 4♠ and obtain an excellent result. At this level a double should be for takeout of hearts, not just to show clubs. Naturally, if you double 4♣ and partner passes over 4♡, so will you. With a stronger hand

♠ AKxx ♡ x ◇ Axxx ♣ KQJx,

you would double again. And finally, you have a chance to make a penalty double. Just pass 4♣ and wait for the opponents to bid 4♡. Then you can double with

♠ xx ♡ KQJ9 ◇ AK ♣ xxxxx,

as you have been wanting to do ever since Chapter One.

PENALTY DOUBLES

A high level double after several rounds of uncontested bidding by the opponents has to be for penalty. What sort of hand would justify it? Usually it is a bad suit break that the opponents don't know about. If the bidding goes

WEST	NORTH	EAST	SOUTH
—	—	1♠	Pass
2♠	Pass	4♠	?

no one has to tell you to double with

♠ QJ108x ♡ Axx ◇ Axx ♣ xx.

The opponents may have bid quite reasonably, and their contract would make with a 3–2 trump break. Since the trumps split 5–0, 4♠ will have no play. No one has a problem in doubling with the setting tricks in his own hand. Suppose you hold the same spades but lack the two aces. You should still double. Partner will turn up with a trick or two, and you have two more trump tricks than the opponents were counting on. There is a possibility that the opponents will run to a better contract, but this danger is very remote because they have bid nothing but spades. Which opponent can logically run? And if the opponents run to 4NT, where will their tricks come from? That reminds me of a hand from an international match. The bidding went something like:

WEST	NORTH	EAST	SOUTH
—	—	2♠	2NT
Pass	3♠	Pass	4♡
Pass	6♣	Pass	6◇
Pass	Pass	?	

East held ♠ K109xxx ♡ x ◇ QJ109 ♣ xx and elected to double. South thought 3♠, followed by 6♣, asked for a choice of the minors. The bidding is peculiar enough so that East should have suspected a misunderstanding. Upon being doubled North ran from a no play contract to a cold 6NT. There is no resemblance between this situation and the previously discussed example where a double was recommended.

As West, you hold ♠ QJ98 ♡ xx ◇ xx ♣ xxxxx.

WEST	NORTH	EAST	SOUTH
—	1◇	Pass	1♠
Pass	3♠	Pass	4NT
Pass	5◇	Pass	5♠
?			

You should double, especially if your opponents are good bidders. South stopped at 5♠ after bidding Blackwood, because two controls were missing. He didn't know about the bad trump break. The North–South hands are:

NORTH	SOUTH
♠ 10xxx	♠ AKxxx
♡ KQx	♡ x
◇ AKQJx	◇ xx
♣ x	♣ KQJxx

As East, you hold ♠ KJ10x ♡ x ◇ Axxx ♣ xxxx.

WEST	NORTH	EAST	SOUTH
—	—	—	1♡
Pass	1♠	Pass	2♡
Pass	3♡	Pass	4♡
Pass	Pass	?	

Unlike the previous examples, a double here is not a "sure thing." The worst holding from your point of view is five small spades in dummy and a singleton or void in declarer's hand. However, the opponents shouldn't have any extra values since North merely invited game, and a two trick set is more likely than that the contract will be made. Partner might have a surprise trump trick (J10xx), and if the opponents need a spade finesse or need to establish the spade suit, it won't work. There is better than an even chance that the contract will be set whether you double or not.

Considering everything, a double will increase your chances of setting the contract. The double suggests that you have dummy's suit under control and may persuade partner to lead a spade rather than a club from the king or queen. It is possible, but unlikely, that declarer will avoid a trump loser by playing you for a singleton. This type of double suggests that the trumps are not breaking evenly, but you may have either length or shortness. Maybe even Qx if you are really diabolical!

You hold ♠ KJ10x ♡ xx ◇ KQJxx ♣ xx.

WEST	NORTH	EAST	SOUTH
—	—	—	1NT
Pass	2♣	Pass	2♠
Pass	2NT	Pass	3NT
?			

Declarer's spades are stacked against him, and it is unlikely that either opponent has four diamonds. The opponents have 26 points, at most, between them and quite likely 25. Even if the opponents have a double diamond stopper, you may still set the hand. A two trick set is probable—provided the diamonds run. If North had jumped to 3NT over 2♠, a double would be far too dangerous. Dummy might have 13 or 14 points, in which case he would surely redouble.

You hold ♠ QJ9x ♡ x ◇ J109x ♣ K109x.

WEST	NORTH	EAST	SOUTH
—	—	—	1NT
Pass	2♣	Pass	2♠
Pass	2NT	Pass	3NT
?			

Despite a lower point count and no long, establishable suit, you have an excellent double. You have a safe lead (◇J) and all the suits are breaking badly for the declarer. If the opponents could run several heart tricks you would have difficulty discarding, but there is no indication that hearts will run. I would expect this contract to be set at least four times out of five and would be disappointed if the set was only one trick.

You hold ♠ Ax ♡ Jxxx ◇ 10xxx ♣ Axx.

WEST	NORTH	EAST	SOUTH
—	—	—	1♠
Pass	2◇	Pass	3◇
Pass	3♠	Pass	4♠
?			

At matchpoints I would double. Partner probably has three spades and a diamond singleton or void. With a diamond lead the contract should be set more often than not, and the extra 50 points will be worth a lot of matchpoints. At IMPS the odds are not so good. If any of your assumptions is incorrect, or if the opponents run (perhaps for the wrong reason) to 5◇, you will lose much more than you might have gained.

IMPS, Not Vulnerable vs. Vulnerable
You hold ♠ Kxx ♡ xx ◇ KJxxx ♣ K10x.

WEST	NORTH	EAST	SOUTH
—	2♡	3◇	Pass
3♠	Pass	4◇	Pass
4♠	Pass	Pass	?

I actually held this hand and passed. Result: +300. My partner accused me of extreme cowardice, and he was right. Obviously, I have diamonds well under control. Since dummy can't run a suit, we will eventually get all our tricks. ♠K appears to be poorly placed, but dummy probably has a singleton spade, in which case declarer won't be able to avoid losing a spade trick. In fact, he might take a deep finesse and lose to partner's ten. The cards lay very favorably for us, but that should have been predictable! That partner had his bid at this vulnerability was the only unpredictable factor!

AMBIGUOUS DOUBLES

I have discussed all the doubles whose meaning is clear, whether the doubles were for penalty or takeout, and I mentioned a few borderline cases: penalty doubles of preemptive bids to show transferable values; Negative Doubles at the two level to show some defense, not

♠ x ♡ x ◇ QJxxx ♣ Q10xxxx.

At the three level they show enough defense so partner can afford to pass with a minimum balanced hand.

The way bridge developed, and the way your convention card is designed, all doubles after partner has bid or doubled are supposed to be for penalty unless they fall within a specific exception. If your double is not clearly for penalty, partner is required to alert. However, the modern tendency is to play many "descriptive doubles" that show a certain type of hand, and it is hard to put a label on them. If you had to use a label, it would be easier to define penalty doubles and refer to all other doubles as takeout, or perhaps as optional.

When Is A Double Penalty?

1. When the double is made late in the auction.

WEST	NORTH	EAST	SOUTH
—	—	—	1♠
Pass	2♠	Pass	4♠
Double			

If West couldn't double 1♠ for takeout, he could hardly ask East to bid at the five level.

2. When the doubler's partner has accurately described both his strength and distribution.

According to this rule, when South opens 1NT or 2NT and West overcalls, North's double should be for penalty. Ironically, some players do not play that way.

WEST	NORTH	EAST	SOUTH
3♠	4♡	Double	

When partner opens a preempt, everyone plays a penalty double of an overcall—even though his 3♠ bid may vary from ♠ Qxxxxxx ♡ xx ◊ xx ♣ xx to ♠ KQJxxxx ♡ x ◊ Q10x ♣ xx.

3. **When either of us has redoubled earlier.**
4. **When either of us has earlier made a penalty. double or a penalty pass of a takeout double.**
5. **When an artificial bid has been doubled.**
6. **When the major suit response to a preempt has been doubled.**
7. **In borderline cases, when the doubler is behind the original bidder.**

Recall a few pages back I said double of a Namyats 4♣ opening bid (showing hearts) should be a takeout double of 4♡. Technically it is a penalty double of clubs. But there is a wide difference between a penalty double showing ♠ xx ♡ xxx ◊ xx ♣ AQJxxx (mostly to indicate a lead) and a penalty double of clubs showing ♠ Axxx ♡ x ◊ Axxxx ♣ AQx (and encouraging partner to bid). So if you play as I recommend, partner should alert your double and, if asked, explain that your double is equivalent to a takeout double of 4♡, but it could be somewhat light.

WEST	NORTH	EAST	SOUTH
—	1◊	1♠	Pass
Pass	Double	2♣	Double

South's double should show that he was planning to make a penalty pass of the double of 1♠ AND he has reasonable defense against clubs—perhaps

1. ♠ KJ10xx ♡ Kxx ◇ xx ♣ Qxx or
2. ♠ AQ108x ♡ Qxxx ◇ xx ♣ J10.

Technically your double is for penalty. Partner should have club length for his reopening double; you intend to lead trumps to prevent spade ruffs in dummy, and you expect to set the contract. Whether you intend to set the contract with lots of good trumps or with your side values and partner's implied club length, it is still a penalty double. With ♠ Ax ♡ Jxxx ◇ xxx ♣ KQ10x, you would have made a Negative Double the previous round, so logically, you have to have good spades for this double. But if partner doesn't alert, you may have trouble with a protest committee, especially if your opponents are inexperienced.

Any double made on a later round of bidding is affected by what happened or failed to happen earlier.

WEST	NORTH	EAST	SOUTH
—	—	—	1◇
4♡	5◇	Pass	Pass
Double			

The double means that 4♡ was bid in the hope of making it rather than as a preempt. Perhaps West has

1. ♠ Kx ♡ AKQxxxxx ◇ x ♣ Kx or
2. ♠ AJx ♡ AKQJxxx ◇ x ♣ Kx.

With an ace (other than in diamonds) East should bid 5♡. With a yarborough or a couple of queens, he should pass and hope for the best.

As South, you hold ♠ x ♡ Ax ◇ KQJxx ♣ AQ10xx.

WEST	NORTH	EAST	SOUTH
—	—	1♠	2NT
3♠	Pass	Pass	Double

You should be unwilling to sell out to 3♠ since the opponents' bidding marks partner with some values.

With ♠ xxx ♡ Jxxxx ◇ xx ♣ Kxx partner should bid 4♣. When he has ♠ Q9xx ♡ K10xx ◇ xx ♣ xxx the double will pay off.

WEST	NORTH	EAST	SOUTH
—	—	1◇	Double
3◇	Pass	Pass	Double

South's second double just shows a good takeout double, perhaps ♠ AQxx ♡ AQxx ◇ x ♣ AJ10x.

WEST	NORTH	EAST	SOUTH
—	1◇	1♠	Double
3♠	Pass	Pass	Double

South's second double shows a good Negative Double, but he is prepared for North to pass with

♠ Kxx ♡ Kxx ◇ AJxx ♣ Qxx.

As South, you hold ♠ AKx ♡ Kx ◇ AQJx ♣ Q10xx.

WEST	NORTH	EAST	SOUTH
—	—	1♡	Double
Pass	1♠	2♡	Double

Your second double shows a very good defensive hand with only three card spade support. Partner would pass with ♠ Jxxx ♡ xxx ◇ xxx ♣ Kxx but I wouldn't define your second double as penalty.

As South, you hold ♠ xx ♡ AQxxx ◇ AJx ♣ xxx.

WEST	NORTH	EAST	SOUTH
2♠	Double	Pass	4♡
Pass	Pass	4♠	?

Double to show your 4♡ bid was based on high cards rather than distribution ♠ x ♡ KQxxxx ◇ J10xx ♣ xx.

Now for the seventh rule which is not obvious. The ideal penalty double occurs when you have trumps stacked behind the declarer. With Q10xx behind the bidder you will usually win two trump tricks. With such a holding in front of the bidder you will usually take one trick, at most, and perhaps no tricks especially when declarer is warned of a bad split by your penalty double. With these factors in mind, you seldom have a good penalty double at a low level when the bidder is on your left. Consequently low level doubles in front of the bidder should mean,"I have a good defensive hand, considering my previous bidding. Pass if you have trumps."

As South, you hold ♠ Q10xx ♡ Ax ◇ AKxx ♣ Axx

WEST	NORTH	EAST	SOUTH
—	—	—	1NT
2♡	Pass	Pass	?

Your 1NT bid showed a balanced hand and described your strength within narrow limits. As a general rule. if partner can't bid, neither should you. But you have a better hand offensively than partner could expect. If partner holds

1. ♠ Jxxx ♡ xxx ◇ Qxx ♣ Q10x or
2. ♠ Jx ♡ xxx ◇ Qxx ♣ Kxxxx,

it could still be your hand—even though partner couldn't bid over 2♡. So you double, mainly for takeout. However, if partner holds ♠ xxx ♡ 10xxx ◇ xxx ♣ Kxx, he will pass and hope for the best. If the bidding goes

As South, you hold ♠ Axx ♡ KQ10x ◇ AK ♣ 10xxx.

WEST	NORTH	EAST	SOUTH
—	—	—	1NT
Pass	Pass	2♡	?

This time, since you are sitting over the bidder, your double is for penalty.

As South, you hold either

1. ♠ Ax ♡ Q10xxx ◇ Ax ♣ K109x or
2. ♠ AKx ♡ AJxxx ◇ xx ♣ QJx.

WEST	NORTH	EAST	SOUTH
—	—	—	1♡
Pass	2♡	3♣	Double

Again, since you are sitting over the bidder, your double is penalty. With ♠ xxxx ♡ KJxx ◇ Jxxx ♣ x, partner should pull the double. If partner has a semi–balanced raise, he will pass.

Suppose the bidding goes

WEST	NORTH	EAST	SOUTH
—	1♡	Pass	2♡
3♣	Pass	Pass	Double

What would you expect South to hold? He should hold a hand like: ♠ Kxxx ♡ Qxx ◇ Axxx ♣ xx. He has enough strength to bid 3♡, but a double is more flexible since he has good defensive values. All he is lacking is clubs. If you hold

1. ♠ Ax ♡ AJxxx ◇ Qxx ♣ Q10x or
2. ♠ Qx ♡ AKxxx ◇ Kx ♣ J10xx,

you will be delighted to pass.

You hold ♠ 10xx ♡ xx ◇ AJ10xx ♣ AQx.

WEST	NORTH	EAST	SOUTH
—	1♡	Pass	2◇
2♠	Pass	Pass	?

Your 2◇ bid promised another call, but what call can you make? A double here has to mean no other action is appealing. You hold a mild to severe misfit with partner, no strong suit of your own, and no assurance of doing better if you play the hand. You might have even held ♠ Jxx ♡ x ◇ AQxxx ♣ KQxx. When partner leaves the double in, it usually means that he has a misfit, and the opponents can be set two or three tricks instead of you being minus your way. Double is best even when you have a spade stopper but no source of tricks once it is knocked out (♠ Axx ♡ xx ◇ AJxxx ♣ Kxx). Since you are sitting under the bidder, partner won't expect a spade stack, but in this sequence, where there was a Two Over One response to a major, you will usually have three, rather than two, in the opponents' suit. However, ♠ Qx ♡ xx ◇ AJxxx ♣ AJxx is possible.

Now that we have seen that a low level double in front of the bidder does not guarantee trumps, what should the following double show?

WEST	NORTH	EAST	SOUTH
—	1◇	Pass	1♠
2♡	Pass	Pass	Double

The best use of the double is to show 9+ HCP with a balanced hand—usually a doubleton in the opponents' suit. Opener can afford to pass the double with

♠ Kx ♡ Q9xx ◇ AKxx ♣ Jxx,

while if responder could hold a singleton, a pass would be too dangerous. Defending doubled contracts at the two level when the opponents have eight trumps seldom works out well. A second advantage is the negative inferences that allow you to find your best fit, especially when these doubles are used with Support Doubles.

WEST	EAST
♠ AJ9xx	♠ Qx
♡ xx	♡ xxx
◇ Kxx	◇ AQxx
♣ Qxx	♣ AJxx

WEST	NORTH	EAST	SOUTH
—	—	1♢	Pass
1♠	2♡	Pass	Pass
Double	Pass	2♠	Pass
Pass	Pass		

By not making a Support Double of 2♡, East practically denied three card spade support. So he can afford to bid 2♠ on high honor doubleton. With a strong five card suit West is willing to play a 5–2 fit.

WEST	EAST
♠ AJxx	♠ Qx
♡ xx	♡ xxx
♢ Kxx	♢ AQxx
♣ Qxxx	♣ AJxx

WEST	NORTH	EAST	SOUTH
—	—	1♢	Pass
1♠	2♡	Pass	Pass
Double	Pass	2♠	Pass
3♣	Pass	Pass	Pass

West doesn't want to play a 4–2 fit, so he runs to clubs. Since the double shows a balanced hand, East would look for a better spot without four card support. If opener's hand were ♠ Qx ♡ xxx ♢ AQxxx ♣ AJx, he would bid 3♢ over 3♣.

There are a few miscellaneous "descriptive" doubles that don't fit into any category previously described. Suppose you are playing "Hamilton" over the opponents' opening notrump and the bidding goes

WEST	NORTH	EAST	SOUTH
1NT	2♣	2♠	?

Partner's 2♣ bid shows a one suiter (any suit), and you hold ♠ xxx ♡ Kxx ♢ Kxxx ♣ Q10x. A double in this sequence says, " I have some useful high cards. Go ahead and bid your suit." Whatever suit he has, your hand should be good in support. Quite likely partner is short in spades, and your honors are well placed. If you pass, partner may lose his nerve and pass also if he holds

♠ x ♡ AJxxxx ◇ QJx ♣ Kxx.

You hold ♠ xx ♡ xxx ◇ AJxx ♣ KJxx.

WEST	NORTH	EAST	SOUTH
1♡	2♡	3♡	?

Partner shows spades and a minor, but which minor? Perhaps if you bid 4♣ partner will correct to 4◇ if his second suit is diamonds, but he might think you have an independent club suit. A double would not be for penalty just as either

WEST	NORTH	EAST	SOUTH
1♡	2◇	3♡	Double?

WEST	NORTH	EAST	SOUTH
1♡	Double	3♡	Double?

would not be for penalty. It should merely show some high card strength and suggest that partner bid his minor, jumping to game if he has extra values.

You hold ♠ Ax ♡ xx ◇ Kxxx ♣ Q10xxx.

WEST	NORTH	EAST	SOUTH
4♡	4♠	4NT	?

East could be bidding 4NT as a bluff, hoping to escape into 5♡, undoubled. On the other hand, it could be partner who has a weak hand

♠ KQJxxxx ♡ x ◇ Q10x ♣ xx.

A double will show partner that you have a few high cards so when 5♡ is passed around to him, he can bid 5♠ or double with a good hand or pass with a bad hand.

The 4NT bid made it easy for you to show strength without risk. (I can't imagine that East will decide to play

4NT doubled.) If East had bid 5♡, you would probably bid 5♠ with the example hand, but it could easily work out badly. Without spade support, but with a few scattered points

♠ x ♡ Jxx ◊ AQxxx ♣ J10xx

you would double 5♡, but partner, with an independent suit and a good offensive hand, would be allowed to pull your double.

Many people say you should decide whether a double is for penalty or takeout simply by listening to the bidding and applying the agreed partnership rules. As a practical matter, I strongly advise looking at your hand.

WEST	NORTH	EAST	SOUTH
—	—	—	1♡
Pass	2♡	Pass	3♡
Double	Pass	?	

If partner couldn't make a takeout double of 1♡, he can't ask you to bid at the three or four level. His double must be for penalty, and he must have an extremely good double. Not only does he risk doubling the opponents into game, but he was so sure that North would have to pass that he didn't pass in the hope of getting to double 4 ♡. I would be delighted to pass with

♠ Axxx ♡ None ◊ xxxx ♣ xxxxx

since my hand has an ace partner doesn't know about. I would not be delighted to pass with

♠ xxxx ♡ None ◊ xxxx ♣ xxxxx.

But I would still pass. Partner should know what he is doing. But suppose I held

♠ AJxx ♡ Jxxx ◊ Qx ♣ xxx.

Something has gone wrong. I don't think responder would raise hearts with a void. Would opener psyche an opening bid with a singleton, then rebid the suit upon being raised? Perhaps that is what I should assume if I had blind confidence in partner. And I do mean BLIND. Partner has done something strange, but he gave me credit for being able to figure it out. He has

♠ Qxxx ♡ None ◇ KJxxx ♣ QJxx.

Whether or not I approve of his bidding, I am not going to punish him (or myself). I'll simply bid 3♠. With

♠ AJ10xx ♡ Jxxx ◇ Qx ♣ xx,

I would bid 4♠, which should make, and it would surely cause confusion in the enemy ranks. If the opponents ask you what partner's double means, you can truthfully say that it is a penalty double. You don't have to add, "I can tell from my own hand that it was intended for takeout."

For that matter, it is possible to play two–way doubles in some sequences.

WEST	NORTH	EAST	SOUTH
—	—	—	1♠
Pass	1NT	Pass	2♠
Double	Pass	?	

Partner is usually doubling for takeout but he might be doubling for penalty. How can you tell? By looking at your own hand! If partner is doubling for takeout with

♠ x ♡ KJxx ◇ Qxxxx ♣ Kxx,

you will usually have at least three spades. If he is doubling for penalty with

♠ QJ98x ♡ Ax ◇ Axxx ♣ J10,

you will usually have a singleton or void in spades. The rule: Partner's double is takeout when you have two or more spades; it is penalty when you have a singleton or a void. Exciting, isn't it?

A 2♢ opening with a minimum opening and any 4–4–4–1 distribution is fairly popular now. Many years ago, the first time I encountered it, this convention broke up a partnership (which was on its last legs anyway).

WEST	NORTH	EAST	SOUTH
—	Pass	2♢	Pass
2♡	Double	Pass	?

When this new convention was sprung, the opponents alerted how they responded in an uncontested auction. Opener would pass 2♡ if that was one of his four card suits; otherwise he would bid 2♠. We had no opportunity to discuss a defense. Should the double be for takeout or penalty? I thought it should be for takeout. The auction was at the two level and partner hadn't bid. Why shouldn't the general rule apply? Partner passed, saying that since I was a passed hand, I couldn't be strong enough to force him to bid, knowing our suits would split badly. But if I had very strong hearts I might double for the lead, just as I would double a Stayman response. I said that since 2♡ was non–forcing (2NT being the only force), partner was marked with some high cards and if I had 4–1–4–4 distribution, I could afford to compete. There is probably some merit in both arguments but, at the time, neither of us could see the other's point of view. To me the clincher was that partner had ♡Jxx . If I really had a penalty double, opener would have a singleton heart, and he surely wouldn't pass 2♡ doubled with a singleton. How would his partner know to run? I had to write this book to get in the last word!

WEISS DOUBLES

I should mention an alternate treatment. In standard bidding each of the following doubles is basically for takeout:

WEST	NORTH	EAST	SOUTH
—	—	2♠	Double

WEST	NORTH	EAST	SOUTH
—	—	2♠	Pass
Pass	Double		

WEST	NORTH	EAST	SOUTH
—	—	3♡	Double

WEST	NORTH	EAST	SOUTH
3◇	Pass	Pass	Double

Partner can pass, but only when he has a strong holding in the opponents' suit. Larry Weiss has suggested that doubles of opening two and three bids guarantee at least two cards in the opponents' suit. With a singleton or void you bid the cheaper minor for takeout. That way, when the bidding goes

WEST	NORTH	EAST	SOUTH
3♡	Double	Pass	?

you can afford to pass with

1. ♠ Axx ♡ 10xxx ◇ Qxx ♣ Jxx or even
2. ♠ Qxx ♡ K10x ◇ Axx ♣ Jxxx.

If partner has ♠ KJxx ♡ None ◇ KJxx ♣ AQxxx, a pass might result in the opponents' making game. Playing the Weiss convention and knowing that partner can't have that hand makes a pass quite safe. You can nip the opponents for a two trick set when you have nothing your way, and perhaps a four trick set when opener has Qxxxxxx with nothing on the side. A typical hand for a Weiss double of a weak two bid is a strong notrump opening. Consequently a 2NT bid over the opponents' 2♡ bid shows a CLUB overcall. (3♣, the cheaper minor, implies a 4–1–4–4 pattern). The weakest part of the convention is that over a 3♢ bid you have to bid 4♣ for takeout and can't find a major suit fit at the three level. Also, in fourth position, I would like to double 3♢ with

♠ AJxx ♡ AJxx ♢ x ♣ KQxx,

hoping partner can pass for penalty.

REDOUBLES

The natural meaning of a redouble is, "The opponents have made a mistake. Let's increase our score." You are gambling that they don't have a better spot or they won't run. Like the double, the redouble seldom has its natural meaning at the present time. Among the possible meanings are

1. "It is our hand; if the opponents bid more we should either bid more ourselves or double them."
2. "I have three card support for your suit." (Support Redouble)
3. "I have a useful control in their suit."
4. "I am doubtful about this contract; run unless you have a suitable holding in the doubled suit."
5. "You should definitely run from this contract."

Just as doubles become more penalty oriented as the bidding level increases, redoubles tend more and more to their natural meaning as the bidding level increases.

Let's start with the most common sequence. Partner opens one of a suit; the next hand makes a takeout double and you redouble. The theory is that if you have enough high cards, you can make a redoubled contract at the one level, even with a poor trump holding (like four opposite two or five opposite one), and if the opponents run out, you can double them for penalty and set them badly. The traditional requirement was 11 HCP or more. Later, as inflation set in and everything was worth less than it used to be, the redouble showed 10 or more points. Any other bid was natural and non–forcing, perhaps quite weak, but it showed at least a five card suit. A suit bid implied that you had a weak hand and were rescuing partner. Experts eventually decided that LHO rarely passed for penalties, and when he did, it was more logical for opener to rescue himself than for responder to bid 1♠ over 1♣ Double when holding

♠ Q10xxx ♡ xxx ◊ xxxx ♣ x.

Thus, the modern practice is to play new suits at the one level constructive and forcing. By "constructive," I mean good enough so that you would have made the bid if there had been no takeout double. Since the bid is forcing, responder might bid 1♡ with

1. ♠ xx ♡ KQJxx ◊ AQxxx ♣ x or
2. ♠ xx ♡ AQJx ◊ xx ♣ AQxxx

on the theory that it would be harder to describe these hands after a redouble and a preempt by LHO in spades. The failure to redouble does not deny 10+ HCP, but in later rounds of bidding opener should consider partner's failure to redouble in deciding whether the later bid is forcing. Also, it is the general consensus that if your hand is primarily offensive with a long suit of your own or great trump support for partner, a redouble could create problems and a loss of bidding rounds since LHO would often preempt over a redouble. Therefore, a redouble implies your hand is primarily defensive, and it suggests that partner double for penalty if he can. Otherwise, he should let the bidding come around to you so that you can double. All doubles by either opener or responder are for penalty after a redouble. The redouble also creates a force. In fourth position each partner is obligated to do something if he can't double. However, if you have an exceptionally strong hand, redouble anyway like with

♠ AK10x ♡ AJxxx ◇ x ♣ Kxx

after partner opens a major and the next hand doubles. While partner tends to let the bidding come around to you, when he isn't planning to sit for a double, he should bid right away. First, he wants to describe his hand before he gets preempted. Second, if he does describe his hand by rebidding, he can then afford to leave a double in with a singleton if the opponents are foolhardy enough to bid again since partner has been warned.

Ed Manfield made a suggestion which many experts have enthusiastically adopted. When your hand and partner's are both balanced, the opponents' hands tend to be balanced, and you may penalize them at the two level or higher when both of you have three of their suit. But if you double for penalty with three of their suit, and partner leaves the double in with one or two, the result may be disastrous. His suggestion was that if responder passes the takeout double and doubles next round, he is showing 10+ HCP with a balanced hand and at least three cards in the opponents' suit. At the two level opener would need three cards in the opponents' suit to leave the double in, and even at the three level, he would need a suitable balanced hand to pass with a doubleton. Therefore, a redouble would imply four or more cards in each of two unbid suits.

You hold ♠ AJxxx ♡ xx ◇ Qx ♣ K10xx.

WEST	NORTH	EAST	SOUTH
—	1♡	Double	?

This would be an ideal redouble. You intend to double if the opponents bid a black suit, and you hope partner can double if they bid diamonds. No matter what you do, partner shouldn't pass a double with a singleton in the opponents' suit unless he has had an opportunity to warn you.

You hold ♠ x ♡ AKxxx ◇ KQ10xx ♣ xx.

WEST	NORTH	EAST	SOUTH
—	—	—	1♡
Double	Redouble	1♠	?

Bid 2◇. Even if partner should double 1♠, you wouldn't leave it in, so why not use the opportunity to describe your hand? Some players say that bidding immediately is weak; passing and pulling the double shows a stronger hand. I don't make that distinction. With a really good offensive hand, I would jump, which must be forcing. But I would rebid 2◇ with

1. ♠ x ♡ AKxxx ◇ KJxxx ♣ xx or
2. ♠ x ♡ AKJxx ◇ KQJxx ♣ xx

on the theory that the sooner partner knows about my hand pattern, the better placed he will be. I do recommend that a distinction of sorts be made by responder with somewhat balanced hands so that the opponents are not likely to preempt us. If responder's pass, followed by a double, shows 10+ balanced points, what does a pass, followed by some other action mean? When you have a weak hand, you will either want to stay out of the auction altogether or bid right away. Thus a pass, followed by later action, shows a fair hand of some kind.

You hold either

1. ♠ Qxx ♡ xx ◇ Kxxx ♣ xxxx or
2. ♠ Qxx ♡ Ax ◇ K10xx ♣ xxxx

WEST	NORTH	EAST	SOUTH
—	1♠	Double	?

With the first hand you would bid 2♠. It would be too dangerous to conceal your spade support and plan to show it later, probably at a higher level. If you bid the second hand the same as with the first hand, partner won't know what to do. The recommended action with the second hand is to pass, intending to support spades later. Since you have 9 HCP and a balanced hand, it is very unlikely that LHO will preempt you. If you have to show your spade support at the three level (unlikely), it should still be safe. With FOUR card support (except with 4–3–3–3) or an unbalanced hand, you will tend to bid right away to avoid the danger of being preempted. Holding

♠ xxxx ♡ Axx ◇ Axx ♣ Qxx

you don't anticipate a preempt, so it looks safe and best to pass and plan to support spades next round at the three level, if necessary. Bid a Jordan 2NT with

♠ QJxx ♡ x ◇ Kxxxx ♣ Q10x,

so partner will know what to do if LHO bids 4♡. Take away either queen while leaving the same distribution, and you should jump to 3♠. You would also bid 3♠ with a weaker hand, but it is more important to crowd the bidding, while showing support, than to try to show exactly how many points you have or don't have.

Pass, followed by a bid of a new suit, shows a fairly good hand. It requires good bidding judgment to know when to try this approach since you risk having to bid at a higher level than you intended.

You hold ♠ xxx ♡ xx ◇ Ax ♣ AQ98xx.

WEST	NORTH	EAST	SOUTH
—	1♡	Double	?

If you bid 2♣ you might miss a game. Partner would pass with ♠ Axx ♡ AKxxx ◇ xxx ♣Kx, expecting you to be about an ace weaker. If you redouble, you will create a forcing situation. After

WEST	NORTH	EAST	SOUTH
1♡	Double	Redouble	2◇
Pass	Pass	3♣	

ths 3♣ bid would be forcing. An immediate 3♣ bid would be preemptive although some people play 3♣ shows a limit raise in partner's suit with values in clubs. So what is left? The solution is to pass and bid clubs next round. There is no reason to believe that you won't be able to bid clubs at the two or three level, which you won't mind doing if the bid isn't forcing.

Over 1◇ doubled it is safe to pass, and plan to bid spades next round with ♠ AJ9xxx ♡ Kx ◇ xx ♣ Jxx. Exchange your majors and it is better to bid 1♡ right away rather than risk having to bid hearts at the three or four level.

The same principles apply, even more strongly, when the opponents redouble. Presumably the opponents have the balance of strength. Any jump bid is preemptive.

You hold ♠ J10xxxx ♡ xx ◇ xxx ♣ Jx.

WEST	NORTH	EAST	SOUTH
1◇	Double	Redouble	?

Bid 2♠. So what should you do with a good hand? You can hardly have a good hand if the other players all have their bids, but when you do, pass and bid later. With

♠ Qxxx ♡ Kxxx ◇ xx ♣Qxx,

pass and raise whatever suit partner bids. Exchange your ♣Q for the ♣A and you would let partner rescue himself and give him a jump raise if he bids a major, and cue bid if he bids 2♣.

You hold ♠ xxxxx ♡ K10x ◇ AJx ♣ xx.

WEST	NORTH	EAST	SOUTH
—	—	1♣	Pass
1♠	Double	Redouble	?

Assume that the redouble was not a Support Redouble. Partner shows the red suits, and you have a super hand, perhaps even a ruffing value in clubs. Either responder is extremely light for his bid or the redouble was a bluff. Your most logical action is to pass and let partner rescue himself. If he bids 2♡, he must have at least five, and you can raise to 4♡ or cue bid to show a very strong raise to three. If he bids 2♢, cue bid to show an interest in greater things. Partner actually held

♠ Q ♡ AQxxx ♢ K10xx ♣ Axx,

which is roughly what you would expect—except that he could have held five diamonds and only four hearts. Since partner has to rescue himself, you have no reason to make an immediate cue bid. You can save your cue bid till next round. Consequently,

WEST	NORTH	EAST	SOUTH
—	—	1♣	Pass
1♠	Double	Redouble	2♣

should show clubs. It would be nice to hold a good six card suit, but ♠ Jxxx ♡ xx ♢ xx ♣ KJ10xx would be sufficient to suggest a club contract. North would be glad to pass with the hand shown above.

A few paragraphs back I said when the bidding went

WEST	NORTH	EAST	SOUTH
—	—	—	1♣
Double	Pass	Pass	?

South could rescue himself. If his hand were either

1. ♠ AKxx ♡ Qxx ♢ Jxx ♣ Kxx or
2. ♠ AKxx ♡ Qx ♢ xxx ♣ Axxx,

South would assume that clubs were badly stacked, and there was probably a better spot. This is a logical place for a S.O.S. Redouble. If South really had a hand with which he expected to make 1♣ doubled

1. ♠ AKx ♡ xx ◇ xx ♣ KQJ10xx or
2. ♠ xx ♡ AQJx ◇ x ♣ AQ108xx,

not that either hand is likely on the bidding, it wouldn't make good sense to redouble in the hope of playing it there. Suppose you hold either balanced hand and the bidding goes

WEST	NORTH	EAST	SOUTH
—	—	—	1♣
Pass	Pass	Double	?

Now it would unwise to redouble. For one thing, West may not pass for penalties, and if he does, partner is the logical person to run if anyone should run. If he has no good suit, he can run by redoubling! A redouble by opener here should mean, "I have a very strong hand. Despite the fact that you couldn't keep the bidding open, it is possible that we can outbid or penalize the opponents." Typical hands for the redouble would be

1. ♠ AKxx ♡ KQxx ◇ x ♣ AKxx or
2. ♠ KQ10x ♡x ◇ AKx ♣ AQxxx.

Partner can now cooperate in the bidding if he holds

♠ Jxxxx ♡ xx ◇ Qxxx ♣ Jx

for example. You might even get to game. Suppose the bidding goes

WEST	NORTH	EAST	SOUTH
—	—	—	1◇
Pass	Pass	Double	Redouble
?			

A pass should mean you were planning to pass 1◇ doubled for penalty. Otherwise, the opponents could bluff you. The fact you are sitting behind declarer makes your pass penalty. Don't confuse this auction with

WEST	NORTH	EAST	SOUTH
—	—	—	1◇
Double	Redouble	?	

In this position you don't get a hand suitable for a penalty pass one time out of 100. A pass merely means that you have no decent suit to bid or it could mean that you have a fair hand and want to let partner rescue himself, after which you will raise him or bid a suit of your own. You will recall that many low level doubles are for penalty when sitting over the bidder but are for takeout when sitting under the bidder. A pass of a redouble should be treated the same way.

A few pages ago I said that after an opening bid and a takeout double, responder could redouble to show high cards, even when short in his partner's suit. The high cards would compensate for a weak trump holding. In theory this could be very dangerous when the opening bid is a minor. Suppose the hands are as follows:

[SEE THE NEXT PAGE]

Would you like to play this hand in 1♣ redoubled? Of course not! Does that mean that responder shouldn't redouble? Or that opener must run if East passes? No, not unless the opponents change their system and play East's pass for penalty. West, the takeout doubler, will be short in the suit. Even when North–South are in trouble, he won't know it. As a practical matter, responder can afford to redouble to show a good defensive hand and South can afford to pass with a three card suit since the opponents' conventions are not designed to cater to this situation. If they change their system, it will cost them in the long run. Incidentally, West should alert you if East's pass is for penalty since that is not the standard treatment.

NORTH
♠ AQ10x
♡ KJxx
◇ Jxxx
♣ x

WEST		EAST
♠ Jxxx		♠ xx
♡ Q10xx		♡ x
◇ AKx		◇ xxx
♣ Kx		♣ QJ10xxxx

SOUTH
♠ Kxx
♡ Axxx
◇ Qxx
♣ Axx

While responder can afford to redouble a natural bid without trump support, the situation is entirely different when the opening bid is artificial. Suppose South opens 2◇, Flannery, or showing a three suiter with a singleton or void in diamonds. In that case the redouble must logically show a willingness to play 2◇ redoubled and would guarantee diamond length and strength.

Another reason the redouble must show length is that a double of a natural opening bid is a takeout double. A double of an artificial bid usually shows the suit and is a penalty double—or it may show a strong, balanced hand. In either case the defenders know opener doesn't have a diamond suit himself and diamonds may be the defenders' best suit. Consequently, responder cannot afford to redouble an artificial 2◇ opening with

♠ Kxx ♡ Kx ◇ Axxx ♣ Kxxx,

merely to show a good hand.

As North, you hold ♠ xx ♡ x ♢ Jxxxxx ♣ Jxxx.

WEST	NORTH	EAST	SOUTH
—	—	—	2♢*
Double	?		

* Flannery

You should pass. This hand is a nightmare, and 2♢ doubled is probably the least odious contract. With

♠ Axx ♡ x ♢ KJ9xx ♣ Q10xx,

2♢ redoubled is the only probable game. The play will be exciting, but the reward would justify the risk. If the opponents lose their nerve and run, you know you have taken the right action and you will double!

Some people play all low level redoubles in fourth position after Double–Pass–Pass for rescue. The theory is that making any doubled contract will be a top or tie for top and, at matchpoints, you don't need to redouble. As a general rule, this is true. At IMPS you might want to try for a big score. Making 1NT doubled would gain 3 IMPS compared to making 1NT undoubled. Making 1NT redoubled would gain 10–12 IMPS. This will be discussed in more detail later.

Recall my suggestion that a redouble here

WEST	NORTH	EAST	SOUTH
—	—	—	1♣
1♠	Pass	3♣	Double
Redouble			

would show game interest in spades, but with length in the opponents' suit. You may prefer some other meaning. But I don't think you would want to suggest playing 3♣ redoubled when you have a known spade fit and the opponents, not only bid clubs, but doubled the cue bid.

When a cue bid, suggesting slam, is doubled, a redouble should show a useful control in the suit.

WEST	NORTH	EAST	SOUTH
—	—	—	1♡
Pass	3♡	Pass	4♣
Pass	4◇	Double	?

Partner probably has the ◇A. If he has Axx, he may be worried about a diamond lead. A redouble by you, besides showing continued slam interest, should show a diamond control, probably a second round control. Since East should have a high diamond honor for his double, your second round control is more likely to be a singleton than the king.

WEST	NORTH	EAST	SOUTH
—	—	—	1♡
Pass	4♣	Double	

If 4♣ is a splinter bid, the ♣K would be a wasted card. In this sequence a redouble should guarantee the ace.

You hold ♠ Axx ♡ Kx ◇ Jxx ♣ KQxxx.

WEST	NORTH	EAST	SOUTH
—	—	—	1♣
Pass	1♡	Pass	1NT
Pass	3NT	Double	?

You should redouble. Otherwise partner would run with

♠ Kx ♡ 109xx ◇ AQx ♣ Axxx.

I would have responded 2NT immediately with this hand, but that is beside the point. Some players would redouble any time they held a heart stopper, even with a weaker hand such as ♠ Qxx ♡ Kx ◇ QJx ♣ Axxxx. That looks rather dangerous, but there is an advantage in knowing, if responder has no heart stopper and opener fails to redouble, responder must run.

Suppose opener passes the double and the bidding comes back to responder. What should he do with

♠ KQ ♡ Qxxx ◊ xx ♣ AJxxx?

Playing as recommended, he knows opener doesn't have a heart stopper, but he could hold ♡Jx or xxx. A redouble by responder should express doubt saying "Unless you have some help in hearts, we had better run." If opener runs, it should be to clubs having supposedly shown a balanced hand. Responder can then correct to diamonds with

♠ Ax ♡ 10xxxx ◊ AK109x ♣ J.

In some sequences, such as a few just described, it is logical to redouble 3NT to show doubt that we are in the right contract unless partner has a crucial holding.

What should a redouble mean here?

WEST	NORTH	EAST	SOUTH
—	—	—	1NT
2♠	3NT	Double	?

Incidentally, you are playing Lebensohl. Partner's 3NT bid shows the values for 3NT but denies a spade stopper. If partner denies a spade stopper, and you don't have one either, you obviously don't belong in 3NT. Opener should run, and if he passes, he should guarantee a stopper. A redouble should show a DOUBLE spade stopper. Suppose opener holds

♠ QJ9x ♡ A10x ◊ KQx ♣ K10x.

He wants to play 3NT. If he passes, partner, with

♠ x ♡ QJx ◊ Jxx ♣ AJxxxx,

might get nervous and run to 4♣. East probably doubled with the ♠ Ax or ♠ Kx. From partner's point of view, even a single stopper might not be good enough unless you reassure him by redoubling. In this sequence a redouble should mean, "I want to play 3NT redoubled." What else could it mean? You may not remember this specific sequence. What is important is that when a bid can have only one logical meaning, you should trust partner to figure out what that meaning is. I would rather be set 1600 than to insult partner by pulling the redouble. Incidentally I was set 1600!

Some players like definite rules such as redoubles in fourth position at the one or two level are for rescue; redoubles at higher levels are natural. Redoubles in second position show strength. These are good general rules, but I prefer to rely upon logic.

WEST	NORTH	EAST	SOUTH
—	—	—	1NT
Double	2♣	Double	Pass
Pass	Redouble?		

Whatever notrump range South has, there is something strange–sounding about this sequence, and the weaker the notrump range, the stranger it is. The opponents both bid strongly. On the first round partner would have passed or redoubled with a decent hand. His 2♣ bid showed weakness. If partner thought he could make 2♣ doubled, would he be so greedy as to redouble? I don't think so. Partner might have

♠ Jxxx ♡ xxxx ◇ xxxx ♣ x,

and he figured that 1NT doubled would be a poor spot, and we probably could do better elsewhere. It is perfectly safe for partner to bid this way, and I won't let him down.

WEST	NORTH	EAST	SOUTH
—	—	—	1◇
4♡	4♠	Double	?

A redouble could not possibly request partner to run. You don't know as much about his hand as he knows about yours. Perhaps he has nothing but a long spade suit and nowhere else to play the hand. If I held ♠AQ10, almost regardless of the rest of my hand, I would redouble. Perhaps partner has

♠ xxxxxx ♡ Ax ◇ Jxxx ♣ A,

and if you don't redouble, he may run to 5◇.

WEST	NORTH	EAST	SOUTH
—	—	—	1NT
Pass	2◇*	Double	Pass
Pass	Redouble		

*Jacoby transfer

This sequence should be discussed with your regular partner. It is very unlikely that East would double if North's second suit were diamonds. Many experts play this as a heart transfer despite the fact that South has shown a doubleton, after which new suits are forcing and notrump bids guarantee diamond stoppers. Immediate bids by North are weaker or deny a diamond stopper.

When the opponents double for penalty or make a penalty pass of a takeout double, a redouble says either, "The opponents have made a mistake," or, "Perhaps we should run," or "We definitely should run to another contract." Examples have been given of all three situations, and a few rules plus logic should tell you which meaning applies.

Suppose the opponents make some sort of takeout double which includes a Responsive Double, Maximal Double or Support Double. If the opponents are not doubling for penalties, and a leave–in is remote, a redouble should suggest what to do on the next round of bidding.

You hold ♠ xxx ♡ xx ◇ Kxx ♣ QJxxx.

WEST	NORTH	EAST	SOUTH
1♠	2◇	Double	?

You would bid 3◇ right away as a mild preempt, possibly suggesting a diamond sacrifice. Suppose you hold

♠ xxx ♡ Ax ◇ Kxx ♣ QJxxx.

You think you can outbid the opponents. If partner bids 5◇, he should bid it to make, not as a sacrifice. You can get that message across by redoubling.

You hold

1. ♠ x ♡ AK109xx ◇ QJ10xx ♣ x
2. ♠ Ax ♡ AJxxx ◇ AQxx ♣ xx

WEST	NORTH	EAST	SOUTH
—	—	—	1♡
2♡	3♡	Double	?

With the first hand bid 4♡ or 5♡ immediately. With the second redouble so as to invite game or suggest doubling the opponents. The redouble shows extra values and requests partner's cooperation.

You hold ♠ AJx ♡ Jx ◇ AKxx ♣ K10xx.

WEST	NORTH	EAST	SOUTH
—	3♡	Double	?

If you pass the most likely continuation is 3♠ all pass, back to you. You are pretty sure the opponents can't make 3♠, with your strength behind the doubler, but if partner has

♠ x ♡ KQxxxxx ◇ Qxx ♣ xx,

you might be giving up the game you are entitled to for +100 or –530. A redouble of a takeout double should ask for partner's cooperation and allow him to bid again, even though he has opened with a preempt. In that respect a double and a redouble have similar meanings.

You hold ♠ Kx ♡ Axx ◇ AKxx ♣ Q10xx.

WEST	NORTH	EAST	SOUTH
Pass	3♠	Double	?

East's double is for takeout, not penalty, and West should have close to a yarborough. If partner has

♠ QJ10xxxx ♡ x ◇ xxx ♣ Kx,

your optimal contract will be 4♠. If he has

♠ Jxxxxxx ♡ xx ◇ Jx ♣ Kx,

it is better to let the opponents play some contract doubled, probably hearts, at the four level. The redouble should create a force. If the bidding continues:

WEST	NORTH	EAST	SOUTH
Pass	3♠	Double	Redouble
Pass	Pass	4♡	Pass
Pass	?		

North must bid or double.

Here is another controversial hand:

As East, you hold ♠ KJ9xx ♡ Qx ◇ xxx ♣ KJx.

WEST	NORTH	EAST	SOUTH
4♣*	4NT**	?	

* Namyats, a good 4♡ opening
** Takeout for minors

East doubled and when North pulled to 5◇ he doubled again for penalties. The East–West hands were:

WEST	EAST
♠ Axx	♠ KJ9xx
♡ AKJ10xxx	♡ Qx
◇ None	◇ xxx
♣ xxx	♣ KJx

Since North had 1–1–6–5 distribution, East–West took a trick in each major and a club trick to set 5◇ down one, but they were cold for 5♡. If North were 1–1–5–6, a club ruff would defeat 5♡, but East–West would be cold for 5◇. So East–West belong in 5♡.

Both players have close decisions, and the lack of diamond duplication was hard to predict. However, West thought he wasn't allowed to bid—only to pass or double. That is not the way to play! It is hard to imagine a hand with which he would double one minor but not the other. With a purely defensive hand East would just pass 4NT and double the final contract. A double tells partner you think it is your hand, but you aren't sure whether you should double the opponents or bid 5♡. Partner can double, pass or bid 5♡. The situation would be similar if North bid 4♡ for takeout. If North had made a takeout double, a redouble by South would get the same message across; if the opponents bid beyond the 4♡ level, you want partner to share in the decision–making.

The rule: When partner preempts and the opponents double for takeout, redouble allows partner to take action, including rebidding his suit. A double when partner preempts and the opponents cue bid or bid notrump for takeout has a similar meaning. Partner is allowed to bid, pass or double unless he is in fourth position, in which case he is not allowed to pass.

Quiz Four

1. Both Vulnerable
   You hold ♠ 7 ♡ AKJ4 ◇ 64 ♣ AQ8742.

WEST	NORTH	EAST	SOUTH
—	—	—	1♣
2◇	Pass	2♠	Pass
Pass	Double	Pass	?

What do you bid?

2. None Vulnerable
   You hold ♠ 1074 ♡ AK8542 ◇ None ♣ K1092.

WEST	NORTH	EAST	SOUTH
—	1◇	1♡	Pass
1♠	Pass	Pass	?

What do you bid?

3. Not Vulnerable vs. Vulnerable
   You hold ♠ 754 ♡ 1087642 ◇ J107 ♣ 6.

WEST	NORTH	EAST	SOUTH
—	1◇	1♠	Pass
3◇	Double	4♠	?

What do you bid?

4. North–South Vulnerable, IMPS
   You hold ♠ AJ74 ♡ 6 ◇ 985 ♣ KQJ96.

WEST	NORTH	EAST	SOUTH
—	—	—	1♣
1♡	Double	2♡	2♠
Pass	2NT	Pass	?

What do you bid?

5. IMPS, Not Vulnerable vs. Vulnerable
You hold ♠ Q6 ♡ KQ75 ◇ Q109 ♣ 10862.

WEST	NORTH	EAST	SOUTH
1♣	Double	Pass	1♡
1NT	Pass	Pass	Double
Pass	Pass	2♣	?

What do you bid?

6. None Vulnerable
You hold ♠ QJ6 ♡ A9743 ◇ KQ6 ♣ 74.

WEST	NORTH	EAST	SOUTH
—	—	—	1♡
Pass	3♣	3◇	?

What do you bid?

7. Both Vulnerable
You hold ♠ 4 ♡ A64 ◇ QJ7 ♣ KQ6542.

WEST	NORTH	EAST	SOUTH
—	—	—	1♣
Double	1♠	Pass	2♣
Pass	2♡	Pass	?

What do you bid?

8. None Vulnerable
You hold ♠ 7 ♡ 543 ◇ 97653 ♣ AJ107.

WEST	NORTH	EAST	SOUTH
—	—	1♣	Pass
1♠	Pass	3♠	Pass
4NT	Pass	5♠	Pass
6♠	Pass	Pass	?

What do you bid?

9. Both Vulnerable, IMPS

You hold ♠ QJ84 ♡ 62 ◇ K10864 ♣ Q6

WEST	NORTH	EAST	SOUTH
—	1♡	Pass	1♠
Pass	2◇	Pass	Pass
2♠	Double	Pass	?

What do you bid?

10. None Vulnerable, Matchpoints

You hold ♠ 8 ♡ AK765 ◇ J862 ♣ AQ7

WEST	NORTH	EAST	SOUTH
—	—	—	1♡
Pass	1NT	2♠	Pass
Pass	Double	Pass	?

What do you bid?

11. Both Vulnerable, IMPS

You hold ♠ K653 ♡ 6 ◇ AJ642 ♣ QJ8

WEST	NORTH	EAST	SOUTH
—	—	1♡	Pass
Pass	Double	Redouble	Pass
Pass	?		

What do you bid?

12. Vulnerable, Matchpoints

You hold ♠ 106 ♡ KQ7 ◇ A975 ♣ AQ62

WEST	NORTH	EAST	SOUTH
—	2♠	Double	?

What do you bid?

Answers

1. **THREE CLUBS**. Partner undoubtedly had a penalty pass over 2♢. The question is how good he needs to be in spades to double. A tolerance for spades is enough. Therefore, you shouldn't leave the double in without length or strength in spades. Partner actually held

♠ 108xxx ♡ xxx ♢ AQJx ♣ K,

and passing the double would have worked out well while the 3♣ bid was down one (with a horrible club split). But partner should not have doubled.

2. **DOUBLE**. This is my idea of what a double of spades should look like. The result was a two trick set, with no game making our way on this horrible misfit. If partner should bid 2♡, it would be to play since he knows you have hearts.

3. **FIVE DIAMONDS**. Partner wouldn't double just to get a diamond lead. If he has an offensive hand such as

♠ x ♡ KQx ♢ AKQxxx ♣ Jxx,

you should have a good sacrifice.

4. **PASS!** Partner should have four spades, but not very good ones, and he should be very strong in hearts. Being the case, 2NT should be safer than 3♠, and at IMPS safety is more important than an extra 20 points. Several players preferred 3♣ but the clubs look good for notrump, and partner might bid over 3♣; he can't bid over a pass. His actual hand was ♠ xxxx ♡ AK109 ♢ xx ♣ Axx.

5. **DOUBLE.** My partner didn't agree, but you should double again. If the hands were distributional, your aceless hand might not be worth much on defense. When West bid 1NT and partner passed your double, it looks as though everyone is fairly balanced and dummy will have a near yarborough. Your fourth club gives you assurance that West doesn't have a long suit, not even five. With trump leads, the opponents will soon run out of tricks. And if the opponents make it, it isn't game. Won't someone please explain to my partner that our –180 was a fluke?

6. **DOUBLE.** Partner has the high cards for slam interest. Unless his hand is quite unbalanced the opponents should be set at least three tricks. Your cards don't look very good for slam. That's what a double should mean: that you expect to set the opponents for more than the value of game, and you doubt a slam can make.

7. **PASS.** Ordinarily new suits by responder are forcing, but partner has limited his hand by failing to redouble or jump on the second round. Expect partner to hold something like: ♠ Kxxxxx ♡ KJxxx ◊ xx ♣ None.

8. **PASS OR DOUBLE.** This is a borderline decision. A club lead looks like your best chance to set the contract. You might take the first two club tricks or win the ace and give partner a ruff. A club lead may avoid a costly lead of a red suit. But there is no assurance that a club lead will beat the contract. At matchpoints I would probably pass but double at IMPS.

9. **THREE DIAMONDS.** A 1♠ bid implies a five card suit or a good four card suit when you are playing Flannery although I approve of the 1♠ bid in this case, and you only have four. Your diamond length cuts down on the tricks partner was counting on for defense. Partner's double here in this auction merely shows better than a minimum

in high cards, not length or strength in spades. His hand is ♠ xx ♡ AQ10xx ◇ AQJx ♣ Kx.

10. **FOUR DIAMONDS OR THREE SPADES**. Partner's double, in front of the bidder, is for takeout and shows a good hand for his notrump response. You have a very good hand for this sequence, and it probably hurt you to pass last round. At least bid 4◇, or perhaps cue bid. A 3◇ bid completely misses the boat. Partner holds

♠ xxx ♡ x ◇ AQ10xx ♣ K10xx.

11. **PASS.** You should be delighted to pass. If your ◇ A were exchanged for the queen, you might be slightly nervous, but running out with this hand would show no confidence in partner.

12. **REDOUBLE.** This redouble has almost the opposite purpose from when partner's one bid is doubled. In the latter case the redouble strongly suggests penalizing the opponents. You hope you can double them for penalty, and if you can't, you hope that partner can. In this sequence, with a misfit for partner and a defensive hand, you would pass knowing that partner couldn't bid more on his own and plan to double next round. Occasionally the doubler will raise his partner's bid and you would get to double a contract at the four level. With

♠ x ♡ QJxx ◇ KQxx ♣ AKxx,

for example, you would pass. Do not redouble with

♠ xx ♡ QJxx ◇ AQxxx ♣ Ax,

for example, hoping that partner could double a 3♣ bid, since it is so unlikely partner would have club length and an appropriate holding. A redouble in this sequence should say, "I don't know whether to double for penalties or try for game. It depends upon whether you have a good suit and an offensive hand."

Partner should bid 4♠ with

1. ♠ KQJxxx ♡ x ◇ xxx ♣ Kxx or
2. ♠ AQ98xx ♡ xx ◇ x ♣ J10xx.

With 6–3–2–2 distribution partner will tend to double unless his honors are mostly in spades. With a broken suit, but an otherwise offensive hand

♠ KJ8xxx ♡ x ◇ A10x ♣ xxx

partner will pass, and you would double because of the weak spade support.

Chapter Five

BIDDING THE ENEMY'S SUIT

NOT OFTEN WILL YOU CHOOSE THE SUIT the opponents bid as your own. Seldom will you have enough length in their suit to be tempted. Even when you do, the predictable bad split should dissuade you. With no opposing bidding ♠ Kxxx in dummy opposite ♠ AJxx, spades might be your most desirable trump suit. When LHO opens 1♠, the probable 5–0 trump split would make the spade suit undesirable. A bid of the opponents' suit then is usually a cue bid, either showing a control in the suit, asking for a stopper, or showing extra values with slam interest. Sometimes a cue bid is just the most convenient forcing bid. Rarely do you want to play in the opponents' suit.

BIDDING THEIR SUIT TO PLAY

However, modern bidding style permits opening with weak minors and responding with weak majors. The standard opening bid with either

1. ♠ AQxx ♡ Axxx ◇ Jx ♣ Qxx or
2. ♠ AJxx ♡ Axxx ◇ Ax ♣ xxx

is 1♣. Playing a Precision style strong club and five card majors 1◇ might be opened with

1. ♠ AKxx ♡ Ax ◇ Jx ♣ xxxxx or
2. ♠ AKxx ♡ Axxx ◇ xx ♣ Kxx

depending upon the opening notrump range. When the opponents open a minor, that suit could well be your best trump suit.

Also, an opponent, with entirely innocent motives, would respond 1♡ to their partner's minor opening with

♠ Kxx ♡ xxxx ◇ xx ♣ QJxx.

Yet hearts may be your best trump suit. Sometimes an opponent's motives are not so innocent. He might psyche your suit to create confusion especially when your side is known to have a great preponderance of strength such as after a strong artificial 1♣ or 2♣ opening, or after his partner has preempted; your opponent will know they have little defense, and will return to partner's suit if doubled for penalty.

Not Vulnerable
You hold ♠ x ♡ Q10x ◇ Jx ♣ KQ10xxxx.

WEST	NORTH	EAST	SOUTH
—	—	1♣	?

Bid 3♣. One of a minor by the opponents—three of the same minor by you—should be natural and preemptive. Although it is dangerous, some players might make the same bid even vulnerable; others require more playing strength. With ♠ x ♡ AQx ◇ Jx ♣ KQ10xxxx the same 3♣ bid might be made but switch the ◇ A for the ◇ J and the hand is too strong. With this good a hand you are very unlikely to be shut out of the bidding by an auction such as

WEST	NORTH	EAST	SOUTH
—	—	—	1♣
Pass	1♠	Pass	4♠
?			

so you pass and plan to show your clubs later. After the auction

WEST	NORTH	EAST	SOUTH
—	—	—	1♣
Pass	1♠	Pass	2♠
?			

bidding 3♣ would describe this hand. If opener rebids 1NT, jump to 3♣ since 2♣ could be bid with

♠ xx ♡ Ax ◇ Axx ♣ KJ109xx.

Both the delayed 2♣ and 3♣ are natural bids since it would be illogical to pass the first round with a strong hand without club length.

Since most opponents play five card majors, you will seldom wish to play in their major. So the auctions:

WEST	NORTH	EAST	SOUTH
—	—	1♠	3♠

WEST	NORTH	EAST	SOUTH
—	—	1♠	Pass
Pass	3♠		

both show a solid minor and a desire to play 3NT if partner has the opponents' suit stopped. Over 1♠ bid 3♠ with

♠ xx ♡ Ax ◇ AKQJxxx ♣ Jx.

If partner has a spade stopper, you are willing to gamble the opponents can't set 3NT off the top. With no spade stopper partner will usually bid 4♣, allowing you to correct to 4◇. This contract could be down two, but if partner has nothing, the opponents can probably make a major suit game.

Note EIGHT QUICK TRICKS are needed so that partner can cash them after his spade stopper is knocked out. With ♠ xx ♡ KQ ◇ AKQJxxx ♣ Jx just bid 2◇ (or 3◇ if playing intermediate jump overcalls.

You hold ♠ KQ108xx ♡ Ax ◇ x ♣ Qxxx.

WEST	NORTH	EAST	SOUTH
1◇	Pass	1♠	?

Despite East's bid there is a good chance of making 2♠, perhaps even 4♠. But by passing now, you may be faced with an unpleasant choice later.

WEST	NORTH	EAST	SOUTH
1◇	Pass	1♠	Pass
1NT	Pass	3NT	?

Should you double? Partner may have no spade to lead, and even if he does, 3NT may be cold. It would have been safer to bid right away.

Nor would you have an easy decision over

WEST	NORTH	EAST	SOUTH
1◇	Pass	1♠	Pass
2◇	Pass	3◇	?

WEST	NORTH	EAST	SOUTH
1◇	Pass	1♠	Pass
2♣	Pass	3♣	?

The solution is to bid a natural 2♠ immediately.

In the following sequence:

WEST	NORTH	EAST	SOUTH
1◇	Pass	1♠	2◇?

2◇ should be natural also. A cue bid is not needed. With a hand strong enough to cue bid you should double and bid your suit later or bid 2NT with a true two–suiter.

WEST	NORTH	EAST	SOUTH
—	—	1♣	Pass
1♡	Double	Pass	2♣

The 2♣ bid here should be natural. It is hard to imagine the kind of hand that would pass over 1♣ and want to cue bid later. If you had passed with a good hand, it would be because of your club length.

An even more persuasive reason for treating 2♣ as natural is that two cue bids are not needed. 2♡ is obviously a cue bid since if you thought you could make 2♡ you would pass and defend 1♡ doubled. Some experts play 2♣ as a weak cue bid and 2♡ as a game–forcing cue bid. But this is a mistake in priorities. A natural bid is needed more than an extra cue bid.

WEST	NORTH	EAST	SOUTH
—	—	1♣	1♡
Pass	1♠	Pass	2♣

Again 2♣ should be natural. A cue bid is not needed. Suppose you hold either

1. ♠ x ♡ AKJx ◊ xx ♣ AJ10xxx or
2. ♠ None ♡ AQ10xx ◊ xx ♣ K109xxx.

A 1♡ overcall with either hand is compulsory. To make game partner needs little more than good heart support. After partner bids 1♠, what are you going to do? You have to pass unless partner will interpret 2♣ as natural. But he should.

Suppose you hold a good hand:

1. ♠ K10 ♡ AQxxxx ◊ AKx ♣ xx or
2. ♠ AJ ♡ AQ10xx ◊ AQxx ♣ xx.

You could hardly hold a better hand than these; if so, you would have doubled. These hands present a problem, but the solution is to raise to 3♠.

Partner should have one of two types of hands: A bad hand with a decent spade suit such as the first hand (partner thought he could improve the contract) or a hand such as the second or third where partner wanted to make some kind of constructive bid in case you had a maximum overcall.

1. ♠ QJ9xxx ♡ x ◇ xxx ♣ QJx
2. ♠ AQ10xx ♡ x ◇ QJxx ♣ xxx
3. ♠ A109xx ♡ Kx ◇ J10x ♣ xxx

In the first case he will pass. In the second case he will happily bid game. With the third hand he should bid 4♡ to give you a choice.

You hold ♠ J10xx ♡ QJ108xx ◇ xx ♣ x.

WEST	NORTH	EAST	SOUTH
—	1♣	1♡	Pass
1♠	2♣	Pass	2♡

2♡ must be natural. With a hand strong enough to cue bid you would have acted sooner. Only with a good holding in the overcaller's suit would you pass with a good hand, hoping partner could reopen with a double. Your hand is worthless as a dummy to partner, but at hearts it is worth four or five tricks, and you can use partner's high cards. In the unlikely event you hold

♠ Axx ♡ KQJ98x ◇ Jxx ♣ x,

you should bid 3♡.

As South, you hold ♠ AJxx ♡ Kxx ◇ xx ♣ KQxx.

WEST	NORTH	EAST	SOUTH
—	—	1◇	Double
1♠	Double	2◇	2♠

This is a typical hand for South's bidding. If North can double 1♠ for penalty, South can bid 2♠ to play. North needs ♠ Kxxx ♡ Qxx ◇ xxxx ♣ Jx or the equivalent to double. If he is much stronger he will bid again. West may be psyching or simply be bidding a weak suit. Since East rescued, it is probable West has his bid. After a penalty double, a spade bid by either North or South is natural.

BIDDING THEIR SUIT TO FIND A STOPPER

Most bids of the opponents' suit are cue bids. The meaning varies with the bidding level and the available alternatives. In general, a cue bid by a defender merely shows more strength than raising partner's suit to the same level. Any cue bids by opener's side below 3NT are "Western Cue Bids." They are forcing, but suggest partner bid notrump with a stopper in the opponents' suit. Cue bids do not show, or even imply, controls in the opponents' suit unless bid beyond the game level. An ambiguous cue bid, followed by a slam try, shows RETROACTIVELY that the cue bidder had a control in the opponents' suit.

For example:

WEST	NORTH	EAST	SOUTH
—	1♢	Pass	1♠
2♡	Pass	Pass	3♡
Pass	3NT	Pass	5♢

North assumed South was looking for a 3NT contract until South removed 3NT. South has heart control, probably a singleton, and slam interest.

WEST	NORTH	EAST	SOUTH
—	1♢	Pass	1♡
1♠	Pass	Pass	2♠

At this stage it is impossible to tell what South has in mind. North's assumes South is trying to get to 3NT with

♠ xx ♡ AJxx ♢ KJx ♣ Axxx.

With a weaker hand (exchange the ♣ A for the ♣ Q) he would double 1♠. With a spade stopper, quite likely South would have bid some number of notrump himself. So the cue bid suggests South's hand either lacks a spade stopper or is unbalanced. South isn't likely to have a spade void since the opponents, with nine or ten spades between them, would have bid higher. However, if South does have a spade void, knowing whether North has a spade stopper will be useful information. Absence of a stopper would be encouraging since this would mean lack of duplication. If partner bids 2NT over your 2♠ bid, a 3♢ bid by you would be forcing. You could have bid 3♢ directly over 1♠ to INVITE.

As South, you hold either

1. ♠ AQx ♡ Ax ♢ AQ10xxx ♣ xx or
2. ♠ AQx ♡ xx ♢ AQ10xxx ♣ Ax.

WEST	NORTH	EAST	SOUTH
—	—	—	1♢
2♣	2♢	2♡	?

When the opponents have bid two suits and you are looking for a notrump contract, it is conventional to cue bid the suit you have stopped. Thus, you would bid 3♡ with the first hand and 3♣ with the second. I carefully avoided a problem by giving you aces in the opponents' suits. With

♠ AKx ♡ xx ♢ AQ10xxx ♣ Kx,

if you cue bid, you are supposed to bid 3♣ and hope partner, with

♠ Jxx ♡ Axx ♢ Kxxx ♣ xxx,

would bid 3♡ to allow you to bid 3NT. In this case 3♡ would show a stopper since you implied you didn't have a heart stopper, and if partner had no heart stopper, you wouldn't belong in 3NT. If partner's heart stopper is the king, it would be dangerous for either of you to play 3NT. With

♠ AKx ♡ xx ◇ AQ10xxx ♣ Kx

bid 2♠ rather than 3♣. In the unlikely event partner has both of the opponents' suits stopped, he will bid notrump himself. If he has a good raise, including the ace of either of the opponents' suits, he will cue bid it, and you will know what to do.

Choosing between a Western Cue Bid and bidding a new suit, can be a problem.

1. ♠ AKx ♡ xx ◇ AKJxxx ♣ Jx
2. ♠ x ♡ AQx ◇ AQJxxx ♣ Kxx
3. ♠ Axx ♡ Ax ◇ AKJxxx ♣ xx

WEST	NORTH	EAST	SOUTH
—	—	—	1◇
2♣	2◇	Pass	?

With the first hand you should have enough winners to take nine tricks at notrump but lack stoppers in two suits. Sometimes you don't worry about unbid suits because partner may have a stopper or enough length so that the opponents can't take the setting tricks off the top, or even if the opponents could take the setting tricks off the top, they may not lead your weak suit. However, the level is low enough in these examples for you to be scientific. Bid 2♠ with the first hand. The partnership needs stoppers in three suits, one of which has been bid by the opponents. When you can cue bid at the two level, bid the suit you have stopped. With stoppers in the remaining suits partner will bid notrump. With a stopper in only one suit, he will bid his stopper. There is a complication. Partner may treat 2♠ as natural and raise with four card support. His failure to make a Negative Double does not deny major suit length when there are two unbid majors. But partner should only raise to 3♠ (forcing), not 4♠.

With the second hand if I didn't trust my partner, I would bid 3NT, which is a reasonable gamble. With a good partner you should bid 2♡. If partner bids 2♠, you can bid 3NT.

With the third hand 3♣ bid is best. All you really want from partner is a club stopper. Why be subtle or devious?

WEST	NORTH	EAST	SOUTH
—	—	—	1◇
2♣	2◇	Pass	2♠
Pass	3♣		

Is partner showing a club stopper or asking you for one? This question was answered earlier. He is showing a club stopper. Perhaps he has

♠ Qx ♡ xxxx ◇ Kxxx ♣ Kxx.

If you hold

1. ♠ AKJx ♡ QJx ◇ AJ10xx ♣ Q or
2. ♠ AJxx ♡ Ax ◇ AKxxx ♣ Qx,

you can bid 3NT and possibly have a double club stopper. Over 2♠ partner would bid 3♡ with

♠ Qx ♡ AKx ◇ xxxxx ♣ xxx

because he has a maximum raise and and concentrated heart strength.

As South, you hold ♠ Ax ♡ Axx ◇ AKxxxx ♣ xx.

WEST	NORTH	EAST	SOUTH
—	—	—	1◇
2♣	2◇	Pass	3♣
Pass	3◇	Pass	?

Pass. Partner not only denied a club stopper but also a good raise. With a good raise he could have bid notrump with stoppers in both majors, he could have bid a major with concentrated strength, or could have jumped to 4 ♢ with some shape. This is a rare sequence where opener's side can cue bid and pass. The bidding can stop short of game despite an earlier cue bid when you have no major fit and neither partner has shown a singleton or a stopper in the opponents' suit.

BIDDING THEIR SUIT TO SHOW SUPPORT

Many modern players like to play all jump raises in competition as preemptive. A cue bid shows a limit raise or better. After the auction

WEST	NORTH	EAST	SOUTH
—	1♠	2♢	3♢

South could hold either

1. ♠ Qxxx ♡ Axx ♢ xx ♣ Kxxx or
2. ♠ Qxxx ♡ AJx ♢ xx ♣ AKxx

With the latter hand South would insist on game. If opener would bid game over a limit raise, he must jump to game or bid a new suit over the ambiguous cue bid.

I play this way with a majority of my partners, but I am not convinced that it is best. You have to cue bid more often with hands that do not clearly belong to your side. LHO can double your 3♢ bid in the above sequence with

♠ xx ♡ Axxx ♢ Qxx ♣ xxxx

but wouldn't risk a 4♢ bid over 3♠. Also, opener's side has less need for a preempt than the defenders because opener, on an average, has more high card strength than the overcaller. In an earlier chapter I recommended a "limit raise" on a hand some players would consider preemptive, with a high ratio of offensive to defensive values, such as ♠ Qxxx ♡ x ◇ xxx ♣ KJ10xx. Finally there is the range uncertainty. If opener has

♠ AQxxx ♡ Axx ◇ x ♣ KJ10x,

he has a mild slam try over a forcing raise but not over a limit raise. Suppose he cue bids 4♣. Should responder cooperate by cue bidding below game with a limit raise? Or should he sign off unless he was strong enough for a forcing raise? For all he knows, opener may have had a slam try over a limit raise.

Admittedly, when partner's 1♠ bid is overcalled, it is nice to be playing preemptive jump raises when you hold

♠ Kxxxx ♡ x ◇ xxx ♣ Jxxx.

But it is also nice to be playing cue bids forcing to game when you hold

♠ KJxx ♡ AQx ◇ xx ♣ KQxx.

Whatever strength a cue bid shows, it denies a side suit worth mentioning. So after a cue bid, all further new suit bids show controls or concentrations of strength, not suits. This is particularly important after a minor suit opening.

WEST	NORTH	EAST	SOUTH
—	1◇	1♠	2♠

South must deny four or more hearts. With five or more, and enough strength to cue bid, bid 2♡. With four hearts either bid 2♣, your longest suit, planning to show hearts later, or make a Negative Double. After a cue bid a heart bid by either North or South shows heart values, not a suit or desire to play in hearts.

You hold ♠ AKQJxx ♡ None ◇ Qxx ♣ Kxxx.

WEST	NORTH	EAST	SOUTH
—	1◇	1♡	?

Hopeless confusion would be caused if you should bid 2♡ rather than 1♠. An immediate cue bid by responder shows good support for opener's suit.

You hold ♠ x ♡ AQ10xx ◊ Ax ♣ AJxxx.

WEST	NORTH	EAST	SOUTH
—	1♠	4◊	?

I don't know what to bid (perhaps 5NT?), but you should not bid 5◊. Partner will not interpret the cue bid as asking for a choice of the remaining two suits. He will expect spade support and jump to 6♠ with

♠ AQxxxx ♡ Kx ◊ x ♣ KQxx.

You won't know whether to leave it there or not.

WEST	NORTH	EAST	SOUTH
—	1◊	4♡	5♠

Is South denying a heart control and asking North to bid 6♠ with one? Of course not! Since 5♡ promises diamond support, no cue bid was possible. When only one or two bids are available, you cannot be so specific about what you are showing or what you want from partner. North should bid six with a reasonable number of controls and fit.

♠ Kx ♡ xxx ◊ AKxxx ♣ KJx

would be enough. South must have a heart control to bid at the five level with so many other key cards missing. The 5♠ bidder might hold

1. ♠ AQ10xxxx ♡ None ◊ Qx ♣ Axxx or
2. ♠ AQJxxx ♡ x ◊ Qxx ♣ AQx.

You hold ♠ K ♡ AJ10xxxx ◊ AKJ9x ♣ None.

WEST	NORTH	EAST	SOUTH
—	1♠	4♣	?

I submitted this hand from a home team game to a bidding panel. Some panelists suggested 6♣, thinking a JUMP cue bid should ask for a choice of the remaining two suits. A 5NT bid seems more logical as a request for partner to choose one of the unbid suits although, in this case, there is quite a disparity in the suit lengths. If partner has a doubleton in each red suit, you greatly prefer to play in hearts. My choice was a "simple" 6♡. One panelist was afraid partner would raise to 7♡ with the singleton ♡ K whatever else he might hold. My contention is in a crowded auction, bids cannot have such specific meanings. If you want to play that 1♠, pass, 6♡ asks for a raise with the ace or king of hearts, that is okay by me although the opportunities to use it will be rare. The logic is if you want to find out about anything else in an uncontested auction, you bid more slowly. When you can't bid slowly and scientifically, you simply have to assign the limited bids available their most logical meaning and hope that partner is on the same wave length. Likewise

WEST	NORTH	EAST	SOUTH
—	1♡	Pass	5NT

5NT is clearly the grand slam force.

WEST	NORTH	EAST	SOUTH
—	1♡	5♢	5NT

is not.

You hold ♠ AQxxxx ♡ Axx ♢ None ♣ Kxxx.

WEST	NORTH	EAST	SOUTH
—	—	—	1♠
2♢	3♠*	Pass	?

*Limit Raise

A 4♢ cue bid in this sequence has the old-fashioned meaning of no diamond losers, probably a void. Partner will know diamond values are wasted and

♠ K10xx ♡ Kx ♢ xxxx ♣ QJx

is a very good hand, because no values are wasted, even though 3♠ seemed like a stretch when it was made.

You hold ♠ AKxxxx ♡ AKJx ♢ x ♣ xx.

WEST	NORTH	EAST	SOUTH
—	—	—	1♠
2♢	3♠	Pass	?

Bid 4♡, neither showing nor denying a diamond control. Partner needs extra values or a good fit to cue bid past the game level, but if he bids 5♣, you should bid 5♢ so that, if partner holds

♠ J10xx ♡ Qxx ♢ xx ♣ AKxx,

he won't worry about losing the first two diamond tricks. You also bid 4♡, saving the cue bid in diamonds till next round, with

♠ AQxxxx ♡ AQJx ♢ Ax ♣ x.

Since 4♢ shows no diamond losers, the failure to cue bid diamonds does not deny a control.

With no room for several cue bids, the opponents' suit is the biggest worry, and with either a first or second round control in that suit and enough strength to suggest a slam, you should cue bid the opponents' suit.

You hold ♠ AKxxxx ♡ AKx ♢ xx ♣ Ax.

WEST	NORTH	EAST	SOUTH
—	—	—	1♠
4♢	4♠	Pass	?

Note that the bidding is one level higher than before. You and partner have no room to exchange cue bids, showing your long suit first. Some players would cue bid 5♣ the cheapest first round control. Others would bid 5♠ since partner's club holding is not of critical importance. You could hardly make a slam try with two losing diamonds and no ace outside of spades, so failure to cue bid implies BOTH aces.

With ♠ AKxxxx ♡ AJx ◇ x ♣ Axx you can't show all your controls, so bid 5◇. Partner will then bid slam with ♠ Q10xx ♡ KQxx ◇ xxx ♣ Kx but bid 5♠ with ♠ QJxx ♡ QJx ◇ Kx ♣ Qxxx. Opener's side usually has several forcing bids at its disposal such as new suits by responder, fourth suit forcing, etc. Often several invitational bids are available.

WEST	NORTH	EAST	SOUTH
—	1◇	Pass	1♡
1♠	Pass	Pass	?

South can double with a good balanced hand, followed by a pass, a raise or a cue bid. In standard bidding 2♣ is forcing although I later suggest that it not be; 3♣ is forcing; 3♡ and 3◇ are invitational. So if you cue bid 2♠, you guarantee another bid. If partner then bids 2NT, 3◇, and 3♡ by you should be forcing.

The defending side does not have so many options. New suits are usually not forcing. A cue bid may be the only available force. It may be the only strength showing bid at the appropriate level. Earlier I said the cue bid

WEST	NORTH	EAST	SOUTH
1♡	1♠	Pass	2♡

presumably shows a good raise to 2♠. If West simply rebids 2♠, East will probably pass. 3♡, a jump cue bid, shows a four card raise to 3♠, but obviously does not promise another bid.

When the opponents artificially show a suit, a bid of the suit they show is a cue bid.

WEST	NORTH	EAST	SOUTH
—	1♠	2NT	?

Since 2NT shows both minors, 3♣ and 3♢ are cue bids. UNUSUAL OVER UNUSUAL is a popular convention, with clubs showing hearts and diamonds showing spades, or clubs showing the unbid major and diamonds showing a limit raise or better of partner's major. After the auction

WEST	NORTH	EAST	SOUTH
—	1♢	2♢	?

showing the majors, act as though the opponents had bid both majors. Therefore, 2♡ or 2♠ would show a stopper in the suit bid and be forcing to the 2NT level or 3♢.

WEST	NORTH	EAST	SOUTH
—	—	—	1NT
Pass	2♡*	2♠	

*Jacoby transfer

East's bid is equivalent to a takeout double of 2♠.

WEST	NORTH	EAST	SOUTH
—	—	—	1♢
Double	Pass	?	

The only forcing bid is a cue bid. The force continues until East limits his hand. A jump response shows a good, but limited hand.

WEST	NORTH	EAST	SOUTH
—	—	—	1♢
Double	Pass	2♢	Pass
2♡/2♠	Pass	3♡/3♠	

could show ♠ Kxxx ♡ Kxxx ♢ xx ♣ Kxx. You hope partner won't bid 3♣, but if he does, raise to 4♣ since partner usually needs more high cards to double without a major. East's cue bid should guarantee another bid. If he cue bids with

♠ Kxxx ♡ Qxxx ◇ xx ♣ xxx,

intending to pass partner's rebid, the situation becomes chaotic. Suppose the doubler holds

♠ Axxx ♡ Kx ◇ Ax ♣ AKxxx.

Should he jump in spades to show extra values? Or make a return cue bid? The only exception to the later force, is that the cue bidder can pass a 2NT rebid.

You hold ♠ Qxx ♡ Kxxx ◇ Q10xx ♣ A10.

WEST	NORTH	EAST	SOUTH
—	—	—	1◇
Double	Pass	?	

A 2NT bid describes your high cards and balanced shape, but you might miss a heart fit. Bid 2◇ and, if partner bids 2♠, bid 2NT, NON–FORCING.

You hold ♠ AQxx ♡ None ◇ A10xx ♣ KQxxx.

WEST	NORTH	EAST	SOUTH
—	—	—	1♡
Pass	Pass	?	

Quite likely partner is hoping you will double so he can pass for penalty. But I wouldn't oblige him. The void in the opponents' suit hurts your defense. You can never lead a trump through declarer. Also, your offense is better. If you double, partner will pass with

♠ Kx ♡ QJ9xx ◇ Kx ♣ Jxxx,

not realizing how great your offensive potential is. My suggestion is to play a reopening cue bid to imply a void in the opponents' suit with a wide range of strength from

♠ AJxx ♡ None ◇ Qxxx ♣ Qxxxx

on up. Needless to say, the cue bidder doesn't promise another bid, and his partner should jump or cue bid with appropriate hands.

While a reopening cue bid implies a void, it can also be made with a very strong one–suited or two–suited hand, with offensive strength too great to risk a penalty pass from partner. For example,

1. ♠ AKQJxxx ♡ x ◇ AJ109 ♣ x or
2. ♠ AQ109x ♡ x ◇ None ♣ AKJ10xxx.

As South you hold ♠ AK10xxx ♡ AKxx ◇ x ♣ AQ.

WEST	NORTH	EAST	SOUTH
—	—	1◇	Double
Pass	1♠	Pass	2◇

South may cue bid with a hand too strong for a raise to 4♠. He wants to suggest a slam by jumping to 4♠ next round or he may have a very strong hand, but not know what to bid such as

1. ♠ AQ ♡ AKJx ◇ xxx ♣AKQx or
2. ♠ AKx ♡ AKxx ◇ x ♣ AQJxx
3. ♠ Kxx ♡ AKQ ◇ xxx ♣ AKQx.

Most pairs haven't decided whether the cue bidder promises another bid and what East's various bids mean. Is rebidding the same suit, say with xxxx, his weakest bid? Is East obligated to bid again? The following rules are somewhat arbitrary. Perhaps you can think of something better, but Ed Davis and I play East's cheapest bid is an artificial negative, denying five working points, and all other bids show some values. After an artificial negative either hand can pass. After any other bid, both partners are obligated to bid again.

WEST	EAST
♠ AKx	♠ 10xxx
♡ AQJx	♡ xxx
◇ xx	◇ xxx
♣ AKxx	♣ Jxx

WEST	NORTH	EAST	SOUTH
—	—	—	1◇
Double	Pass	1♠	Pass
2◇	Pass	2♡	Pass
2♠	Pass	Pass	Pass

WEST	EAST
♠ AKQx	♠ xxx
♡ AJ	♡ xxxx
◇ xxx	◇ Jxx
♣ AKJ10	♣ xxx

WEST	NORTH	EAST	SOUTH
—	—	—	1◇
Double	Pass	1♡	Pass
2◇	Pass	2♡	Pass
2♠	Pass	Pass	Pass

WEST	EAST
♠ AQx	♠ Kxxx
♡ AKQxx	♡ xxx
◇ x	◇ xxx
♣ AJ10x	♣ Qxx

WEST	NORTH	EAST	SOUTH
—	—	—	1◇
Double	Pass	1♠	Pass
2◇	Pass	3◇	Pass
3♡	Pass	4♡	Pass
Pass	Pass		

What do you expect this sequence to mean?

WEST	NORTH	EAST	SOUTH
1♡	Double	Pass	3♡

South shows a long, solid minor and asks North to bid notrump with a heart stop; otherwise bid 4♣ which South may convert to diamonds. Typical South hands:

1. ♠ xx ♡ xx ◊ AKQxxxx ♣ xx or
2. ♠ xx ♡ xx ◊ AKQxxx ♣ Kxx.

I don't see many articles written by Ed Manfield, but every one I've read is excellent. In the July 1985 Bridge World he suggested a "Choice Of Games" cue bid. In competitive auctions where you haven't found a suit fit, and you are already at the three level or higher, a cue bid merely seeks a suit fit rather than implying slam. We have already considered one specific sequence:

WEST	NORTH	EAST	SOUTH
—	—	—	3◊
Double	Pass	4◊	Pass
4♡	Pass	4♠	

to show a four card spade suit and longer clubs. Ed Manfield carries this idea much further. For example,

WEST	NORTH	EAST	SOUTH
—	—	—	1♠
Double	Pass	2♣	2♠
3♠	Pass	4♣	Pass
4♡			

West's bids suggests an alternate contract, obviously 5♣ in this sequence.

WEST	NORTH	EAST	SOUTH
—	2♣	3♣	Pass
Pass	3♠	Pass	4♣

The 4♣ bid, instead of showing slam interest, would suggest another trump suit. South can't bid a four card suit at the four level without misleading his partner. The ideal distribution for this cue bid would be 1–4–5–3, 2–4–4–3 or 2–4–5–2. Opener has had only one chance to show a suit, and he could easily have 5–5 in the majors or 5–4–3–1 or 5–3–4–1. There is no doubt the cue bid would be best if partner wouldn't expect a strong hand.

West holds ♠ KJx ♡ Axx ◇ x ♣ AKxxxx

WEST	NORTH	EAST	SOUTH
1♣	1♡	Double	3♡
?			

West can bid 4♡ to say, "I'm willing to gamble on game somewhere, but I don't know where." With four good spades or possibly four bad spades opener would bid 4♠. So if responder holds either

1. ♠ Axxx ♡ x ◇ QJxxx ♣ xxx or
2. ♠ xxxx ♡ x ◇ AQxxxx ♣ Qx,

he knows 4♠ is not the right spot. If he had four clubs, he would bid 5♣. Bidding 4NT denies four good spades or four clubs. It would ask opener to choose between diamonds and clubs, and obviously the diamonds are longer. With the hand above opener would bid 5♣. If he had ♠ KJx ♡ A ◇ Kxxx ♣ AKxxx he would bid 5◇.

You can adopt the basic concept and make up your own rules on when a cue bid is "COG" (choice of games), as distinguished from a slam try. Ed's rules are as follows: A three–level or four–level cue bid of the opponents' suit is COG if a forcing pass is not available AND the cue bid is below game in at least two of the partnership's possible strains, AND we have bid or implied at least two suits, OR the bidding is already at the four–level, OR the cue bidder is limited.

Quiz Five

1. Matchpoints, None Vulnerable
You hold ♠ K10 ♡ AKJ85 ◇ AJ32 ♣ J7.

WEST	NORTH	EAST	SOUTH
—	—	1♣	1♡
Pass	1♠	Pass	?

What do you bid?

2. IMPS, Not Vulnerable vs. Vulnerable
You hold ♠ QJ542 ♡ 7 ◇ 53 ♣ AK875.

WEST	NORTH	EAST	SOUTH
—	—	1♣	1♠
Pass	2♣*	Pass	2♠
Pass	3◇	Pass	?

*You are not playing transfer responses.
What do you bid?

3. IMPS, Both Vulnerable
You hold ♠ AJ83 ♡ K7 ◇ J9642 ♣ AQ.

WEST	NORTH	EAST	SOUTH
—	—	—	1◇
Pass	1♡	1♠	1NT
Pass	2♠	Pass	?

What do you bid?

4. Matchpoints, None Vulnerable
You hold ♠ None ♡ KQ874 ◇ 92 ♣ AJ10873.

WEST	NORTH	EAST	SOUTH
—	—	1♣	1♡
Pass	1♠	Pass	?

What do you bid?

5. IMPS, None Vulnerable
You hold ♠ Q1065 ♡ AKQJ4 ◇ 1054 ♣ 6.

WEST	NORTH	EAST	SOUTH
1◇	1♠	2♡	Pass
3◇	Pass	?	

What do you bid?

6. Matchpoints, None Vulnerable
You hold ♠ KQ54 ♡ KQ85 ◇ 9 ♣ 10742.

WEST	NORTH	EAST	SOUTH
1♣	Pass	1◇	Pass
1NT	Pass	Pass	?

What do you bid?

7. Matchpoints, Vulnerable vs. Not Vulnerable
You hold ♠ AJ8 ♡ KJ1076 ◇ A5 ♣ J52.

WEST	NORTH	EAST	SOUTH
—	1♣	Pass	1♡
2◇	Pass	Pass	?

What do you bid?

8. Matchpoints, None Vulnerable
You hold ♠ 6 ♡ 10854 ◇ 643 ♣ J9653.

WEST	NORTH	EAST	SOUTH
—	2♣	Pass	2◇
3◇	3♠	Pass	?

What do you bid?

Answers

1. **THREE SPADES**. Partner must have a good suit, and a 2♣ bid would be natural. 2♢ risks a pass by partner holding ♠ QJxxxx ♡ x ♢ xxx ♣ Axx.

2. **THREE NOTRUMP**. What else can you do? If you were playing transfer responses to overcalls, a 2♡ "cue bid" would guarantee spade support. As it is, the cue bid only implies spade support, and the implication disappears when partner bids a new suit. This sequence means that partner has diamonds and wanted to make a forcing bid. With a good hand, partner probably has something in hearts. Since you are forced to bid, it is logical to bid notrump when you have the opponents' suit stopped. How else can you get to 3NT when partner has

♠ xx ♡ AJxx ♢ AKQJxx ♣ x?

3. **THREE SPADES**. You might have been opened 1NT but it looks as though your choice is going to turn out well. You have a very good hand the way the bidding has gone, but no outstanding single feature like a powerful diamond suit or exceptionally good heart support. A cue bid implies a good hand without drawing attention to a specific feature. When this hand was dealt South bid 3NT, and his partner gave up on slam, holding

♠ None ♡ QJxx ♢ AK10xx ♣ Kxxx.

Over the cue bid, North would show his diamond support, and a slam would be reached.

4. **TWO CLUBS**. Make your natural bid. Even if partner forgets your agreement, he should suspect from looking at his own hand and listening to the bidding that you have club length.

5. **THREE NOTRUMP**. Since a 3♠ bid would ASK partner to bid notrump with a spade stopper, which he is unlikely to have, simply bid 3NT yourself. Your hand looks much better for notrump than in support of diamonds, so don't let the singleton club bother you. Partner has

♠ 9xx ♡ x ◇ AKJxxx ♣ KQx,

and a spade ruff defeats even 4◇. In the unlikely event the opponents could run the club suit against 3NT, would West be likely to lead a club from ♣ Qxxxxx and no outside entries?

6. **TWO DIAMONDS**. You can risk a reopening call, but not 2♣. Partner will have enough length in diamonds to recognize 2◇ as a cue bid. If partner has a singleton club, he might think your 2♣ bid was natural. Why take the chance? By the way, a double would be too dangerous. Partner might leave it in, expecting you to have a better defensive hand including a diamond stopper.

7. **TWO SPADES**. You could double (for takeout), figuring that partner is unlikely to leave it in—and if he does, you might set the contract enough to compensate for your game. However, my choice is 2♠. If partner bids 2NT, you will gladly raise to game. If partner bids 3♣ or 3♠, you can bid 3NT yourself, which clearly shows no more than a single stopper in diamonds and encourages partner to look for a better contract with a hand unsuitable for notrump. The trouble with bidding 3◇ is that partner, with either

1. ♠ Kxx ♡ xx ◇ Jx ♣ AKQxxx or
2. ♠ xxxx ♡ A ◇ Jxx ♣ AKQxx,

would have to bid 4♣, which would by–pass your best game contract.

8. **FOUR DIAMONDS**. You and partner should agree to play Manfield cue bids (or COG's). Even in the absence of an agreement bidding 4♢ is best! Opener will probably make his natural rebid, waiting for you to clarify what you have in mind, but unless he cue bids himself or bids 4NT, both of which will probably result in disaster, you plan to pass. Bidding 4♣ is also possible, the risk being that partner would expect a better suit and might jump to 6♣ with ♠ AKxxx ♡ AKQx ♢ x ♣ AKx.

Chapter Six

UNSUAL NOTRUMP BIDS

THE FIRST UNUSUAL NOTRUMP CONVENTION was Blackwood. After the bidding goes

WEST	NORTH	EAST	SOUTH
—	1♠	Pass	3♠
Pass	4NT		

or

WEST	NORTH	EAST	SOUTH
—	1♢	Pass	1♡
Pass	3♡	Pass	4NT

it is unlikely that the 4NT bidder would want to play 4NT or suggest a raise to 6NT. Consequently the 4NT bid should be given an artificial meaning.

THE UNUSUAL NOTRUMP

The next unusual notrump was recommended by Roth and Stone. Whether they were the first players to use it or the first to write it up I don't know. Probably both. When a player couldn't logically want to play notrump, a notrump bid should ask partner to choose a suit. Usually the choice is between the lower unbid suits but in some auctions partner can choose any of three suits. For example:

WEST	NORTH	EAST	SOUTH
—	—	Pass	1♠
Pass	2♠	2NT	

Since East didn't open the bidding, he can not want to play 2NT or invite his partner to raise to 3NT. East should hold

♠ x ♡ x ◇ KQJxx ♣ Kxxxxx.

WEST	NORTH	EAST	SOUTH
—	—	—	1♠
Pass	2♠	Pass	Pass
?			

When your opponents, despite finding a fit, make no effort to reach game, your side probably has about half the high cards. 2NT can be bid with a far weaker hand than in the previous sequence–perhaps

1. ♠ x ♡ xx ◇ KJxxx ♣ QJxxx or
2. ♠ Axx ♡ x ◇ KQxx ♣ 10xxxx.

WEST	NORTH	EAST	SOUTH
—	—	Pass	1◇
Pass	1♠	1NT	

It would be suicidal for East, in a live auction, to bid 1NT with a balanced hand to show a maximum pass. East shows hearts and clubs. Why didn't East double? The double shows more high cards and less distribution than an unusual notrump. He might double with

♠ x ♡ KQxx ◇ xxx ♣ AJxxx

and bid 1NT with

♠ x ♡ QJ10xx ◇ x ♣ KJxxxx.

Whenever a bid or double shows a major and a minor below the game level, if either suit is longer than the other, it should be the minor. With a longer major, bid the major. Incidentally, at favorable vulnerability, you might bid 2NT with the latter hand, not because 1NT would be ambiguous, but to preempt the opponents.

In the beginning Roth and Stone treated a notrump bid as unusual only when the previous bidding showed it could not have its natural meaning. Suppose RHO bids 1♠. You could have a very strong balanced hand with which you would like to bid 2NT (either stronger or weaker than doubling and bidding 2NT next round). Or you might want to bid 2NT as a natural bid with a good minor suit

♠ Kx ♡ xx ◇ AKQJxx ♣ KJx,

reserving a double to show a more balanced hand and better support for the unbid major. However, modern methods treat an immediate 2NT overcall as unusual. Strong balanced hands occur less often than two–suiters, and with strong balanced hands you can simply double and bid 2NT the next round. You would make the same calls (double, followed by 2NT) with

1. ♠ Kxx ♡ AK ◇ AQxx ♣ Kxxx
2. ♠ KQx ♡ AKxx ◇ AQxx ♣ Kxx
3. ♠ Kx ♡ Ax ◇ Jxx ♣ AKQxxx

which is a rather wide range of strength and shape.

WEST	NORTH	EAST	SOUTH
—	—	1♡	2NT

This auction shows the minors.

WEST	NORTH	EAST	SOUTH
—	—	1◇	2NT

This auction shows hearts and clubs. Where modern players disagree is WHEN to bid an unusual notrump. A good ratio of offense values to defense values is needed; also, a reasonable chance of buying the bid. Otherwise, your bidding will accomplish nothing except to help declarer play the hand. Over 1♠, bid 2NT with any of the following hands:

1. ♠ x ♡ xx ◇ KQJxx ♣ AQJxx
2. ♠ Ax ♡ x ◇ AQJxx ♣ KQxxx
3. ♠ x ♡ x ◇ KJxxxx ♣ KQ10xx.

Since the range varies so widely, partner should bid 4♣ with ♠ xxx ♡ xxxxx ◇ Ax ♣ A10x or bid 5♣ with ♠ xxx ♡ xx ◇ Qxx ♣ KJxxx.With the latter hand 5♣ will be a good sacrifice if it doesn't make.

TWO NOTRUMP OVERCALLS

Most jumps to 2NT over the opponents' bids and most 2NT bids in fourth position after both opponents have bid are unusual.

WEST	NORTH	EAST	SOUTH
1◇	Pass	1♠	2NT

However, when the opponents open a weak two bid, a 2NT overcall is natural, showing roughly an opening 1NT bid. After

WEST	NORTH	EAST	SOUTH
2♠	2NT	Pass	?

I suggest playing the same stucture as though partner had opened 2NT, even though the range is different. In other words, 3♣ would be Stayman, 3◇ would be a transfer to hearts, etc.

When the opponents open a Flannery 2◇, the standard defense is to bid 2♡ as a takeout of hearts; 2♠ as natural; double to show a strong notrump (so that occasionally partner can double the run–out for penalties) and 2NT as natural, but implying more offense and less defense than a double:

1. ♠ Axx ♡ Kx ◇ AKQxx ♣ Jxx or
2. ♠ Jx ♡ Kx ◇ Axx ♣ AKJ10xx

TWO NOTRUMP IN THE BALANCING SEAT

WEST	NORTH	EAST	SOUTH
1♡	Pass	Pass	?

In reopening position 2NT is natural. Most players bid 1NT with as few as 10 HCP. Mike Lawrence and I think a 1NT bid over a major should show 12–16 HCP (12–14 over a minor since we can probably double and bid 1NT with 15–16). A double followed by bidding 2NT over a two level response shows 17–18 HCP (or the equivalent with a long suit) and bidding an immediate 2NT shows 19–21. Whatever range you use, 2NT is needed as a natural bid.

FOUR NOTRUMP FOR TAKEOUT

A 3NT bid is almost always natural, so when 2NT would also be natural you may have to jump to 4NT to ask partner for a choice of suits. If the opponents open 2♠, 3♠ or 4♠, bid 4NT with either

1. ♠ None ♡ Kx ◊ KJxxx ♣ AQxxxx or
2. ♠ Ax ♡ x ◊ AQJxx ♣ AKQxx.

As you can see, there is a very wide range of strength. It is more important to show your hand pattern and find the right suit than to show your exact strength. That is one reason why partner should be very conservative about bidding a slam.

There is another reason to be conservative.

WEST	NORTH	EAST	SOUTH
—	—	4♠	4NT
Pass	5♣	Pass	5◊

This auction shows South has the red suits, possibly

♠ x ♡ AKxxxx ◊ KQ10xx ♣ x.

A holding of ♠ xxx ♡ xx ◇ Ax ♣ AQ10xxx is a very good North hand when partner has both minors, but if you jump to 6♣ and partner has the red suits, you will surely be too high.

THREE NOTRUMP BIDS

Suppose RHO opens 1♡ and you hold

♠ Qx ♡ Kx ◇ AKQJxxx ♣ xx.

Since 2NT would be unusual, you must bid either 2◇ or 3NT. The latter bid is my choice. You might make 3NT (if partner has an ace). If you can't make 3NT, and if you can hold the set to one trick, the opponents could probably make a partscore, and down one will be a good result. LHO doesn't know how much of a gamble your 3NT bid is. You would make the same bid with

♠ Ax ♡ Ax ◇ xx ♣ AKQJxxx,

so he doesn't know whether to bid, pass or double. When he elects to defend he must guess what to lead. It isn't always to his advantage to lead his partner's suit.

Even a 3NT bid can be unusual.

WEST	NORTH	EAST	SOUTH
—	—	—	1♠
Double	3♠	Pass	Pass
Double	Pass	?	

You, East, probably hold close to a yarborough. If you happen to hold ♠ QJ10x ♡ Qxx ◇ xxx ♣ xxx, you would pass. Admittedly you could hold

♠ Kx ♡ xxx ◇ KJxxx ♣ xxx,

which, opposite

♠ x ♡ AQxx ◇ AQxx ♣ AQxx,

would make 3NT. A much likelier hand for you is

♠ Jxx ♡ xx ◇ Jxxx ♣ xxxx,

in which case you would like to bid 3NT asking for a choice of the minors. Partner might hold

1. ♠ x ♡ AQxx ◇ AQxxx ♣ AJx or
2. ♠ x ♡ AQxx ◇ AQx ♣ AJxxx,

and if you guess to bid the wrong minor, it won't turn out well. When making 3NT is extremely remote, it pays to treat 3NT as unusual. By definition, 3NT is extremely remote when the takeout doubler has to double a second time to get his partner to bid.

WEST	NORTH	EAST	SOUTH
—	—	—	1♠
Pass	2♠	Pass	Pass
Double	Pass	?	

Most likely partner didn't take action the first round because he was too weak. He might hold either

1. ♠ x ♡ Kxxx ◇ Kxxx ♣ QJxx or
2. ♠ xx ♡ Kxxx ◇ KJx ♣ QJxx.

Partner reopened because you are marked with some high card strength. Another possibility is that partner was strong enough to take immediate action, but he had a distributional flaw. For example, he might hold

1. ♠ xxxx ♡ AK10x ◇ x ♣ KJ10x or
2. ♠ xxx ♡ KQxx ◇ AKxx ♣ xx.

He was afraid to double for fear you would bid his short suit. With the first hand after spades are raised he is pretty sure that you have a singleton spade. If so, there is bound to be a 4–4 fit unless you have precisely 1–3–6–3 distribution. He can risk a reopening double if you will bid 2NT whenever you have both minors like

1. ♠ x ♡ Qxx ◇ AJxxx ♣ Qxxx or
2. ♠ x ♡ Axx ◇ QJxx ♣ Jxxxx.

If he thinks you will automatically bid your longest suit, a reopening double is too dangerous.

DELAYED UNUSUAL NOTRUMPS

In the examples shown, the unusual notrump was that side's first BID (as distinguished from a pass or double). When the unusual notrump bidder has bid a suit previously (or his partner has bid) it can still be unusual, but the meaning is affected by the previous bidding and what alternatives are still available.

WEST	NORTH	EAST	SOUTH
—	—	—	1♠
2♡	Pass	Pass	2♠
?			

WEST	NORTH	EAST	SOUTH
—	—	—	1♠
2♡	2♠	Pass	Pass
?			

In either sequence, suppose you hold

1. ♠ x ♡ AK10xxx ◇ AQxx ♣ Qx or
2. ♠ x ♡ AQ98xx ◇ xx ♣ AKJx.

You have to risk bidding again since the cost might be 6 IMPS or lots of matchpoints to sell out to 2♠, making, when you can make nine tricks in a partscore. Partner needs very little for you to make 3♡.

♠ Jxx ♡ Jx ◇ Qxxxx ♣ Qxx

would be enough opposite the second hand with normal breaks; yet partner can't bid. Probably you belong in hearts, but if partner has a heart singleton or void, rebidding 3♡ could be disasterous. You would like to show your side suit for additional safety, but partner might think you had 5–5 shape and leave you in the side suit with just three card support only a doubleton heart or a singleton honor.

Despite partner's pass you could belong in game—but the game will be in hearts or the side suit, not 3NT. So 2NT should be unusual, showing a great disparity between your first and second suit. After the 2NT bid East should bid 3♢ with

♠ xxx ♡ xx ♢ J109xx ♣ Kxx.

If West's second suit is diamonds, he will pass, but if his second suit is clubs, he will bid 3♡.

WEST	NORTH	EAST	SOUTH
—	—	—	1♠
2♢	Pass	Pass	2♠
2NT			

West's second suit must be clubs. Since he was strong enough to bid again with no encouragement, he would have doubled instead if his second suit were hearts.

♠ x ♡ AQxx ♢ AK10xxx ♣ Qx.

There is an inference the diamonds are very strong. With ♠ x ♡ Kx ♢ AJ9xxx ♣ AKxx West would bid 3♣ directly. Since he would have bid 2NT the first time with most 5–5 or 6–5 hands, the 3♣ bid implies much shorter clubs. If he holds

♠ x ♡ Ax ♢ AKJ9xx ♣ Q9xx,

he can show an even greater disparity between the two suits by bidding 2NT.

WEST	NORTH	EAST	SOUTH
—	—	—	1♠
2♣	2♠	Pass	Pass
2NT			

simply shows six clubs and four diamonds. With

♠ x ♡ AQxx ◇ xx ♣ AK10xxx

West would have bid 2♠, Michaels, originally. By the way, if the partner of the Michaels bidder bids 2NT, it asks the Michaels bidder to bid his minor.

WEST	NORTH	EAST	SOUTH
—	—	—	1◇
1♠	Double	2♠	3♣
4♠	Pass	Pass	?

You, South, hold ♠ None ♡ x ◇ AQ10xxxx ♣ KQxxx. You can't be sure of taking the right action, but since partner didn't double 4♠, it is probably right to bid again. But what should you bid? If you bid 5♣ partner will leave you there with

♠ Jxx ♡ AQxxx ◇ Jx ♣ xxx,

and spade leads may force you to lose control. Like in the sequences previously mentioned, an unusual notrump bid, 4NT in this case, would imply a two card difference in length. The fact that you bid 3♣, which was likely to be passed, followed by 4NT, means that you are very distributional rather than strong.

WEST	NORTH	EAST	SOUTH
—	—	—	1◇
Pass	1♡	1♠	3♣
4♠	Pass	Pass	4NT

4NT should not be Blackwood in this sequence because no suit has been agreed upon. Besides, how can South blast into a slam by himself over a 1♡ response? Could it show

♠ A ♡ None ◇ AKJxxxx ♣ KQxxx,

which would be analogous to the previous hand? I'll admit I wouldn't know what to do with this hand, but since 3♣ showed a strong hand, not just a distributional hand, 0–3–5–5 distribution is more likely. South held

♠ None ♡ AQx ◇ KQJxx ♣ KQ109x

and was offering a choice of three contracts.

With ♠ Qxx ♡ Kxxx ◇ xx ♣ Jxxx North would bid 5♣ over 4NT. He wouldn't bid 5♣ the previous round for fear of overstating his hand (and getting to a slam). With

♠ xxxx ♡ KJxxx ◇ Ax ♣ xx

North should bid 6♡. South's hand is as weak as it could be. He might hold

♠ None ♡ AQx ◇ KQJxx ♣ AKxxx,

in which case you would belong in 7♡, although you wouldn't get there over interference.

LEBENSOHL AFTER ONE NOTRUMP

George Boehm in a Bridge World article (Novermber 1970) suggested a new unusual notrump. His theory was when the opponents bid, 2NT is seldom the right contract. If they can get their suit established in time, probably you won't take eight tricks. If they can't get their suit established in time, you can often take nine or ten tricks. The odds are against your taking exactly eight tricks, and there is no game bonus to reward you when you do. So why not use 2NT in competition for other purposes?

WEST	NORTH	EAST	SOUTH
—	1NT	2♡	?

The old way was to play 2♠ as weak and 3♠ as forcing. 3♣ and 3♢ were also weak. The only way to INVITE game was to bid 2NT.

WEST	NORTH	EAST	SOUTH
—	1NT	2♠	?

Now the problem was even worse. Many players played 3♣ and 3♢ as weak, but 3♡ as forcing. With

♠ xx ♡ AQxxx ♢ Kxx ♣ Jxx

you would like to bid 3♡ forcing to give partner a choice between 4♡ and 3NT. With

♠ x ♡ Qxxxxx ♢ Kxx ♣ xxx

you would like to bid 3♡ rather than sell out to 2♠, but you certainly wouldn't be happy to hear partner rebid 3NT. If partner raised to 4♡ OVER YOUR NON–FORCING THREE HEART BID, you should have a play.

The solution was to bid 2NT as a relay to 3♣. He would pass 3♣ with

♠ xx ♡ Kxx ♢ xx ♣ QJxxxx

or bid 3♢ or 3♡, WEAK, with

1. ♠ x ♡ Qxx ♢ QJ10xxx ♣ xxx or
2. ♠ x ♡ K109xxx ♢ J10xx ♣ Jx.

An immediate bid at the three level would be forcing.

WEST	NORTH	EAST	SOUTH
—	1NT	2♡	?

Since 2♠ would be weak, 2NT followed by 3♠ would be invitational, and an immediate 3♠ bid would be forcing.

The main benefit of Lebensohl is to distinguish between weak and strong hands while allowing responder to bid with both. However there is a secondary benefit.

WEST	NORTH	EAST	SOUTH
—	—	—	1NT
2♡	2NT	Pass	3♣
Pass	3NT		

would guarantee a stopper in hearts while a direct 3NT bid over 2♡ would deny a heart stopper. For the latter sequence North might hold

♠ Ax ♡ xx ◇ KQ10xxx ♣ xxx.

If South held ♠ KQx ♡ xxx ◇ Axx ♣ AKxx, he could avoid the embarrassment of allowing the opponents to take the first six tricks by bidding 4♣. With the hand shown, responder would correct to diamonds. (It is close whether he should bid 4◇ or 5◇.) Also,

WEST	NORTH	EAST	SOUTH
—	—	—	1NT
2♡	3♡		

would be "Stayman," asking opener to show a four card spade suit if he had one, but denying a heart stopper.

WEST	NORTH	EAST	SOUTH
—	—	—	1NT
2♡	2NT	Pass	3♣
Pass	3♡		

would ask opener to show his four card spade suit, but would also guarantee a heart stopper. The rule is, "Slow shows; fast denies," a stopper in the opponents' suit.

Almost all experts play some variation of Lebensohl. Some think they have improved upon it by bidding directly with the weak hands and bidding 2NT first with strong hands. Others play fast shows and slow denies. The original version looks best to me. Lest you get confused by details, the basic idea is to give up a natural 2NT bid in order to show how strong your hand is.

LEBENSOHL AFTER A WEAK TWO BID

You hold ♠ xx ♡ AJ10xx ◇ Kxx ♣ xxx

WEST	NORTH	EAST	SOUTH
—	—	—	2♠
Double	Pass	?	

What should you bid? You have 8 HCP and a good five card suit; you could have held a yarborough. A jump would punish partner when he has doubled with

♠ Kx ♡ KQxx ◇ AQxx ♣ Jxx.

Suppose you hold ♠ xx ♡ Axx ◇ AQxxx ♣ xxx. Since you could hold a yarborough, should you bid 4◇ to show your values? And possibly bypass your only game when partner holds

♠ Kx ♡ KQxx ◇ Kxx ♣ Axxx?

The solution is to bid 2NT with all bad or mediocre hands. A simple response at the three level shows about 7–11 HCP. Naturally, with hands near the top or bottom of the range you use your judgment. Over 2NT the doubler will usually bid 3♣. With either

1. ♠ x ♡ AQ109x ◇ AKxx ♣ AJx or
2. ♠ x ♡ AJx ◇ AKQJxx ♣ Q10x

the doubler will refuse the transfer and bid 3♡ or 3◇, strongly inviting game. Giving up the natural 2NT pays in the long run, since showing the strength of your hand will almost always be helpful, while not being able to make a natural 2NT bid will only cost occasionally. But when the bidding goes

WEST	NORTH	EAST	SOUTH
—	—	—	2♠
Double	Pass	?	

or

WEST	NORTH	EAST	SOUTH
—	—	—	2♠
Pass	Pass	Double	Pass
?			

I would feel very uncomfortable not to be able to bid 2NT with ♠ KJx ♡ xxx ◊ KQxx ♣ Jxx. While 2NT may not be a desirable final contract, it is nice to be able to bid 2NT to invite 3NT, while still allowing partner to sign off in a suit if notrump does't appeal to him. Not being able to bid 2NT as a natural bid may hurt occasionally, but by showing your strength you can often recover.

WEST	EAST
♠ xx	♠ KJx
♡ AJ10x	♡ xxx
◊ Axxx	◊ KQxx
♣ AKx	♣ Jxx

The old way:

WEST	NORTH	EAST	SOUTH
—	—	—	2♠
Double	Pass	2NT	Pass
3NT			

The new way:

WEST	NORTH	EAST	SOUTH
—	—	—	2♠
Double	Pass	3◊	pass
3♠	Pass	3NT	

In the latter sequence, since East promises some values, West can make a Western cue bid in an effort to get to 3NT—or to 5◊ if East holds

♠ xxx ♡ x ◊ KQxxxx ♣ QJx.

THE GOOD–BAD TWO NOTRUMP

Marty Bergen carries the Lebensohl principle much farther. You hold:

1. ♠ AJ ♡ xx ◇ AKQJxx ♣ Qxx
2. ♠ Ax ♡ x ◇ KQJxxxx ♣ J10x
3. ♠ x ♡ Kx ◇ AKJxx ♣ AQ10xx
4. ♠ x ♡ xx ◇ AQJxx ♣ KQ10xx.

WEST	NORTH	EAST	SOUTH
—	—	—	1◇
Pass	1♠	2♡	?

With Hand One you would have bid 3◇ if East had passed. If you bid 3◇ over 2♡, will partner realize how strong you are? With Hand Two you would like to bid 3◇, but you are afraid partner will play you for a better hand. If you bid 3◇ and partner bids 3NT, will you pass or rescue? If he bids 3NT with

♠ Kxxxx ♡ Kx ◇ xxx ♣ Kxx,

your predictable result is down three.

You would like to bid 3♣ with hands three and four, but there is a wide variation in strength. Marty's solution is to bid 2NT with the weaker hands such as Hand Two and Hand Four. Partner will bid 3♣ or 3◇ with a mediocre hand. He will asssume that you have a two–suiter and will take a preference. With

♠ Kxxxx ♡ Qxx ◇ Qx ♣ xxx

he will bid 3♣ and, if you have a one–suiter, you will return to diamonds. With

♠ Kxxxx ♡ Qxx ◇ Qxx ♣ xx

he will bid 3◇ himself rather than risk your passing 3♣.

Partner will sometimes have a problem with a good hand. With

♠ AQxxx ♡ xxx ◊ Kx ♣ Kxx

partner would cue bid 3♡. With

♠ QJ109xx ♡ Qx ◊ Qx ♣ xxx

partner would bid 3♣, but if you bid 3◊, he might risk 3♠. This is inferentially a weak sequence since he was willing to play 3♣. With

♠ QJ109xx ♡ Ax ◊ Qx ♣ Jxx

he will bid 3♠ over 2NT, which must show a decent hand plus a good suit, and opener will raise to 4♠ with

♠ Kx ♡ xx ◊ AK10xxx ♣ Kxx.

Responder should simply bid 4♠ with

♠ QJ109xx ♡ Ax ◊ Kx ♣ Qxx.

The worst situation happens when responder holds

♠ AQxxx ♡ Kx ◊ Kxx ♣ Jxx.

He would like to bid 3NT, but since you got the notrump bid in first, and the heart lead will go through his hand, he doesn't know what to do. I don't claim this gadget is infallible, only that it gains more than it loses.

You hold ♠ xx ♡ Qxxx ◊ AKxx ♣ Axx.

WEST	NORTH	EAST	SOUTH
—	—	—	1◊
Pass	1♡	2♠	?

You would like to show heart support, and you would prefer a 3♡ bid to a pass. However it is desirable to distinguish between this hand and

♠ Kx ♡ KQxx ◊ AKxxx ♣ Jx.

The solution is to bid 2NT with the first hand and correct 3♣ or 3♢ to 3♡. This means you were stretching to bid. An immediate 3♡, when you have the alternative of a good–bad 2NT, should guarantee full values.

THE GOOD-BAD TWO NOTRUMP USED BY RESPONDER

The good–bad 2NT can also be used by responder.

WEST	NORTH	EAST	SOUTH
—	1♢	Pass	1♠
2♡	Pass	Pass	?

With ♠ KJxxx ♡ xx ♢ Kxxx ♣ Jx, bid 2NT, planning to sign off in diamonds. Incidentally, you know you don't belong in spades because partner did not make a support double. With

♠ AJxxx ♡ xx ♢ KQxx ♣ Jx

bid 3♢ immediately. Invitational! 3♠ would be forcing since, with an invitational hand and long spades, you would bid 2NT followed by 3♠. The latter sequence cannot be weak since a 2♠ bid was available. With

♠ KJxx ♡ Kxx ♢ Ax ♣ 109xx

you cannot bid 2NT since it would be unusual. Simply double. It is unlikely that partner can leave your takeout double in, but if he does, you will be delighted. Partner's most probable rebid is 2♠ to show a doubleton honor. If he does that, you can still make your natural 2NT bid one round later. The only bad situation will be when partner bids three of a minor, and you are forced to guess whether to bid 3NT or not. My inclination would be to gamble it out if partner bids 3♢. Maybe you can take five diamond tricks. If he bids 3♣ I would pass because I don't know where our tricks will come from.

You hold ♠ Ax ♡ Q10xxx ◊ x ♣ KJ9xx.

WEST	NORTH	EAST	SOUTH
—	1◊	Pass	1♡
Pass	1NT	2◊	?

The bidding has taken a surprising turn. Bid 3♣, showing a good hand and a willingness for partner to take a preference; he might bid 4♡ with an appropriate hand. If you held

♠ Axx ♡ Qxxx ◊ x ♣ Q10xxx,

you would bid 2NT, transfering partner to 3♣.

You hold ♠ Kxx ♡ Jxx ◊ Kxxx ♣ Jxx.

WEST	NORTH	EAST	SOUTH
—	—	—	1♠
Pass	1NT	2♣	2♡
?			

If you pass, 2♡ will probably conclude the auction. You'd like to push the opponents higher, and partner might even make 3♣. But you surely don't want to encourage partner to bid more, competitively or otherwise. So bid 2NT. Unless partner has an unusual hand, he will bid 3♣. Suppose you hold either

1. ♠ Axxx ♡ x ◊ Qxxx ♣ Jxxx or
2. ♠ Kx ♡ xxxx ◊ KJxx ♣ Qxx.

It may easily be your hand. If partner wants to bid more, you won't mind. So you should raise to 3♣.

WEST	NORTH	EAST	SOUTH
—	1♣	2♠	Pass
Pass	Double	Pass	?

Partner doesn't know whether you have a good hand with spades, a hopeless hand or a distributional hand unsuitable for a negative double. With

♠ Jxxx ♡ xxxx ◇ Qxx ♣ xx,

bid 2NT and correct partner's 3♣ bid to 3♡. This may not be a good contract, but at least partner is unlikely to raise to 4♡. With

♠ xxx ♡ Q10xxx ◇ A10x ♣ xx,

bid 3♡ immediately to show a good hand, considering your failure to make a negative double the previous round.

With a few exceptions, when you and partner might or might not be interested in game, AND when the last BID (as distinguished from a pass or double) was made by your opponents, a 2NT bid by you is good–bad rather than natural.

Let's consider the exceptions.

WEST	NORTH	EAST	SOUTH
—	—	—	1♠
2◇	2NT		

The 2NT bid is non–forcing and shows about 10–11 HCP and describes hands of this type:

1. ♠ xx ♡ Axx ◇ Kxxx ♣ A10xx or
2. ♠ 10x ♡ Qxx ◇ KQx ♣ K109xx.

With new suits forcing, negative doubles and preemptive jump responses available, a good–bad 2NT is not needed to define your strength.

WEST	NORTH	EAST	SOUTH
—	—	—	1◇
1♠	1NT	2♠	2NT

North's free 1NT bid shows his strength within a very narrow range. South simply has to place the contract. 3◇ should mean you wanted to play 3◇. When South holds a good five card diamond suit, his hand is worth an extra trick offensively and is poorer defensively than when his hand is completely balanced. Suppose the four hands are as follows:

	NORTH	
	♠ KJx	
	♡ Kxx	
	◊ Qxx	
	♣ 10xxx	
WEST		EAST
♠ A109xx		♠ Qxx
♡ Qxx		♡ J10xx
◊ x		◊ Jxxx
♣ Axxx		♣ KJ
	SOUTH	
	♠ xx	
	♡ Axx	
	◊ AK10xx	
	♣ Qxx	

North–South can make 2NT, East–West would make 2♠. Bidding will usually be better than passing when EITHER contract will make. After a free 1NT bid, 2NT by opener is merely competitive, not good–bad. You could play the same way after

WEST	NORTH	EAST	SOUTH
—	—	—	1♣
Pass	1NT	2♡	2NT

if you play a narrow range 1NT response over 1♣ (like 8–10 HCP). If the 1NT response could show 6–10 HCP or possibly an even stronger hand (like a forcing notrump response to a major), then 2NT should be good–bad.

WEST	NORTH	EAST	SOUTH
—	—	—	1♠
Pass	2◊	2♡	Pass
Pass	?		

A 2NT bid in this sequence would be natural. One reason is that North can't be weak. His Two Over One response guaranteed a rebid and showed game–invitational values or better. So a good–bad 2NT is not needed to distinguish between invitational and weak bids.

WEST	NORTH	EAST	SOUTH
—	—	—	1♠
Pass	2♢	2♡	2NT

Again, after the 2♢ response North cannot be weak. Since he promises a rebid. South can simply pass to show a non–descript minimum hand or a hand too weak to bid 3♣. Besides, how could South want to sign off in 3♣?

THE GOOD–BAD TWO NOTRUMP DOES NOT APPLY AFTER A TWO OVER ONE RESPONSE.

WEST	NORTH	EAST	SOUTH
—	—	—	1♡
1♠	Pass	1NT	2♡
?			

The 1NT bid after partner has overcalled shows a fairly narrow range, similar to a free 1NT bid by the partner of the opening bidder. A 3♣ or 3♢ bid would be to play, and there is no need for a good–bad 2NT here. Thus, a 2NT bid should be natural and invitational, probably based upon a good six card suit such as

1. ♠ AKQxxx ♡ Jx ♢ Kxx ♣ xx or
2. ♠ AQJxxx ♡ xx ♢ Ax ♣ Qxx

We have run out of exceptions. Perhaps there should be more, but I can't think of any.

You hold:

1. ♠ AQxx ♡ Kxx ♢ AQx ♣ A10x
2. ♠ AKx ♡ Kx ♢ AQxxx ♣ Axx
3. ♠ AQxx ♡ x ♢ K10xx ♣ Axxx
4. ♠ AQxx ♡ xx ♢ Kx ♣ KQJxx
5. ♠ AQxx ♡ xx ♢ Kx ♣ AKQ10x

WEST	NORTH	EAST	SOUTH
—	—	—	1♡
Double	Pass	2♢	2♡
?			

With the first hand you have to double again instead of bidding 2NT as you had originally intended, since 2NT would be good–bad. With the second hand you might bid 3NT, gambling that partner has the ♢K or the ♠Q as entry for a diamond finesse. With the third hand you were planning to pass 2♢, but can now bid 2NT to get to 3♢ (as compared with raising to 3♢ directly with

♠ AQxx ♡ x ♢ K10xx ♣ AQ10x).

You might bid 2NT with the fourth hand expecting partner to bid 3♣. With a stronger hand, such as the fifth hand you would bid 3♣ immediately. Incidentally, over 2NT partner should bid 3♢ rather than 3♣ with

♠ Jx ♡ xxxx ♢ QJ9xxx ♣ x.

You hold ♠ KJx ♡ xxx ♢ Qxx ♣ A10xx.

WEST	NORTH	EAST	SOUTH
—	—	—	1♠
Pass	1NT	2♢	2♠
?			

you would like to bid 2NT, but you have to bid 3♢. Perhaps partner, with

♠ xx ♡ AJx ♢ AK10xxxx ♣ x,

will bid 3♠ himself. The good–bad 2NT requires a while to get used to. Until you have played it for several sessions, you will probably forget and bid 2NT, natural, in a sequence where it is supposed to be good–bad. In some undiscussed sequence you may think the good–bad 2NT applies and partner won't, or vice versa. Keep a record of your results. The idea is good, but you may want to adopt different rules as to when it applies. I don't pretend to have the final answers.

Quiz Six

1. IMPS, None Vulnerable, you hold:
♠ 7 ♡ Q654 ◇ J873 ♣ A973

WEST	NORTH	EAST	SOUTH
1♡	1♠	2♡	Pass
Pass	Double	Pass	?

What do you bid?

2. Matchpoints, Both Vulnerable, you hold:
♠ A75 ♡ J9 ◇ 10875 ♣ J752

WEST	NORTH	EAST	SOUTH
1♠	2♡	2♠	Pass
Pass	2NT	Pass	?

What do you bid?

3. You hold ♠ AJ64 ♡ K8 ◇ Q10865 ♣ 75.

WEST	NORTH	EAST	SOUTH
—	1NT*	2♣**	Pass
2◇	Pass	2♡	?

*15–17
**Hamilton showing any one suited hand
What do you bid?

4. You hold ♠ A98 ♡ K ◇ AKJ1072 ♣ A52.

WEST	NORTH	EAST	SOUTH
—	—	2♡	Double
Pass	2NT	Pass	?

What do you bid?

5. You hold ♠ KQ87 ♡ 763 ◇ 10854 ♣ A9.

WEST	NORTH	EAST	SOUTH
—	1◇	Pass	1♠
2♡	2NT	Pass	?

What do you bid?

6. You hold ♠ Q73 ♡ Q74 ◇ A875 ♣ K92.

WEST	NORTH	EAST	SOUTH
—	—	1♣	Pass
1♠	2♡	2♠	?

What do you bid?

7. You hold ♠ J1083 ♡ AJ8 ◇ J652 ♣ K8.

WEST	NORTH	EAST	SOUTH
1♠	2NT	3◇*	?

*Limit raise in spades or better

What do you bid?

8. You hold ♠ J ♡ AQ10 ◇ K1097652 ♣ K5.

WEST	NORTH	EAST	SOUTH
—	—	1♠	2◇
2♠	3◇	3♠	?

What do you bid?

Answers

1. **TWO NOTRUMP**. If this were matchpoints or if you were on lead, you might leave the double in. Under the conditions given, it is too close to risk it. If partner has 5–4–3–1 distribution, you want to find your 4–4 fit.

2. **THREE HEARTS**. If you bid 3♣ and that is not partner's side suit, he will bid 3♢. So there should be no problem in finding your 4–4 fit. However you have a good hand for partner. Even if you could do a trick better in a minor, your +130 would lose to the +140's. Sometimes your 4–4 does not do better; it does worse than the 6–2 fit. So simply bid 3♡.

3. **TWO NOTRUMP**. This situation will be discussed in more in the next chapter. I can't see any reason why Lebensohl should not apply here. When you bid 3♡ next round you will show four spades and a heart stopper.

4. **THREE NOTRUMP**. It is a gamble, but I would bid 3NT. The opening lead will probably be a small heart, and if partner has the queen of diamonds or it falls, you will have nine tricks.

5. **FOUR DIAMONDS**. Whether partner has a one–suiter or both minors, you have a pretty good hand for him. It will be a great hand if he has a singleton heart but only a fair hand if he has a singleton spade. My inclination is to bid 4♢, but it is close.

6. **THREE HEARTS**. You can show three degrees of strength for a raise to 3♡. Bidding 2NT is the weakest; bidding 3♡ is the middle action; bidding 3♣ is the strongest. Your queen of spades is probably worthless and you have no ruffing values. But you do have nine working points. 3♡ looks about right to me.

7. **FOUR DIAMONDS**. Your problem is more complicated than usual. If your high cards were all in the minors, you could jump to game, figuring that it would be a good sacrifice if it did not make. Here with very good defense values you might even be able to set 3♠. 4♢ is my choice. This shows a fair offensive hand. With a weaker hand diamonds could have been shown simply by doubling.

8. **FIVE DIAMONDS**. Partner has shown a sound raise since his alternative was to bid 2NT. Most of the missing high cards should be in declarer's hand and your finesses will work.

Chapter Seven

THE ONE NOTRUMP BATTLE

AN OPENING NOTRUMP BID HAS MANY ADVANTAGES whatever the range used. The opponents have been preempted. If they want to overcall, they have to do so at the two level. If they do overcall, partner has a very good idea of both his offensive and defensive prospects. If they don't overcall, it is much easier for you to play 1NT than for the opponents to defend. The opening leader doesn't know where his partner's strength is located. Should he lead aggressively or passively? If he avoids leading his best suit so as not to give declarer an undeserved trick, how will his partner know to lead the "best suit" rather than return the suit led originally?

This book is not concerned with defense, but when you realize the defensive problems an opening 1NT bid creates, you can see some of its advantages. Many experts want to bid 1NT more frequently than they could playing a 15–17 point range. As the range is lowered, the bid becomes more dangerous. The questions are: Does opening 1NT more frequently with a weaker hand compensate for the greater risks in the opening bid itself? Also, what problems are created on other hands where the "standard" 15–17 point notrump can't be used.

Let's consider the strong notrump opening first.

AFTER A STRONG ONE NOTRUMP OPENING

As mentioned in the last chapter, I favor Lebensohl when the one notrump bid is overcalled. Two of a higher ranking suit is weak or non–invitational. A three level bid, whether a jump or not, is forcing. A two notrump response is a transfer to 3♣. This may be the start of a weak sequence when responder passes 3♣ or bids a lower ranking suit at the three level. It may start an invitational sequence.

WEST	NORTH	EAST	SOUTH
1NT	2♢	2NT	Pass
3♣	Pass	3♡/3♠?	

This is an invitational sequence since responder could have bid 2♡ or 2♠. The 2NT response may be the start of a game forcing sequence. Two notrump followed by Three notrump shows a stopper in the opponents' suit while an immediate 3NT bid denies a stopper. 2NT followed by a cue bid is "Stayman with a stopper" while an immediate cue bid is "Stayman without a stopper." This assumes the overcall was natural. If the overcall shows the suit bid plus another suit, Lebensohl still applies. Thus, if a 2♡ overcall shows hearts and a minor, 2NT would still be a transfer to 3♣, and an immediate 3NT bid would deny a heart stopper.

You don't worry about the unknown suit which is probably a four card suit anyway. Even when the second suit is known, you only show the absence or presence of a stopper in the long suit. If, by any chance, the 2♡ overcall was a spade transfer, showing a spade suit, Lebensohl would apply, and you would bid as though the overcall had been 2♠. Three notrump would deny a spade stopper.

If the opponents are playing the convention called "Hamilton" in some parts of the country and "Capelletti" in others, where a 2♣ bid asks partner to bid 2♢, after which the 2♣ bidder shows his suit, responder can wait until the real suit is bid and use Lebensohl over the real suit. Some players say that if partner of the 2♣ bidder passes, perhaps with

♠xx ♡xx ♢xx ♣J10xxxxx

opener must bid. They alert the pass over 2♣, saying that opener is required to take action if the next hand passes. I don't like this method as it allows fourth hand to pass in order to show a very weak hand and, if the 2♣ bidder's suit was clubs, to play at the two level instead of the three level. If opener can pass or double when fourth hand passes 2♣, you won't have to alert the opponents and fourth hand will seldom be willing to gamble a pass since he doesn't know how strong his partner is. By the way, Fred Hamilton recommends using the double of 2♣ as Stayman. Other players prefer a double of 2♣ to show a good defensive hand so opener can double if responder can't. If the double shows values, 2♢ is "Stayman" and two of a major is natural but weak.

Suppose the opening bidder's LHO doubles. If the double has some sort of conventional meaning such as a transfer to 2♣, responder can disregard the double and bid as though there was a pass or he can redouble with a strong balanced hand. Traditionally a double of 1NT is penalty. The ideal penalty double is a hand with a good suit and stoppers

♠ Ax ♡ xx ♢ KQJ10xx ♣ AJx.

This is a good second position double since you will be on lead. It would not be a good penalty double in fourth position since, without a diamond lead, declarer can probably establish his tricks before you can establish yours.

The ideal penalty double is seldom dealt, so if you play the double for penalty, it is usually on a strong balanced hand—as strong as the opening notrump or stronger. In theory, the doubler has an advantage since his strength lies over the notrump bidder. In practice, this advantage is outweighed by the fact that declarer knows what his combined assets are, while the defenders do not. The balanced hand doubler is gambling his partner will have more strength than his left hand opponent and he won't lose too many tricks by making the wrong opening lead and not knowing where to attack later. His partner can pull the double with a weak hand and a five card suit or longer.

With a balanced hand his partner should leave the double in regardless of strength. With a yarborough, he passes and simply hopes his partner has an exceptionally strong hand (perhaps 22 points instead of 17) or a good suit. A rescue to a four card suit is like jumping from the frying pan into the fire. –180 is not always a bottom—not when other pairs with your cards are taking 200, 300 and 500 point sets. Few opponents have a way to redouble for business to make you pay heavily for your transgressions.

Second hand will not often have a good penalty double of 1NT. Almost never will fourth hand have a good penalty double of 1NT. His strength is located in front of the notrump bidder, and his partner will have no idea what to lead. While I have my doubts about playing a penalty double of a strong notrump in second seat, I'm sure there is a better use for a double in fourth position. Unless you adopt the Woolsey convention, which will soon be explained, my suggestion is to play a double of a strong notrump by fourth hand to show a good overcall. Thus, with

♠KQ10xxx ♡Ax ◊Q10xx ♣x

you would double; partner would relay to 2♣ and you would bid 2♠.

With ♠ xxx ♡ Kxx ◊ AKJ ♣ 10xxx partner should bid 3◊ to show a spade raise with a concentration of strength in diamonds, and you would jump to 4♠. If partner had a diamond suit he really wanted to show, he would have bid it over the double.

With ♠ Q10xxxx ♡ x ◊ Q10xx ♣ xx you would bid 2♠ immediately, and even with a somewhat better hand than the previous example say,

♠ Kxx ♡ Kxx ◊ AKJ ♣ 10xxx

partner would pass. That is another factor. With a long suit and any sort of unbalanced hand it pays for fourth hand to bid—almost regardless of strength! Suppose the hands are as follows:

	NORTH	
	♠ AK	
	♡ xxx	
	◊ AQxx	
	♣ Jxxx	
WEST		EAST
♠ Qxx		♠ xx
♡ AKx		♡ QJxx
◊ KJxx		◊ xx
♣ Kxx		♣ Q109xx
	SOUTH	
	♠ J10xxxx	
	♡ xxx	
	◊ 1098	
	♣ A	

or

	NORTH	
	♠ KQxx	
	♡ Ax	
	◇ QJxx	
	♣ Jxx	
WEST		EAST
♠ AJx		♠ 10xxx
♡ KQx		♡ 10x
◇ Axx		◇ K10xxx
♣ Qxxx		♣ Kx
	SOUTH	
	♠ xx	
	♡ Jxxxxx	
	◇ x	
	♣ A109x	

The first hand plays very well in spades since you can use the ♣A and club ruffs as entries to take diamond finesses. Defending against notrump, you could never establish and cash the spade suit, even if North should guess to lead a spade. Passing 1NT would result in –120 or –150. Bidding 2♠ would result in +140.

The second example is less clear–cut. North–South will probably make 2♡, and they may or may not set 1NT. You need a system that allows you to bid in fourth seat with weak–distributional hands, without partner raising to game, just because he has the values you are playing him for.

Suppose 1NT is doubled for penalty. We already mentioned how seldom second hand has a good penalty double. Even when he has 18 or 19 balanced points, he won't know what to lead, and the defenders will often drop a couple of defensive tricks. Or the doubler's partner may rescue with a long suit.

Most people worry too much about playing 1NT doubled and go to costly lengths to avoid a largely imaginary danger. I like a simple system of bidding over the double. All suit bids are natural, and a redouble means the opponents made a mistake because your side has the balance of power.

You hold:

1. ♠xx ♡J10xxx ♢Qxxx ♣xx
2. ♠xx ♡xxx ♢xx ♣10xxxxx

WEST	NORTH	EAST	SOUTH
—	—	—	1NT
Double	?		

Bid 2♡ with the first hand and bid 2♣ with the second. Many experts play a system of run–outs so that a pass requires opener to redouble, and a redouble by responder forces opener to bid 2♣. This way they can play their whole system, just as though there were no double (2♣ is Stayman; 2♢ and 2♡ are transfers, etc.), and they can look for a 4–4 fit rather than play 1NT doubled. It is somewhat more difficult for the opponents to double a suit run–out than to double or leave partner's double in a notrump contract.

"Systems on" over a double may sound like a good idea, but I don't like it. When 1NT is doubled for penalty, it is extremely unlikely your side belongs in 3NT, game in a major, game in a minor, or in slam. The most likely game is 1NT redoubled. A system that won't allow you to play in your most probable game contract has two strikes against it. All of the gadgets to get you to the right games and slams in an uncontested auction are wasted because you won't have the hands with which to use them. Besides, if you can't redouble to show the balance of power, partner won't be able to double the opponents when they run from the double. That is the biggest disadvantage in not being able to redouble with a good hand.

All four suits are needed for run–out purposes. If you play Stayman you can't run to 2♣. If you play transfers, you can't run to 2♢. Half the time, when you are in trouble, your long suit is a minor, so you need some way to run to 2♣ or 2♢.

What is wrong with a system that allows you to pass and forces partner to redouble when you want to run to a minor? There are several things wrong!

First, 1NT doubled may be your best (or least bad) contract. Remember how hard it is to defend 1NT contracts? Even when responder has a yarborough, you can often get out for down one.

Second, there may be no better spot. The run–outs only gain when you find a 4–4 fit and there may be no 4–4 fit or when the opponents fail to double.

Good opponents will probably find a way to double your run–out, especially when your auction tells them you are in trouble. If your opponents are not good, they will surely drop two tricks defending 1NT while expert defenders may drop only one.

Besides needing all four suits for runout, there is another reason for not playing transfers.

East holds ♠Axx ♡xx ♢Kxx ♣10xxxx.

WEST	NORTH	EAST	SOUTH
—	—	—	1NT
Double	2♢	?	

If 2♢ is a heart transfer East can double to show general strength and West may double the heart run–out with a suitable heart holding. If North had bid 2♡, his real suit, East couldn't double unless his double is negative. In other words, it is easier for the opponents to double for penalty when you make a transfer bid than when you bid your real suit.

Suppose the bidding goes

WEST	NORTH	EAST	SOUTH
—	—	—	1NT
2♡	Double		

According to the rules in an earlier chapter, the double here is penalty. Responder knows opener's approximate strength and distribution so there is no great need for a Negative Double. Furthermore, if you play Negative Doubles, after

WEST	NORTH	EAST	SOUTH
—	—	—	1NT
2♡	Pass	Pass	?

South, as opener, is supposed to make a reopening double with

♠AQx ♡Kx ◇QJxx ♣QJxx

in case responder had a penalty double. This seems unsound. Nevertheless, many experts favor Negative Doubles to enable them to compete more effectively at the part–score level at the cost of not being able to penalize the opponents as often. Suppose responder holds

♠Axxx ♡xx ◇Qxxx ♣Jxx.

After a 2♡ overcall, his orthodox call is a pass. But if opener holds

1. ♠KJxx ♡Axx ◇KJx ♣Axx
2. ♠Kx ♡Jxx ◇AKx ♣KQxxx,

a Negative Double would allow your side to buy the bid successfully.

If you don't play Negative Doubles, you have to risk bidding four card suits. Partner opens 1NT and RHO overcalls 2♡. Bid 2♠ with

♠KJxx ♡ x ◇Q10xxx ♣xxx.

This could work out spectacularly badly, but in the long run, it will gain—compared to passing. Heart length on your right increases the probability that partner has three or four spades. Of course, when holding this hand you would prefer to be playing Negative Doubles.

In an uncontested auction

WEST	NORTH	EAST	SOUTH
—	—	—	1NT
Pass	2♡*	Pass	3◇

*Transfer

3◇ should show a good hand with good spade support with a concentration of diamond strength or a doubleton diamond, according to partnership agreement. North guarantees at least five spades; he knows more about opener's hand than opener knows about his; and South has no reason to suggest play in diamonds. However, when the bidding goes

WEST	NORTH	EAST	SOUTH
—	—	—	1NT
2♡	2♠	Pass	?

Opener should bid 3◇ with

1. ♠ Qx ♡ Axx ◇ AK109x ♣ Kxx
2. ♠ Kx ♡ Ax ◇ KQxxxx ♣ Kxx.

In other words, 3◇ should be natural. Responder's spade length is suspect. If the opponents compete further by bidding 3♡, partner will have a better idea what to do than if you had passed.

While it is close, I still prefer Penalty Doubles to Negative Doubles. But my penalty doubles are more tentative than most people's. After partner bids 1NT and RHO overcalls 2♡, I would double with

♠ Kxx ♡ Jxx ◊ Axxx ♣ xxx

since my alternatives are to pass or commit the hand to game. If opener has a doubleton heart he should pull the double unless he has an exceptionally good defensive hand.

These are my recommendations after partner's Negative Double of 2♡:

1. ♠ KQx ♡ Jx ◊ KQxxx ♣ KQx
2. ♠ AQJx ♡ Ax ◊ QJxx ♣ J10x
3. ♠ Qx ♡ Kx ◊ AJxxx ♣ KQxx
4. ♠ Axx ♡ Qx ◊ AKQxxx ♣ Jx

Bid 3◊ with Hand One, bid 2♠ with Hand Two, bid 2NT with Hand Three, and bid 3NT with Hand Four.

Although my preference is to play penalty doubles when the opponents overcall a strong notrump, I feel obligated to present Negative Doubles in their best light.

The following system, using a combination of Negative Doubles and modified Lebensohl, is the brainchild of Lew Stansby and Chip Martel. If you are willing to accept the obligation of opener to reopen with a double after the auction

WEST	NORTH	EAST	SOUTH
—	—	—	1NT
2◊/♡/♠	Pass	Pass	?

with a doubleton in the opponents' suit (unless it is AK, AQ, KQ, KJ or QJ) this system is very good.

Stansby & Martel System After Interference Over Your One Notrump Opening

1. 1NT, 2♠, DOUBLE followed by 3♡ is forcing and shows at least five hearts.
2. Direct three level bids (whether jumps or not) are invitational.
3. 2NT is a transfer to 3♣; when followed by a lower ranking suit, it is to play (non–invitational).
4. 2NT followed by a higher ranking suit is forcing, no stopper in the opponents' suit.
5. Double followed by a higher ranking suit at the three level is forcing and shows a stopper.
6. A direct 3NT bid denies a stopper.
7. 2NT followed by 3NT shows a stopper.
8. Cue bid of opponents' suit shows a singleton in their suit and a four card major (game forcing).
9. 2NT followed by a cue bid shows a singleton in the opponents' suit, no four card major, game force.
10. Double followed by cue bid shows no stopper, no singleton, four card major.
11. Double followed by 3NT shows stopper, no singleton, four card major.
12. If North bids 2NT, East raises West's suit, and the bid is passed around to North, a double shows a 3NT bid (i.e. stopper) and 3NT shows a cue bid (i.e. singleton).

This is a lot to remember. However, if you understand the logic, you may be able to figure out what the bids should mean and not have to rely upon memory alone.

Most doubles are negative showing 6–9 HCP with shortage in the opponents' suit. Typically you double a 2♡ overcall with:

1. ♠AJxx ♡xx ◇Qxxx ♣xxx
2. ♠KQx ♡xx ◇Jxxx ♣Qxxx
3. ♠Jxxx ♡x ◇Axxx ♣Kxxx.

Opener is allowed to pass with a strong holding in the opponents' suit.

A Negative Double is possible with a singleton when not strong enough to take other or further action gambling that partner won't leave the double in or that you will set the contract anyway. But when you plan to describe your hand with two bids, your first bid should not be a double when your defensive strength is poor.

You hold

1. ♠KJxxx ♡Kx ◇Axxx ♣xx
2. ♠KJxxx ♡x ◇Axxx ♣Kxx

WEST	NORTH	EAST	SOUTH
—	—	—	1NT
2♡	?		

With the first hand, a double followed by 3♠ would be natural and forcing and would also show a heart stopper. If partner passes your double you are likely to set the contract for more than the value of your game. With the second hand, you would describe your hand by bidding 2NT followed by 3♠ since you wouldn't like to risk partner's passing your double. Neither a cue bid nor a 2NT bid allows a penalty pass. Also a double implies an unbid four card major while a 2NT bid does not. Now that you know the secrets you don't have to rely on rote memory to distinguish between sequences 4 and 5 or between sequences 8 and 10.

I have switched back and forth from the problems of the side that opens the bidding to the side that does not. The reason for not discussing the problems separately is that they are interwoven. If the defenders seldom get a good penalty double, opener's side shouldn't devote most of its bidding sequences to run–outs. Likewise, the defenders might find a better use for a penalty double, especially in fourth position. If certain types of hands are better for offense than for defense, the system you adopt should enable you to bid with these hands.

There are many defenses to 1NT.

Typical Defenses To One Notrump Openings

1. Natural; doubles are for penalty; all suit bids show the suit.
2. Bids that show a specific two suiters; Landy is an example, where 2♣ shows the majors and all other bids are natural.
3. Bids that show a suit other than the one bid plus another suit. Astro is an example. 2♣ shows hearts and another suit; 2♢ shows spades and another suit.
4. Bids that show the suit bid plus an unspecified suit like bidding spades to show spades and a minor.
5. Transfer bids; 2♢ is a transfer to hearts, showing hearts.
6. Unusual transfer bids; 2♢ is a transfer to hearts showing hearts or the black suits.
7. Complete systems where every bid has a meaning, usually artificial.

Every defense has some shortcomings. Natural bidding doesn't enable you to compete often enough. It is too dangerous to overcall a five card suit unless, at the same time, you can suggest an alternate contract. Yet, with two five card suits or 5–4–3–1 distribution, it usually pays to play the hand rather than defend. Landy is not bad. You only give up one natural bid, and you can show the two most important suits which give you the best chance for game. But most experts think you should compete more frequently than Landy permits.

Hamilton (or Capelletti) is popular in my area. 2♣ shows a one–suiter; 2♢ shows the majors; 2♡ shows hearts and a minor; 2♠ shows spades and a minor. Perhaps this convention is best, but the two things I don't like about it are the 2♣ bid makes it easier for the responder to compete than when you bid your real suit and even though a major suit overcall shows that major plus a minor, it is not often practical to look for the minor fit at the three level. After the auction

WEST	NORTH	EAST	SOUTH
—	—	—	1NT
2♠	Pass	2NT	

Your 2NT bid asks partner to bid his minor. But if you hold

♠x ♡Jxxxx ♢KJxx ♣Jxx,

should you pass 2♠ (which hasn't yet been doubled) or bid 2NT, possibly finding partner with

♠AKJxx ♡xxx ♢x ♣Kxxx?

Ed Davis has a complicated, but well worked out defense against a Hamilton 2♣ overcall (showing an undisclosed one–suiter) after 1NT–2♣– ?.

The Davis System Against Hamilton

1. Pass shows less than invitational values OR a desire to use Lebensohl after the 2♣ bidder bids a suit OR certain game hands with a singleton. However, and this has to be alerted, if the partner of the 2♣ bidder passes, opener must double for penalty or bid a suit. Following the pass, a double by responder is for penalty. Bidding a suit is equivalent to a takeout double since it shows support for that suit and higher ranking suits.
2. Double shows an invitational one suited hand or a balanced hand with at least invitational values. After the opponents bid their suit responder will bid his suit immediately with an invitational one–suiter.
3. 2♢ is game–forcing Stayman, used for hands not interested in penalties or using Lebensohl (such as 5–5 or 6–4 distribution).
4. 2♡ and 2♠ is natural and non–forcing, but willing for partner to raise in a competitive auction.
5. 2NT is a minor suit takeout; opener is not expected to compete; a subsequent major suit bid by responder is a singleton with invitational or better values (and, of course, at least nine cards in the minors).
6. 3♣, 3♢, 3♡, 3♠—preemptive.
7. 3NT, to play.
8. 4♣ is Gerber.
9. 4♢ and 4♡ are Texas transfers.

I like this defense with one exception. I don't think opener should have to bid if East doesn't. East will seldom gamble on a pass unless opener promises to take further action.

I don't know why Astro has lost its popularity. It gives you a reasonable chance to play the minor suit at the two level. I suppose its main weakness is that it is not efficient in showing both majors. Partner can't evaluate his hand if he holds the major not guaranteed.

The choice of defenses against 1NT is largely a matter of taste. The defenses I prefer are Woolsey against a strong notrump and Mohan against a weak notrump. I'll explain Woolsey first.

The Woolsley Defense To One Notrump

1. Double of 1NT shows a five card or longer minor and a four card major. The doubler's partner bids 2♣ to say, "I want to play in your minor." The doubler passes or converts to diamonds.
2. 2♣ shows the majors.
3. 2♢ shows a major one–suiter.
4. 2♡ shows hearts and a minor.
5. 2♠ shows spades and a minor.

Suppose the bidding goes

WEST	NORTH	EAST	SOUTH
—	—	—	1NT
Double	Pass	2♣	Pass
2♢	Pass	2♡	

The 2♡ bid means, "I changed my mind. Let's play in your major." The 2♡ bidder probably has something like

♠Axxx ♡Qxx ♢x ♣10xxxx.

He was willing to play clubs in the unlikely event that clubs were his partner's minor, but rather than play a 5–1 diamond fit, he will risk a 4–3 major fit, hoping, of course, to find a 4–4 fit. A 2♢ response to the double says, "I want to play in your major."

Respond 2♣ to the double with

♠Axxx ♡Qx ♢xxx ♣xxxx

rather than gamble that partner's major was spades. The main objective is to find a playable contract, not necessarily the highest scoring contract. Other pairs, not playing this convention, may not enter the bidding at all, and it is very unlikely they have a way to find their 4–4 major fit. So you shouldn't take undue risks to find the top spot when a good contract is the alternative. If the response is anything but 2♣ or 2♢ it means that the bidder has a good suit which he wants to play rather than one of the doubler's suits. This convention, unlike most others, allows you to play your minor suits at the two level and thus has an added safety feature.

I have already mentioned how seldom you get a good penalty double of a strong notrump. So it doesn't bother me to give it up in order to play this convention. Ironically this convention allows you to defend against 1NT doubled more frequently than when you are playing straight penalty doubles, and when you do defend, your opening lead and subsequent defense will be better. The following is from actual play:

WEST	NORTH	EAST	SOUTH
—	—	—	1NT
Double	Pass	Pass	Pass

	NORTH	
	♠ 653	
	♡ J986	
	◊ 10875	
	♣ 104	
WEST		EAST
♠ KQ42		♠ 987
♡ 542		♡ A73
◊ Q		◊ A642
♣ AK876		♣ J93
	SOUTH	
	♠ AJ10	
	♡ KQ10	
	◊ KJ93	
	♣ Q52	

As East I figured partner would lead his long minor, and I had excellent support for it, no matter which minor partner held. Declarer won the opening club lead with his queen and led the king of hearts. The defense from this point was double dummy. I knew partner's second suit was spades, and by the rule of eleven I knew declarer couldn't beat my ♣ J. So I used my entries to lead spades, and we set the hand two tricks. (It would be a mistake to duck two rounds of hearts; declarer would, in desperation, lead the ◊ K.) This hand came up the first time I used this convention, and I have been sold on it ever since.

The only thing I am in doubt about is whether the double in fourth position should have the same (Woolsey) meaning or whether it is more important to be able to distinguish between sound and weak overcalls by fourth hand. The latter is probably more important, although I hate to give up Woolsey in fourth position. It is a close decision.

A 2♢ bid over 1NT shows a major one–suiter. Normally partner will bid 2♡, which you can pass or correct to spades. However a 2♠ response says, "Pass if your suit is spades. If your suit is hearts, I'm inviting game." A 2NT response shows game interest no matter which major partner has. Another advantage of the transfer is that the 2♢ bidder can bid again with an exceptionally good hand. While

WEST	NORTH	EAST	SOUTH
—	—	—	1NT
2♢			

purportedly shows a one suiter, the bidding could go

WEST	NORTH	EAST	SOUTH
—	—	—	1NT
2♢	Pass	2♡	Pass
3♢	Pass	?	

West's 3♢ bid confirms hearts (he couldn't do this with spades) and shows diamonds are his second suit with a very strong playing hand such as

♠x ♡AKJxxx ♢KQ10xx ♣x.

If East has as much as three small hearts and the ace of diamonds, he can now bid 4♡. Or West could bid 3♠ over the 2♡ response with

♠AQJxxx ♡x ♢KQ10x ♣Kx,

while an immediate 3♠ bid would be more preemptive.

Suppose the opponents are playing a weak notrump (12–14) or a very weak notrump (10–12). Now you don't want to give up the penalty double of 1NT. John Mohan has devised the following defense to a weak notrump:

The Mohan Defense To One Notrump

1. Double is penalty.
2. 2♣ is for the majors.
3. 2♢ is a heart transfer.
4. 2♡ is a spade transfer.
5. 2♠ shows spades and a minor.
6. 2NT shows hearts and a minor.

That's not all! There are some cute follow–ups. After transferring to a major, a minor suit bid shows a six card minor and that the major was only four cards in length. Thus, after the auction

WEST	NORTH	EAST	SOUTH
—	—	—	1NT
2♡	Pass	2♠	Pass
3♢			

West shows ♠KJxx ♡x ♢AK10xxx ♣Jx. East could now jump to 4♠ with

♠AQxx ♡xxxx ♢Qx ♣xxx,

and with a slightly better hand East would have jumped to 3♠ the previous round.

After transferring to the major, a 2NT bid shows a good, balanced hand, probably 6–3–2–2 or 7–2–2–2 distribution. The primary purpose is to describe the hand, not to seriously suggest playing it in notrump. Other bids over the transfer have their natural meaning and show extra values. This way immediate jump overcalls are preemptive and you don't have to double 1NT, just to show strength, with unbalanced hands such as

♠KJxxxxx ♡x ♢AKJ ♣Kx.

If I doubled with this, I would not feel confident of a good result when everyone passed. With this hand I'd much rather risk getting as high as 3♠ to invite a raise to four. There is another unusual wrinkle; when partner doubles 1NT, you will pass with most balanced hands or most reasonably good hands. But when you hold

♠ x ♡ AQxxx ◇ Q10xxx ♣ xx,

you are not anxious to defend, with partner leading a club or spade. If you do pull the double, the unusual follow–up is to act as though partner had opened 1NT. In other words, 2♣ would be Stayman; 2◇ a transfer to hearts, etc.

The only deviation would be, since partner would double with 14 points or 22 points, over 2♣ (Stayman) with 18 or more he would bid 2NT rather than 2◇ or jump to the three level with a major; also take similar strong action over a transfer response. You can find flaws with this treatment, but it works better than anything else I've seen.

The minimum for a double should be 14 points—even when the opponents adopt an opening 10–12 point range. Theoretically you could sell out to 1NT, undoubled, when you and partner each had 13 points. The reason for requiring a little higher strength than the opponents' maximum range is that once you double, you may commit yourself to further action. Some players play once 1NT is doubled, the opponents can't be allowed to play an undoubled two level contract. Others say you can't sell out to two of a minor, undoubled.

The way I play with Ed Davis is the next double by either partner is negative. A double by the partner of the original doubler shows high cards (6 or more), but no more than two of the opponents' suit. If the original doubler doubles again, he merely shows shortage in the opponents' suit, not extra values. The only time the opponents can play an undoubled contract after 1NT has been doubled is when both partners have length in the suit or when the initial doubler has length and his partner was too weak to make a Negative Double with shortness.

For example, suppose West doubles 1NT with

♠ AQ10 ♡ xx ◇ KQxx ♣ K10xx

and North bids 2♠. If East doubles, showing 6 or more HCP and no more than two spades, West can (just barely) leave the double in and will probably set it. If North had bid 2♡ and East and South passed, West would be obligated to double again with his 14 points! That is because partner could not double with

♠ Kx ♡ KJxx ◇ xxx ♣ Qxxx,

and you don't want to let the opponents off the hook. It looks dangerous to keep doubling with 14 points when partner may have nothing, but it usually seems to work.

An alternate method is to play that the initial double by West shows 14 HCP or more, and a balanced hand. A subsequent double by West would show 17 HCP or more like after

WEST	NORTH	EAST	SOUTH
—	—	—	1NT
Double	2♡	Pass	Pass
Double			

A double by East of a suit bid by North shows at least 6 HCP and a balanced hand. Neither can leave the double in without three or more cards in the opponents' suit. This method gives you a greater assurance that when the opponents are doubled, your side has at least half the high cards, with balanced hands, and the opponents have at best an eight card fit. It prevents the opponents from getting away undoubled when you and your partner each hold three cards in the opponents' suit, while the previous method required that one of you have a four card holding. Also, if you double with 14 HCP and partner does nothing, you are not obligated to double again. I prefer the latter method, but it is hard to say which method works better in the long run.

THE KAMIKAZE NOTRUMP

Since the very weak notrump causes us all sorts of problems when the opponents use it, perhaps we should use it. This is the way it works in an uncontested auction: It should only be used when not vulnerable in first, second or third position. (Some players say only in first or second seat.) It shows a balanced hand, but "balanced" includes 4–3–3–3, 4–4–3–2, 5–3–3–2, and some 5–4–2–2 and 6–3–2–2 distributions. Certain negative inferences can be drawn when partner passes—either that he has less than 10 HCP or that his hand is unbalanced. At the risk of diluting these negative inferences, it doesn't pay to open 1NT with a normal opening bid, or concentrated strength, with 5–4–2–2 or 6–3–2–2 distribution, or a six card major. Open 1♠ with

♠ AKxxx ♡ Axx ◇ xx ♣ xxx.

Open 1◇ with

♠ xx ♡ Axx ◇ AKxxxx ♣ xx

You could easily miss a game if you were to open 1NT with either hand. Partner assumes that you don't have a normal opening bid and would pass with either

1. ♠ Qxxx ♡ KJx ◇ Axxx ♣ Kx or
2. ♠ Axx ♡ Kxx ◇ Qxx ♣ KJxx,

and you would miss a good game. It doesn't pay for responder to invite with balanced 13 point hands. Game is unlikely, and even 2NT may be in danger; the best chance for a good score is to pass quickly and hope the opponents reopen; bidding after a 10–12 point notrump opening is not as accurate as after a strong notrump opening; the conventions you use are chosen more for safety than for accurate exploration.

You should pass rather than open 1NT with

1. ♠ AK10xx ♡ xx ◇ QJxx ♣ xx
2. ♠ xx ♡ AQ10xx ◇ xx ♣ KJ10x.

Only with an unusual hand should 1NT be opened with 5–4–2–2 distribution when your five card suit is a major. A 2♡ opening is preferable with

♠ xx ♡ AKQJx ◇ xxx ♣ xxx

These hands are strong enough to compete by overcalling in most sequences, and if partner has an opening bid, you are much more likely to get to the right contract by passing originally. As a practical matter, when you open 1NT with a five card major, you have scattered strength and a maximum of 11 HCP. A typical hand would be:

♠ Qxxxx ♡ Kx ◇ Kxx ♣ Kxx.

In responding, 2♣ is a Stayman type of inquiry and 2◇ is "game–forcing Stayman." But opener's rebids over both 2♣ and 2◇ are considerably different from normal. Over 2♣ he rebids 2◇ unless he has a FIVE card major. Then any bid by responder is supposed to be invitational, but two of a major only purports to show four. Thus, with

♠ Qxxx ♡ Kx ◇ Axx ♣ AJxx

you would bid 2♣ and, over 2◇, bid 2♠. Opener needs four spades and an absolute minimum to pass. Normally, with four spades, he would raise to 3♠ or 4♠. With less than four spades, opener would bid 2NT with a minimum and 3♣ with a maximum, allowing responder to place the contract. 2♣, followed by a jump in a major, is invitational and shows at least a five card suit.

This is only one way to treat a 2♣ response. Some players prefer to play 2♣ as not necessarily invitational. In fact, it may show 0–14 HCP. Opener still rebids 2♢ unless he has a five card major, but

WEST	NORTH	EAST	SOUTH
—	—	—	1NT
Pass	2♣	Pass	2♢
Pass	2♡/2♠		

could be very weak. Opener is allowed to pass or raise to three of the major, but he can't bid four. Whether opener bids 2NT with a minimum or 3♣ with a maximum, he must pass responder's next bid. Responder could hold

♠ xxxx ♡ x ♢ Jxxxxx ♣ Jx

for the following sequence:

OPENER	RESPONDER
1NT	2♣
2♢	2♠
3♣	3♢

In real life the opponents would be doing something with 26–28 HCP.

With a very weak hand a 2♣ response conceals your weakness and makes it harder for the opponents to make a penalty double or to judge whether to compete. However, the auction

WEST	NORTH	EAST	SOUTH
—	—	—	1NT
Pass	2♣	Pass	2♢
Pass	Pass		

tells the opponents that responder has a weak hand, and they are almost certain to reopen.

Pass 1NT with

♠ xx ♡ xx ◇ KQxxxx ♣ Q10x

for two reasons. First, we have a good chance of making it, even though the opponents have more points than we do. Partner might win the opening lead and run six diamond tricks if he has the ◇A. Second, even if partner doesn't have the ◇A we will often do better declaring than defending (like –100 vs –140). The opponents can surely make a part score in one of the majors, and passing 1NT makes it more dangerous for them to reopen than if you bid 2♣ and pass 2◇. Also, there is a possibility that partner has a five card major and wouldn't rebid 2◇.

However, you would surely bid 2♣ if you held

♠ xxx ♡ xx ◇ Qxxxx ♣ Qxx,

Even if partner buys the contract undoubled he would probably be set three or four tricks—more than the value of a part score, and on this bidding it is unlikely the opponents will get to game, even if they can make it so you want to make it easy for the opponents to compete and take the bid away from you. Also, it will be harder for the opponents to double for penalty and make the double stick when you run out to a suit.

Suppose partner opens 1NT and you hold

♠ Kxxx ♡ x ◇ Kxxxx ♣ xxx.

There are four possible approaches:

1. Pass.
2. Bid 2♣ and pass when partner bids 2◇.
3. Bid 2♣ and then bid 2♠ over 2◇.
4. Bid 2♠.

The first thing you should try to decide is whether the hand belongs to you or the opponents. Since they have

22–24 HCP, the hand should belong to them, and they can probably make at least 3♡, perhaps 4♡. What you would like to do is buy the contract undoubled if you can hold the set to two tricks, or let the opponents buy the contract if you would be set more than two tricks. If you play 1NT you can probably take five tricks. In diamonds you should take six or seven tricks. (These are very rough estimates since there is no way to know how well your hand fits partner.) In a spade contract everything will depend upon how many spades partner has, but you would expect to take five to seven tricks, or six tricks on an average. Against double dummy defense the average would be less than six tricks, but you don't expect double dummy defense—the opponents won't realize their best defense is to pull your trumps rather than let you ruff a couple of hearts with your small trumps. With these thoughts in mind, let's analyze the various alternatives.

1. Pass. A very reasonable action. The notrump bid may keep the opponents out of the bidding when their strength is evenly divided; if so, you can probably take five tricks.
2. 2♣ followed by a pass of 2♢. A very "safe" action but not likely to buy the bid. If LHO doesn't bid 2♡ immediately over 2♣, he will almost surely reopen when you pass 2♢.
3. 2♣ followed by 2♠. Very deceptive, but if you buy the bid at the three level (or 2NT) you are apt to be set three tricks.
4. 2♠. This is my choice. It shuts out a 2♡ bid. If LHO bids 3♡, his partner won't know whether to raise to 4♡. The biggest risk comes when partner holds a spade doubleton; the opponents will set you three tricks. Some of my friends, who play the very weak notrump regularly say 2♠ is terrible, and almost anything else is better. Having heard the pros and cons, you can make your own choice. Playing the very

weak notrump will enable you to give full reign to your imagination. However, if you feel uncomfortable with all these "opportunities" perhaps you shouldn't play this convention.

As you will recall, a 2♢ response is game–forcing Stayman. In order to force to game responder must be stronger than opener. Therefore, there is no reason to transfer the play to opener, and there is good reason not to. It is better for opener to describe his hand, then lay his hand down as dummy with responder's hand concealed. Consequently, over a 2♢ response, opener, when holding a four card major, should bid the other major. A 2♡ rebid would show spades and a 2♠ rebid would show hearts. With neither major he should rebid 2NT.

What should opener rebid with both majors or a five card major? He bids 3♣ in either case. Responder puppets to 3♢ after which 3♡ shows five spades; 3♠ shows five hearts, and 3NT shows both majors. That is the system used by most of the West Coast players. 3NT directly over 2♢ shows both majors also and can either be stronger or weaker than 3♣ followed by 3NT. My suggestion is to treat 3♣ and 3♢ as natural, showing a six card minor or a good five card minor. An immediate 3♡ bid (over 2♢) shows five spades; 3♠ shows five hearts and 3NT shows both majors.

Other responses to 1NT are as follows: 2NT, 3♣, 3♢ and 3♡ are all transfers to the next highest bid. They show either a preempt in the suit you transfer to OR a singleton or void! Naturally, when you have a singleton or void, you won't pass partner's puppet bid. You will then bid 3NT or your long minor, depending upon how distributional your hand is. For example, you would bid 2NT (transferring to 3♣) with

1. ♠ Qxx ♡ x ♢ Jxx ♣ KJ10xxx or
2. ♠ AJx ♡ KJx ♢ AQxxxx ♣ x.

With Hand Two, when you bid 2NT followed by 3NT, partner would bid 4♢ with

♠ KQx ♡ Axx ♢ J10xx ♣ Jxx

since he knows you don't belong in 3NT with ♣Jxx opposite a singleton. Likewise you would respond 3♡ with either

1. ♠ KJxxxxx ♡ xx ♢ x ♣ Axx or
2. ♠ x ♡ K10x ♢ AQJ10xx ♣ Kxx.

Opposite the latter hand opener would pass your 3NT rebid with

♠ Q10xx ♡ Ax ♢ xxx ♣ Axxx

or bid 4♣ with

♠ xxx ♡ AQx ♢ Kxxx ♣ Qxx

and you would correct to diamonds.

Usually opener will bid the suit responder transfers him to. But with as much as KQx or KJ10x in the suit opener should rebid 3NT. If responder really has the suit, the super–fit may be enough for game or if not, the opponents can surely make a lot their way. If responder is short, the hand will probably make 3NT. Consequently if responder has

♠ AQx ♡ None ♢ Q10x ♣ KQxxxxx,

he should bid 3♢, transferring to hearts, followed by 4♣ next round. 3NT seems like an improbable contract unless opener bids it directly over 3♢. If opener has

♠ Kxx ♡ Jxxx ♢ KJx ♣ Axx,

a perfect fitting slam can be visualized (after responder bids 3♢, 4♣).

When discussing the strong notrump many people are much too worried about playing 1NT doubled, and go to extreme lengths to avoid it. The worries playing a 10–12 point notrump are not irrational; when the opponents double 1NT you probably ARE in trouble. Even so, a redouble by responder should not be part of a run–out sequence. It should show a good hand so that if the opponents bid, opener may be able to double for penalty.

All suit bids by responder are natural. Pass shows responder has no five card suit OR he has a fair hand and is willing to play 1NT (redoubled, if necessary). Opener should alert the pass and explain if RHO passes, opener must bid. Opener will run to a long suit, if he has one, and if not, he will redouble. That is another reason why responder should redouble with a good hand—to keep opener from running with a five card suit. After opener's redouble, responder can pass if he expects 1NT to make. If he runs, he bids his lowest four card suit, having denied a five card suit, and the partners can try to find a 4–4 fit (or a 4–3 fit if it is not doubled).

I'm unconvinced a system requiring opener to take action rather than pass 1NT doubled when responder has no long suit is best. If you don't find a fit you could be in worse trouble at a higher level. But most people who play the Kamikaze notrump think a system of automatic run–outs is best because of the difficulty the opponents have of doubling for penalty and leaving the double in. The player with extra strength may be short in the suit. When the suit is split 4–3–3–3 each partner is afraid to double for fear that his partner has two and the opponents have found an eight card fit.

As a defender, how can you profit from this discussion? You should question the opponents about the meaning of their delayed bids. When responder has denied a five card suit and has run from 1NT doubled, tend to double any runout with a balanced hand, and partner should pass the double with a balanced hand. When all hands are balanced and the defenders have even a slight preponderance of strength, declarer is very unlikely to take eight tricks. Also the defense is much easier against a suit contract than against notrump.

When the bidding goes

WEST	NORTH	EAST	SOUTH
—	—	—	1NT
Pass	Pass	Double	

the situation is quite different. Responder has denied a five card major; if he has a long suit it must be a minor. Suppose opener has a five card suit. Should he run? If he does, he could be letting the opponents off the hook. Opener should redouble to say that he has a five card suit. With 8 HCP or more responder can gamble a pass. West won't know what to lead, and if opener's five card suit can be established in time, the contract will make for a top, gaining 10–12 IMPS. If responder is weak, he will usually bid 2♣ and opener can bid his suit or pass if his suit is clubs. With a good five or six card diamond suit, responder should bid 2♢.

With no five card suit opener will pass. Now a 2♣ bid by responder means he has a five card minor or 4–4–4–1 distribution (in that order). The main objective is to avoid a doubled contract. Undoubled, he can afford to play 2♣ with a singleton club or when his suit is diamonds, and the opponents must consider this possibility when deciding to double 2♣ for penalty. Your multiple meaning 2♣ bid must be alerted, of course. If 2♣ is doubled, redouble shows 4–4–4–1, and 2♢ simply means that responder's long suit is diamonds. If responder bids 2♢ immediately, he shows diamonds plus a major (four of each). If he bids 2♡ immediately, he shows both majors. Before deciding to run (without a five card suit), responder must consider his suit quality. With

♠ Q109x ♡ J108x ◇ xx ♣ xxx,

he should run to 2♡, showing the majors. With

♠ xxxx ♡ 10xxx ◇ Jx ♣ Qxx,

he should stay in 1NT doubled.

After the auction

WEST	NORTH	EAST	SOUTH
—	—	—	1NT
Pass	Pass	Double	Pass
Pass	?		

what should a redouble mean? There is some logic in saying that 1NT doubled and making should be a good result at match points, and you don't need to be greedy. Consequently a redouble could be used as part of a run–out structure. At match–points the redouble could be used to show four clubs plus another suit.

At IMPS the odds are considerably different. If your opponents are making a part–score with your cards at the other table or are plus 50 or 100, plus 180 will, on an average, gain 3 IMPS. But +560 or +760 (1NT redoubled, making) will gain 10–12 IMPS. In other words, the gain from a successful redouble is 7–9 IMPS. It is not likely that the opponents holding your cards are playing 1NT redoubled, but if you can't take seven tricks at notrump they probably won't get a plus score with your cards. The redouble could change your score from –100 to –200 or from –200 to –400. An unsuccessful redouble would cost you 3 to 5 IMPS. Omitted from the computation is the possibility of a two trick set or a redoubled overtrick. Suffice it to say, the odds favor a redouble when you expect to take six or seven tricks. So at IMPs the redouble should have its natural meaning and not be part of a run–out structure. Responder should redouble with 10 HCP or more. This hand

♠ Axx ♡ Kxxx ◇ Kxx ♣ J10x

would be an ideal redouble, intending to double any run–out. Since you have already shown your high card strength, a penalty double should show at least three of the opponents' suit.

Suppose the opponents overcall partner's very weak notrump. Should you play penalty doubles or Negative Doubles? You will recall that my slight preference was to play penalty doubles after a strong notrump opening, although I was intrigued with the Martel–Stansby complicated system which combined Negative Doubles and modified Lebensohl. There were two primary reasons for my preference.

1. Opener has described his strength and distribution within narrow limits so that responder could usually make the right decision.
2. I didn't like the idea that opener, having described his hand, would be obligated to reopen with a double whenever he was short in the suit, even with a minimum hand.

The first reason is less compelling after a very weak notrump opening. Although the high card range is still three points (10–12 instead of 15–17), the distribution can vary more. You seldom open a strong notrump with 6–3–2–2 or 5–4–2–2 shape. You might open a strong notrump with an otherwise perfect hand containing a five card major, but not with a worthless doubleton or some other flaw. You WOULD open a 10–12 point notrump with

1. ♠ Q10xx ♡ Ax ◇ xx ♣ A109xx
2. ♠ Ax ♡ xx ◇ Qxx ♣ KJxxxx.

Another factor is that your choices will not be duplicated throughout the field.

You hold ♠ Kx ♡ KJ9x ◇ Axx ♣ xxxx.

WEST	NORTH	EAST	SOUTH
—	—	—	1NT
2♡	?		

This looks like an ideal penalty double withexcellent defense, and no game your way. But you have no idea how good your defense is against spades. Partner may have from two to five spades. East, with a borderline decision, might run to spades if 2♡ is doubled and pass otherwise. Presumably at other tables the bidding will go

WEST	NORTH	EAST	SOUTH
—	—	—	Pass
1♡	?		

and you would have no choice but to pass. Quite likely the bidding would continue:

WEST	NORTH	EAST	SOUTH
—	—	—	Pass
1♡	Pass	1NT	Pass
2♣/2◇	?		

WEST	NORTH	EAST	SOUTH
—	—	—	Pass
1♡	Pass	1♠	Pass
2♠	?		

Other North players won't have the option of defending against 2♡. When the strength is fairly evenly balanced and the opponents are in the wrong contract, going down, you will usually get a good result without doubling. With this hand it is unlikely that you could make a partscore your way, other than 1NT which the rest of the field won't get to after West's opening bid. Since setting 2♡ will give you a good result, you don't have to double. For every hand you would like to double for penalty, there will be several hands you would like to double for takeout since, when the strength is fairly evenly divided, both sides can usually make a partscore. So I whole–heartedly accept Martel–Stansby competitive tactics described earlier with one exception: Opener is not obligated to reopen with a double with a doubleton in the opponents' suit when the overcall has been passed around to him. For all practical purposes, you are giving up on penalty doubles or penalty passes of reopening doubles. However, the opening bidder reserves the right to make a reopening double of 2♡ with a maximum and no wasted cards such as

1. ♠ AJ10x ♡ xx ◇ KQx ♣ J10xx
2. ♠ AQx ♡ Ax ◇ Qxxx ♣ xxxx,

but he should surely pass with

♠ Qxx ♡ Kx ◇ QJxx ♣ Q10xx.

Does the 10–12 point notrump pay in the long run? I haven't played it long enough to say so with confidence, but I think so. It doesn't work well when you and partner have most of the strength. You shouldn't use it in a bidding contest. One disadvantage is your range for notrump rebids are forced to be wider. Supposedly

WEST	NORTH	EAST	SOUTH
—	—	—	1◇
Pass	1♡	Pass	1NT

shows 13–16 HCP. As a practical matter, you have to bid this way with a good 12 points, especially when you have a five card suit.

You hold ♠ Axxx ♡ Axx ◇ Qxx ♣ xxx.

WEST	NORTH	EAST	SOUTH
—	—	—	1♣
Pass	1♠	Pass	1NT
Pass	?		

Should you raise in case partner has 16 HCP? Would he like to play 2NT with

♠ Qx ♡ Kxxx ◇ Axx ♣ Axxx?

This sequence

WEST	NORTH	EAST	SOUTH
—	—	—	1♣
Pass	1♡	Pass	2NT

shows 17–19 HCP. There is no way to get to all your 26 point games without getting to some 24 point games or getting to 2NT when the rest of the field is in 1NT. Ed Davis suggests rebidding 2NT with 17–18 HCP, opening 2NT with 19–20 HCP and opening 2♣ and rebidding 2NT with 21–23 HCP. This is probably an improvement since it narrows the range for the most frequently dealt hands, but whatever you do, you have fewer bids to describe a wide range of strength.

Another weakness is that the follow–up bids after the 1NT opening were chosen more for safety and deception than for constructive bidding accuracy. One disaster that sticks in my memory was

WEST	EAST
♠ Qx	♠ AK10xx
♡ xxx	♡ AKxx
◇ Jx	◇ x
♣ AKxxxx	♣ Q10x

Our bidding:

WEST	EAST
1NT	2◇
2NT	3♠
3NT	Pass

Normal bidding:

WEST	EAST
Pass	1♠
3♣*	4♢
6♣	Pass

*Since 2♣ would be Drury

What a terrible contract! Down one in 3NT when we were cold for 6♣! Our result persuaded me that a 3♣ or 3♢ rebid should be natural. My partner was unconvinced. His solution was not to open 1NT with most of my strength in the long suit. You can change the system to avoid one problem while creating others. No matter what you do, the 10–12 point notrump will be a detriment to your constructive bidding.

However, when it is the opponents' hand, especially when everyone but opener is distributional, the 1NT bid makes life very difficult for them. Not only are they deprived of an opportunity to open the bidding. They have also lost a complete round of bidding.

The very weak notrump also works well for you when the strength is evenly divided. It will be much easier for your side to get to the right contract than for the opponents. Here are just a couple of examples to illustrate the competitive advantage.

Normal bidding:

WEST	NORTH	EAST	SOUTH
—	—	—	Pass
1♠	Pass	1NT	Pass
2♠	Pass	Pass	Pass

The new way:

WEST	NORTH	EAST	SOUTH
—	—	—	1NT
2♠	2NT	Pass	3♣
Pass	3♡	Pass	Pass
Pass			

	NORTH	
	♠ Jxxx ♡ KQxxx ♢ Axx ♣ x	
WEST ♠ AQ10xxx ♡ x ♢ Jx ♣ AQxx		**EAST** ♠ x ♡ J10xx ♢ Q10x ♣ KJxxx
	SOUTH ♠ Kx ♡ Axx ♢ Kxxxx ♣ 10xx	

Normal bidding:

WEST	NORTH	EAST	SOUTH
—	—	—	Pass
1♡	Pass	1NT	Pass
2♢	Pass	Pass	Double
Pass	2♠	3♢	Pass
Pass	Pass		

the new way:

WEST	NORTH	EAST	SOUTH
—	—	—	1NT
2♡	Double	Pass	2♠
Pass	Pass	Pass	

NORTH
♠ KJxx
♡ Kx
◇ xxx
♣ K10xx

WEST		EAST
♠ xxx		♠ xx
♡ AJ10xx		♡ xx
◇ KJx		◇ AQ10xx
♣ Ax		♣ Jxxx

SOUTH
♠ AQ10x
♡ Qxxx
◇ xx
♣ Qxx

These are not spectacular hands. If North–South had the ♡ Jin the first example, there would be a double partscore swing. As it is, 3♡ will be down one, undoubled, while East–West are cold for 2♠. In the second example South has a dubious reopening double, but even giving him the benefit of a good guess, he would be outbid in a normal sequence. By the way, when opener pulls the double to 2NT, his bid is for takeout. If his holding in the opponents' suit were strong enough for him to want to play notrump, he would pass for penalty.

Quiz Seven

In the first group of hands the opening 1NT bid shows 15–17 HCP and North–South are playing Jacoby transfer bids.

1. You hold ♠ xx ♡ QJ10xxx ◊ xx ♣ A109.

WEST	NORTH	EAST	SOUTH
—	—	—	1NT
Pass	2◊	Double	Pass
Pass	?		

What do you bid?

2. You hold ♠ Ax ♡ Qxxxx ◊ xxx ♣ A109.

WEST	NORTH	EAST	SOUTH
—	—	—	1NT
Pass	2◊	Double	Pass
Pass	?		

What do you bid?

3. None Vulnerable
You hold ♠ A109x ♡ xx ◊ Kxx ♣ 10xxx.

WEST	NORTH	EAST	SOUTH
—	—	—	1NT
Double	Redouble	2♡	Pass
Pass	?		

What do you bid?

4. Both Sides Vulnerable
You hold ♠ QJxx ♡ Jxxx ◇ Kx ♣ Qxx.

WEST	NORTH	EAST	SOUTH
—	—	—	1NT
Double*	Pass	?	

*Woolsey.

What do you bid?

5. None Vulnerable
You hold ♠ KQJxxx ♡ xxx ◇ Kx ♣ xx.

WEST	NORTH	EAST	SOUTH
—	—	—	1NT
Pass	2◇	?	

What do you bid?

Problems 6–10
The Opening 1NT Shows 10–12 HCP
East–West Are Playing Mohan

6. None Vulnerable
You, West, hold ♠ x ♡ AKxxxx ◇ xxx ♣ xxx.

WEST	NORTH	EAST	SOUTH
—	—	—	1NT
Double	Pass	?	

What do you bid?

7. East–West Vulnerable
You, East, hold ♠ AKxx ♡ AJx ◇ Q10xx ♣ Jx.

WEST	NORTH	EAST	SOUTH
—	—	—	1NT
Double	2♡	Pass	Pass
?			

What do you bid?

8. None Vulnerable
You, East, hold ♠ AKxx ♡ A ◇ KQxxx ♣ Jxx.

WEST	NORTH	EAST	SOUTH
—	—	—	1NT
Double	2♡	Pass	Pass
?			

What do you bid?

9. None Vulnerable
You, South, hold ♠ J10xxxx ♡ x ◇ Qxxx ♣ xx.

WEST	NORTH	EAST	SOUTH
—	1NT	Pass	?

What do you bid?

10. East–West Vulnerable
You, South, hold ♠ Ax ♡ xx ◇ Axxxx ♣ K109x.

WEST	NORTH	EAST	SOUTH
—	—	—	1NT
Pass	3♣	Pass	?

What do you bid?

Answers

1. **REDOUBLE.** If the opponents had stayed out of the bidding you would have transfered to hearts and raised to three. Partner's pass means that he has a doubleton heart, but you don't care since your hearts are so strong. If you bid 2♡ it should mean that you have no interest in game. If you bid 3♡, partner might consider your bid forcing. The solution is to redouble, forcing partner to bid 2♡, then raise to 3♡.

2. **THREE NOTRUMP.** That's what you were planning to bid anyway. Surely you have no interest in a heart contract when partner shows a doubleton heart. Your failure to redouble denies a diamond stopper. It is hard to see how partner can be missing a diamond stopper but if he has ♠ KQx ♡Ax ◊ xxx ♣ KQJxx he can salvage a few points by bidding 4♣. If your ♣ 109 were small cards, you should take a conservative view and bid 2NT. The hearts can't be established, and the opponents will make the most harmful opening lead. Partner can still bid 3NT with a maximum or a double diamond stopper.

3. **TWO SPADES.** Obviously you can't double if partner doesn't double. If partner lacks the ability to double hearts, he is likely to have good spade support. Since you didn't cue bid or jump, your bid isn't forcing. Quite likely the opponents can make 2♡ and you can make 2♠.

4. **TWO DIAMONDS.** It is tempting to pass and try for +200. But you are aceless, and declarer may be able to run the minor suit partner doesn't have. The risk is not worth while since you are almost positive that you can make two of a major—a contract most of the field won't find—for an excellent score. Bid 2◊, asking partner to bid his major.

5. **TWO SPADES**. There is a risk an immediate bid will get you too high, and partner may play you for a better hand. You could pass, intending to bid 2♠ if the 2♡ bid is passed around to you. However, if you pass and the opponents bid more, you won't dare bid at a higher level. You want a spade lead; you might be able to outbid the opponents at the three level, and it will be difficult for either opponent to double. West doesn't know whether his partner is weak or strong. East won't have length or strength in spades. Give partner something like

♠ xxx ♡ x ◇ Axxx ♣ KQxxx

and you may be able to outbid your opponents.

6. **TWO DIAMONDS**. A penalty pass would be a good gamble if you could get partner to lead a heart. He is almost sure to lead a spade instead, and he won't find out where your values are until late in the hand. Even if you beat 1NT a trick or two, you may discover that you are cold for 4♡. My recommendation is to bid 2◇ as a transfer to hearts and raise 2♡ to 3♡.

7. **PASS**. Whatever approach you are using, since partner passed 2♡, you have nothing more to say.

8. **TWO SPADES**. This time a pass would concede defeat. If you are playing Ed Davis' way, double again (for takeout). Playing my way, bid 2♠ (and go to 4♠ if partner raises). On this bidding partner probably has spade length, but you should do well even if he has three card support.

9. **TWO HEARTS!** No, I didn't forget we don't play transfer bids over a weak notrump. The opponents will surely get to game with 25–27 HCP over a 2♠ bid. 4♠ could be down three (doubled), although it is a reasonable choice. 3♡, a transfer to 3♠, would probably be doubled, making it easier for the opponents to find their fit. How can either opponent (or your partner) bid over 2♡? A double would

be for takeout, and neither opponent can make a takeout double with length in hearts and shortness in spades. So you will probably play 2♡, undoubled, down five or six. I don't see how the opponents can double, but if they do, you would, of course, run to spades. Aside from its theoretical merits, a 2♡ bid is fun!

10. **THREE NOTRUMP**. Partner has either a good minor suit and a singleton club (unlikely opposite your diamond holding; also unlikely opposite your club holding) or a preeempt in diamonds (much more likely). A preempt over this 10-12 notrump range may not be hopelessly weak. Partner could hold

♠ x ♡ AQ ◇ KJxxxx ♣ xxxx,

with which you might be able to set four of a major (and might make 3NT). Anyway, with such a good offensive hand and so little defense because of your diamond length, you should bid more than 3◇.

Chapter Eight

ODDS AND ENDS

MANY ARTIFICIAL BIDS ARE USED in modern bidding such as Stayman, Texas, Jacoby Transfers, Namyats, Blackwood, Gerber, Drury, Splinters, Flannery, and Michaels, etc. How should our bidding be modified to profit from the opponents' conventions? Several situations have been discussed such as lead directing doubles of Stayman or transfer responses to a strong notrump as distinguished from doubles showing general strength when the notrump bid is weak and NOT doubling a cue bid of a suit you have previously bid just to ask for a lead. There are too many artificial bids to discuss each in detail, so we need some general rules.

A double of an artificial bid made late in the auction is merely lead–directing. The most obvious example is a double of a Blackwood response.

A double of an artificial bid shows that suit. At a low level it could suggest competing.

WEST	NORTH	EAST	SOUTH
—	—	—	1NT
Pass	2♡*	Double	

* Jacoby Transfer

If the 1NT opening was strong, the double would be primarily lead–directing, but it should show the suit rather than a void since you want partner to compete with the appropriate hand and you don't want partner to lead your void suit against a notrump contract. A double of 2♡ could be made with as little as

♠ xx ♡ AQ109x ♢ Jxxx ♣ xx.

Getting the right opening lead and occasionally allowing partner to compete in hearts will more than compensate for the rare times the opponents will play 2♡ redoubled, making an overtrick. Few pairs have a way to suggest playing 2♡ redoubled, as distinguished from 2♣ redoubled after a lead–directing double of Stayman. Suppose the bidding continues:

WEST	NORTH	EAST	SOUTH
—	—	—	1NT
Pass	2♡	Double	2♠
Pass	Pass	3♢	

East will have shown hearts and diamonds. If East doubles again, instead of bidding 3♢, he shows a good hand with at least five hearts.

♠ x ♡ AQ10xx ♢ Axx ♣ KJxx.

Why five? Because with

♠ x ♡ AQ10x ♢ Axxx ♣ KJxx

he should bid 2♠ on the first round. A bid of the suit shown artificially is equivalent to a takeout double, and shows a fairly good hand. With

♠ x ♡ Q10xx ♢ Axxx ♣ KJxx

East would pass the 2♡ bid and stay out of the bidding altogether if North should make a game try or game bid next round. However, if 2♠ were passed around to him, East should make a reopening double.

Some friends had the following bidding disaster.

IMPS, Both Vulnerable.

WEST	NORTH	EAST	SOUTH
—	—	—	1NT*
Pass	2♠	Pass	3♣
Pass	Pass	3♡	Pass
Pass	Pass		

* Strong

WEST	EAST
♠ AQxx	♠ xxx
♡ Jx	♡ KQ109xx
◊ Jxx	◊ AQx
♣ Axxx	♣ x

The 2♠ bid was alerted as a club transfer. East passed the first time, thinking he would bid 3♡ next round if responder should pass, or stay out of the bidding altogether if responder showed extra values. Most people would blame West for not raising to game when his partner bid at the three level, Vulnerable. West knew he had a good hand, but thought East was playing him for high cards based upon the opponents' bidding, and West had no distributional fit.

The decision was close for both players, but East should have bid 3♡ immediately to show a sound overcall—also he might need a heart lead to defeat 3NT. By passing and bidding later he showed a weaker hand than by bidding immediately. It sounded as though he was only bidding because the opponents' lack of enterprise marked his partner with high cards. East could have held ♠ xxx ♡ KQ10xxx ◊ Q10x ♣ x.

An immediate 3♡ bid is not as dangerous as it may seem. Since responder's hand is unlimited and could be quite weak, opener can't double unless he has an exceptionally good defensive hand including ♡AJxx. Responder won't have the sort of heart holding to make a double attractive. The greatest practical danger is West will play you for a slightly better hand and raise to game when you don't belong there.

The general principle: Immediate action is stronger than delayed action because you might not have taken delayed action if the bidding had proceeded differently.

We have already discussed this sequence.

WEST	NORTH	EAST	SOUTH
—	—	4♣*	?

*Namyats showing hearts

A double, just to show clubs, is less useful than a double to show support for three suits. So double is equivalent to a takeout double of 4♡, but it is much safer than a double of 4♡. If LHO bids 4♡ and partner passes, you can pass with

♠ AJxx ♡ x ◇ Kxxx ♣ Axxx.

A repeat double would show a stronger hand. To make a penalty double of 4♡, you would pass 4♣ and double when the opponents bid 4♡.

I play 4◇ in the following sequence

WEST	NORTH	EAST	SOUTH
—	—	—	4♣*
Pass	4◇		

* Namyats showing hearts

as a slam try, but some people play 4◇ merely as a relay to allow opener to play the hand. If the opponents are playing that way, what should you, as East, bid with

♠ AJxx ♡ x ◇ Kxx ♣ AQxxx?

You should double, as a safe takeout double of 4♡, rather than as showing length or concentration of strength in diamonds. A double followed by a double of 4♡ would show a normal, but good, double of 4♡. With

♠ QJxx ♡ None ◇ KQxxx ♣ KQxx

it might turn out badly, but I would bid 4♡ immediately, implying a great deal more offense than defense. Let's hope partner does not hold

♠ Axx ♡ KJ10x ◇ xx ♣ Jxxx.

(Or if so that he is a very understanding partner.)

WEST	NORTH	EAST	SOUTH
—	—	—	1♡
1♠	Pass	2♡	?

Refrain from doubling here merely to ask for a lead. A double helps the opponents more by releasing West from the obligation to bid. If he bids anyway, his bid will be more descriptive. The double should show an offensive hand and suggest further competition. Doubling with

♠ x ♡ AQ10xxx ◇ KJxx ♣ Ax

seems about right, since it suggests competing to the three level, without the risk. Strengthen your hearts to AQJ10xx and you would bid 3♡ immediately to show an even better offensive hand and to make it more difficult for the opponents to describe their hands. We can now state four more general rules:

1. Bidding a suit is stronger offensively than showing it by means of a double.
2. A double followed by another double is stronger than doubling and passing or passing and doubling.
3. When an artificial bid shows a specific suit, bidding that suit is a "takeout double" showing the strongest offensive action.
4. Doubles of transfer preempts or transfer responses to preempts show an all–around hand, equivalent to

a takeout double of the opponents' known suit; the double does not just show the doubled suit.

The concept of a forcing pass is simple. If partner is forced to bid, and you have no clear–cut message to give, pass in order to give him more bidding room plus the chance to double the opponents. While the concept is simple, determining when a pass is forcing is complicated. Theoretically, every possible sequence should be analyzed to decide whether it should be forcing. The trouble is we won't remember what we decided in each case, and even if we could, we would be afraid partner might forget. It is better to have general rules, which may not be best in a particular case, than to have a thousand specific rules.

Let's start with the most clear–cut cases: Unless you are playing a strong club system, 2♣ is forcing to game except after a negative response and a 2NT rebid, or after a double negative when opener rebids his original suit. This happened to me:

WEST	NORTH	EAST	SOUTH
—	—	—	2♣
Pass	2♢	2♠	3♡
Pass	Pass!	Pass	

Partner said, "I thought you would cue bid 3♠ if you really wanted to force." That doesn't seem practical since partner can't make an intelligent decision until he knows what my long suit is, and I might have a two–suiter. What else could I bid with

♠ None ♡ AJxxxx ♢ AKQxx ♣ AQ?

In any ambiguous situation the force to game applies. That means that opener should pass 2♠ with

♠ None ♡ AQJx ♢ AKQJx ♣ AQxx,

in which case the pass shows a better offensive hand than a double. The double would imply a balanced hand such as

♠ Axx ♡ AKQx ◇ AJx ♣ KQx.

Double would also be correct with

♠ AKQJ9xx ♡ A ◇ KQx ♣ Kx,

to be followed by a spade bid if someone, including partner, runs from the double.

Say you play a strong club system. If the bidding goes

WEST	NORTH	EAST	SOUTH
—	—	—	1♣
Pass	1◇	1♠	?

a double is for takeout when the 1◇ bid is negative because partner is not obligated to bid if you pass. But suppose partner bids 1♡, showing any distribution with 7 HCP+ and less than three controls. Now if you pass the 1♠ overcall partner is obligated to bid, and you would pass with

♠ x ♡ AKJx ◇ Axxxx ♣ AQx.

Therefore, a double is for penalty.

Next case: Partner makes a strong jump shift, forcing to game and showing slam interest.

WEST	NORTH	EAST	SOUTH
—	—	—	1◇
Pass	2♠	3♡	?

Obviously, a pass is forcing and a double is discouraging (so far as bidding slam is concerned). It would show that opener had poor offensive values and a spade misfit.

WEST	NORTH	EAST	SOUTH
—	—	—	1◇
Pass	2NT	3♠	?

If the 2NT is standard (13–15 HCP), it is forcing to game. Consequently you should pass with

♠ xx ♡ Axx ◊ AQ10xx ♣ Kxx.

With only a four diamonds you would double because you have no long suit to establish before the opponents establish theirs and your offensive to defensive ratio would be low.

I don't play Two Over One forcing to game. However, a Two Over One response promises a rebid, so opener can pass an overcall, knowing that responder will either bid or double.

Difficult situations arise when responder's strength is not clearly defined.

WEST	NORTH	EAST	SOUTH
—	—	—	1♠
4♡	4♠	5♡	?

North may have a good hand, just short of a slam try. He may have bid 4♠ as a probable sacrifice with

♠ KJxxx ♡ x ◊ Jxxx ♣ xxx.

He may have bid it with an in–between hand such as

♠ Kxx ♡ x ◊ A10xxx ♣ Jxxx,

not knowing whose hand it was. A pass should not be forcing. However, with no clear–cut action South should pass, knowing that North will usually do something.

WEST	NORTH	EAST	SOUTH
—	—	—	1♠
2♡	3♠	4♡	?

3♠was a limit raise. If you play 3♠ as preemptive, assume that partner bid 3♡, showing a limit raise or better. South's pass should mean that he would not have bid 4♠ if East had passed. This pass is not forcing.

However, when the bidding gets back to North he should double with

♠ Jxxx ♡ xx ◇ A10x ♣ KJxx

since his high card strength is outside opener's suit and 4♡ is unlikely to be made. Perhaps, East bid 4♡ to suggest a sacrifice over 4♠. With

♠ Kxxx ♡ x ◇ QJxxx ♣ Q10x

North should bid 4♠ to avoid a possible double game swing.

It looks strange and inconsistent to bid 3♠ and then 4♠, but the fact that partner did not double 4♡ is the justification for this peculiar sequence. With

♠ KJxx ♡ Qx ◇ KJ10x ♣ xxx,

North should pass.

WEST	NORTH	EAST	SOUTH
—	—	—	1♡
1♠	3♡	4♠	?

This sequence does not force either North or South to bid. Both sides could hold very pure hands. But if South passes, North will take some action 85% of the time. As South I would treat this situation as forcing, even though it isn't!

My inclination is not to adopt a lot of rules. When it is improbable that the opponents can make their bid based upon the sequence, not your hand, which partner can't see, a pass should be forcing. If it sounds as though the opponents might make their bid, a pass is not forcing.

While deciding whether a pass is forcing is the biggest problem, other problems still remain.

WEST	NORTH	EAST	SOUTH
—	—	—	1♡
Pass	2◇	4♠	?

A pass is clearly forcing. Should you make a forcing pass with

♠ xx ♡ AK10xxxx ◇ x ♣ AQx?

If partner has as much as ♡ Qx, you have a very fine offensive hand. But if he holds

♠ xx ♡ x ◇ AKxxxxx ♣ KJx

the pass might persuade partner to bid 5◇, which would be disasterous. Passing would imply a diamond fit. Consequently you should double. (The next problem will be whether to bid a slam if partner bids 5♡ over the double.)

WEST	NORTH	EAST	SOUTH
—	—	—	1♡
Pass	2◇	4♠	?

You might double because you have very good defense against a spade contract or you have a poor offensive hand and/or misfit with partner. Whatever your reasons, the double will discourage partner from bidding more. Offensively, double is your weakest action. Pass, intending to abide by partner's decision, whether it is to bid again or double, is the next action up the line. But experts don't agree upon which of the next two steps should be stronger. To bid 5◇ directly or to pass and bid 5◇ if partner doubles? In my opinion, the latter sequence should be stronger. Suppose you hold

♠ x ♡ AKJxx ◇ AJxx ♣ Kxx.

If partner has wasted values in spades, a slam may not make. If you pass and he bids 5◇, you surely have enough to raise to 6◇. Even if partner doubles, there may be a slam. Perhaps he is doubling, not because of wasted spade strength, but because of his heart misfit.

♠ Jxx ♡ x ◇ KQxxx ♣ AQxx

But when he doubles and you pull, showing the best type of hand, he will bid six. So far you might say that both methods work equally well. If an immediate 5♢ bid shows the best hand, responder would bid six with

♠ Jxx ♡ x ♢ KQxxx ♣ AKxx.

But he might not with

♠ xx ♡ Qx ♢ KQxxx ♣ A10xx

However, he would bid 5♢ over a forcing pass and you would raise to six. Anyway the pass followed by a pull of the double should be the strongest sequence other than bidding slam directly, and that is probably the most popular expert method.

The rule just stated, that pass followed by a pull of partner's double, is the strongest action, only applies when both partners have shown strength.

You hold ♠AQ98x ♡ KQJ10xx ♢ AK ♣ None.

WEST	NORTH	EAST	SOUTH
—	—	—	1♣*
1NT**	Pass	3♣	4♣
5♣	5♠	Pass	?

* Strong and artificial
** Shows minors

If partner has nothing but four or five spades headed by the jack, you should pass. But you should play partner for one key card and bid six. Partner has not shown any strength by his previous bids, and with a very weak balanced hand he would pass and let you make the decision. Double by him would show a little strength somewhere. With

♠ 10xxxx ♡ xx ♢ xxx ♣ xxx

partner should pass over 5♣ and POSSIBLY pull your double to 5♠. His actual hand was

♠ 10xxx ♡ Ax ◇ xxxx ♣ xxx,

which is about what you should play him for.

At lower levels, when partner forces to the three level in a major, bidding at the three level shows no game interest while a pass or anything else shows uncertainty.

WEST	NORTH	EAST	SOUTH
—	—	—	1◇
1♠	Pass	2◇	3◇
?			

East's 2◇ bid just guaranteed a good three card raise to 2♠. No one is obligated to bid 3♠, so a pass would not be forcing. 3♠ would not show a strong game interest since a 3♡ bid is available as a game try. If no game try were available, rebidding the major would show extra values and East might or might not raise to game.

WEST	NORTH	EAST	SOUTH
—	—	—	1◇
1♠	Pass	3◇	Double
?			

3♠ would show no game interest. You could assign whatever meanings you want to 3♡, pass and redouble, but all should show some game interest. Pass should be stronger than 3♠ because more room is allowed for further investigation. Over a pass West can redouble or bid 3♡ as further game tries.

Usually after you preempt, you don't bid again other than to respond to partner's forcing bids. The general rule is that the preempter bids as much as he can the first time; therefore, it is inconsistent for him to take any further initiative. Besides, partner knows more about the preempter's hand than the preempter knows about his partner's hand, and the player who knows the most about the combined assets should make the decisions.

But almost every rule has exceptions.

WEST	NORTH	EAST	SOUTH
—	—	—	1♢
2♠	3♡	3♠	4♡
?			

If North's bid had been 3♢, West would be barred. He has already told his story, and East might expect to make 3♠ and to set 4♢. However, the 3♡ bid was forcing, and there was no danger of the opponents' playing 3♡ if East had passed. There were only two reasons for East to bid 3♠—to request a lead or to suggest a sacrifice. I don't think requesting the lead is important enough to save the bid for that purpose. But with

♠ Jxx ♡ Axx ♢ xxx ♣ KJ10x

East might suspect that there would be a good sacrifice since not all 2♠ bids are the same. If West has

1. ♠ KQxxxx ♡ x ♢ xx ♣ Q98x
2. ♠ AQxxxx ♡ x ♢ Q10x ♣ Jxx
3. ♠ KQxxxx ♡ xx ♢ xx ♣ xxx

He would gladly bid 4♠ with the first hand. He has a good offensive hand with little defense. With the second hand he would pass because he has too much defense for a sacrifice. With the third hand he should pass because his distribution is too sterile, and the penalty might exceed the value of game. In other words, this is a cooperative situation. The 3♠ bid meant that partner didn't know whether a sacrifice would be profitable.

Vulnerable vs Not Vulnerable
You hold ♠ KQ10xxx ♡ None ◇ QJ10x ♣ xxx.

WEST	NORTH	EAST	SOUTH
—	—	—	2♠
3♡	4♠	5♡	?

With unfavorable vulnerability partner bid 4♠ to make, not as a sacrifice. The void in the opponents' suit makes this hand unusually good offensively, and a 5♠ bid is justified. With

♠ Axx ♡ xx ◇ Kxxx ♣ AKxx

partner would surely double if he had to make the decision. Needless to say, when you open a weak two bid, partner should normally make all the decisions, and it could be wrong to bid again with the hand just shown.

When the opponents bid a suit, you are supposed to have a stopper to bid notrump. There are exceptions to this rule also when you may infer partner has a stopper.

You hold ♠ xx ♡ Kxx ◇ Kxxx ♣ QJxx

WEST	NORTH	EAST	SOUTH
—	—	—	1♣
Double	1♠	?	

East has a perfect 1NT bid. For his takeout double partner should be short in clubs and have length and strength in the majors. East only needs to have clubs stopped. Presumably partner can take care of spades.

You hold ♠ Ax ♡ xxx ◇ J ♣ AKQxxxx.

WEST	NORTH	EAST	SOUTH
—	—	—	3◇
Pass	Pass	?	

An earlier chapter mentioned North's failure to raise diamonds plus the fact that South shouldn't preempt with a solid suit suggests West has a diamond stopper. 3NT is East's percentage bid.

You have ♠ 10xxx ♡ A10x ◇ Kxx ♣ Axx.

WEST	NORTH	EAST	SOUTH
—	—	—	1♠
2◇	Pass	?	

A 2NT bid describes your strength and distribution. How else are you going to get to 3NT when partner holds

♠ Jx ♡ Kx ◇ AQJxxx ♣ Kxx?

Even if partner has two small spades, the suit may be blocked or East may fail to lead fourth best from

♠AKQxx.

There are certain holdings which are worth more when you are declarer than when you are dummy. Suppose LHO opens 1♠. Your ♠ Qx will take an extra trick when LHO is on lead and partner holds ♠ Ax, ♠ Axx, or ♠ Kxx. Even if partner has nothing but small spades, your queen MAY take a trick. LHO may lead low from AKxxx and is almost certain to do so with no quick entry. Or he may cash a high spade and shift, not realizing your queen would fall next round. So if partner overcalls, you should tend to bid notrump yourself with Qx rather than try to get partner to bid notrump.

Likewise, when you hold the singleton king, it may take a trick on its own or be worth an extra trick when LHO leads low and partner holds Qxx.

A few examples of lead directing bids have been shown throughout the book. When the bidding went

WEST	NORTH	EAST	SOUTH
—	—	—	1♣
Pass	1♠	3♡	4♠
?			

the main advice was to bid something with

♠ xxx ♡ Kxx ◇ AJ10x ♣ xxx

since your values were in partner's suit and the unbid suit. However, the best bid is 5◇ to get a diamond lead if the opponents should compete to 5♠. When partner opens 4♡, a 5♣ response should be some sort of slam try in hearts, preferably an asking bid. If the bidding goes

WEST	NORTH	EAST	SOUTH
—	—	—	4♡
Pass	Pass	4♠	Pass
Pass	5♣		

you still are not suggesting 5♣ as an alternate contract. You are suggesting a club lead if the opponents bid again, and if they don't, you expect partner to bid 5♡. You might bid this way with

♠ x ♡ xxx ◇ Jxxxx ♣ AKxx.

When partner preempts at the four level or higher, it is very unlikely you can find a better trump suit than his. Therefore, any new suit bid is either a slam try or a lead–directing bid. The logic of the situation, such as your failure to bid more strongly previously, should tell partner which it is.

You hold ♠ xx ♡ Jxxxx ◇ xx ♣ KQ10x.

WEST	NORTH	EAST	SOUTH
—	—	Pass	1♠
2♡	4♠	5♣	

If the opponents compete to the five level, a club lead looks like the best start for the defense. Since you didn't make a preemptive opening bid in clubs, you can't have a strong enough club suit and an otherwise suitable hand to suggest playing 5♣.

You hold ♠ xxx ♡ J10xxx ◇ Qxxxx ♣ None.

WEST	NORTH	EAST	SOUTH
—	—	—	1♠
2♡	2♠	?	

You should risk a 5♣ bid despite not having passed originally. Quite likely South will double, and when you run to 5♡ your intentions will be crystal clear. If South doesn't double, partner will probably have enough clubs to realize what you are doing—combining a lead-directing splinter with a preempt.

After partner's weak two bid and a takeout double on your right, it is unlikely that LHO would leave the double in—or that you could improve the contract by bidding a new suit yourself.

WEST	NORTH	EAST	SOUTH
—	2♡	Double	2♠/3♣/3◇

Many players recommend any suit bid show a raise of partner's suit plus a desire for the lead of the suit bid. Playing that way, you would bid 3♣ with either

1. ♠ xx ♡ Kxx ◇ xxx ♣ KQ10xx or
2. ♠ xx ♡ Jxxx ◇ xxx ♣ AQJx.

West will probably bid 3♠ and East will have to guess whether to raise to four. Whatever the final contract is, a club lead should get the defense off to a good start.

What should you do over an artificial bid that shows widely differing hand patterns? RHO opens 2◇, which shows any 4–4–4–1 distribution and 11–15 HCP. When you hold

♠ AJ10x ♡ x ◇ KQxx ♣ A10xx,

your correct action is to pass. LHO cannot afford to pass unless he has something like

♠ xx ♡ xx ◇ J109xxx ♣ xxx.

About 97% of the time he will bid something because opener's singleton is unknown. Once he bids and opener bids or passes, any ambiguity will be eliminated. Suppose LHO bids 2♡, which is followed by two passes. You know the opponents have at least an eight card heart fit, and LHO is not strong enough to try for game. Double by you is clearly for takeout, based upon heart shortage. If the bidding had gone

WEST	NORTH	EAST	SOUTH
—	—	—	2♢
Pass	2♡	Pass	2♠
?			

you would know opener had the same distribution as you; the opponents have a potential misfit. Therefore, you would stay out of the bidding. Or if the bidding had gone

WEST	NORTH	EAST	SOUTH
—	—	—	2♢
Pass	2NT	Pass	3♣
?			

you would know that opener's singleton was in clubs, but that responder was strong enough to try for game and, again, you don't belong in the bidding. Without clear–cut action you should pass over an ambiguous bid when you are in second position. However, if the bidding goes

WEST	NORTH	EAST	SOUTH
—	—	—	2♢
Pass	2♡	?	

and you, as East, hold the same hand

♠ AJ10x ♡ x ♢ KQxx ♣ A10xx,

you must risk a double, based on the probability that the opponents have an eight card heart fit. Pass is too likely to result in the opponents' making a part score when you could make a part score.

In the finals of a national event, when your opponents come to your table they say, "Pre–alert! We play Octopus. All our bids from 2♢ to 3♠ have alternate meanings. We have a way to distinguish between sound preempts and weak preempts. Here is a chart showing the possible meanings of each bid and our recommended defense." The practical thing to do is to agree with partner that if one of these bids comes up, you will play the opponents' recommended defense. You don't want to study their system and invent a defense of your own to each of eight possible opening bids on the remote chance that one of these bids will come up this round. Besides, I am a trustful soul. The opponents ought to know the best defense to their pet convention, and it is unlikely that they are trying to lead you astray.

But if you are curious or slightly paranoid you might inquire further. You notice a 2♢ opening shows a weak 2♡ bid, spades and a minor, or a balanced 20–21 HCP. Common sense tells you responder will have to keep the bidding open to allow opener to further describe his hand. Common sense also tells you that a 2♡ response would be passed by opener if he has a weak 2♡ bid. To reassure yourself you ask, "What are the responses?" Your opponents reply, "Generally speaking, the cheapest response is negative, denying game interest if that is opener's suit. The next cheapest response is an artificial positive, and other responses are natural."

Partner refuses to play the opponents' recommended defenses because he thinks you and he can do better. RHO opens 2♢ and you hold

♠ AJxx ♡ x ♢ KJx ♣ AQxxx.

It seems unlikely that opener has an opening 2NT bid. It is also unlikely that he has spades and a minor. You are almost sure that he has a weak two heart bid, but partner won't know, and a double by you would be ambiguous. Would it just show diamonds? So the logical action is to pass just as you did over a 4–4–4–1 2♢ bid and allow the opponents clarify their holdings. If the bidding goes as predicted

WEST	NORTH	EAST	SOUTH
—	—	—	2♢
Pass	2♡	Pass	Pass
?			

you will double, and partner will know what you are doing. In the unlikely event that North makes a positive response showing game interest opposite an opening weak two heart bid or South shows some other type of hand, you will be glad you kept quiet. If partner had your hand, he would have to risk a double of 2♡ since you might not be able to reopen over opener's pass.

Somehow you survive this round, and next round RHO again opens 2♢, but this time the opponents are playing "multi", as recommended by Fred Hamilton and others. Opener can have some strong hand or a weak two bid in a major. The practical thing to do is to forget about the strong hand, based on frequency, and assume opener has a weak two bid. LHO could pass and wait for the opponents to clarify their holdings, but the defense most favored by experts is as follows: Double is a takeout double of spades; 2♡ is equivalent to a takeout double of hearts; 3♡ shows a heart overcall (at other tables your hand would have to bid 3♡ over an opening 2♠ bid); other bids are natural.

The way multi works, a 2♡ response shows no game interest opposite a weak 2♡ bid. Conceivably responder would raise if opener rebids 2♠, showing that his suit was spades. A 2♠ response shows game interest if opener's suit is hearts but no interest if it is spades; 2NT shows game interest whatever opener may have. After

WEST	NORTH	EAST	SOUTH
—	—	—	2♢
Pass	2♡	?	

all overcalls should be natural, and a double should just show high cards. It is all right to double with a singleton in one major and length in the other because opener's action should clear things up. If opener passes, partner will assume he has hearts, and if opener bids 2♠ partner will know he has spades. Opener cannot risk passing the double when he has spades for fear of a disaster.

The defense against Flannery mentioned earlier is entirely different. Everyone at the table knows much more about opener's distribution than in the cases previously discussed. The popular defense is to bid 2♡ as a distributional takeout double; 2♠ is natural; 2NT is natural but shows playing strength with a good minor suit; double shows a balanced strong notrump. For a change, fourth hand's decisions are easier than second hand's. When responder bids 2♡ or 2♠, he knows the opponents' strength is limited and that opener is going to pass.

Many players who play Precision, or any type of strong club with five card majors, open 2♢ to show specifically a diamond singleton or void. Typically opener has

1. ♠ KJxx ♡ AQxx ♢ x ♣ Kxxx or
2. ♠ Qxxx ♡ Axxx ♢ None ♣ AKJxx,

but he could hold

3. ♠ KJx ♡ KQxx ♢ x ♣ QJxxx or
4. ♠ AJxx ♡ Kxx ♢ x ♣ AQxxx.

Over this bid a takeout double makes little sense and a double should show diamonds but is weaker offensively than an overcall of 3♢.

Sometimes, merely by staying awake and listening to the bidding, inferences can be drawn that lazy players might miss.

You, East, hold ♠ Q10xx ♡ Axxxx ♢ Axx ♣ x.

WEST	NORTH	EAST	SOUTH
—	—	—	1NT*
Pass	2♣	Pass	2♢
3♣	Pass	?	

*15–17 HCP.

As a general rule, the sooner you bid, the safer it is, and the more it creates problems for the opponents. So if partner was going to bid 3♣, why didn't he bid it sooner? The most logical explanation is that his clubs were solid enough to cash against a notrump contract. On the other hand, since responder's hand is unlimited, it would be dangerous to make a delayed entrance into the auction at this level with less than seven tricks. The winning bid is 3NT since partner has ♣AKQJxxx and nothing else, of course. Responder has a weak hand with 3–4–5–1 shape and was planning to pass any rebid by opener.

None Vulnerable
You hold ♠ Q10xx ♡ xxxx ♢ A ♣ J10xx.

WEST	NORTH	EAST	SOUTH
—	—	—	1♡
Pass	3♠*	Pass	4♡
?			

*Splinter

Bidding looks dangerous, but North has a spade singleton or void, and South didn't make a slam try. Is it because he has a minimum opening bid or because he has lots of wasted spade values? Partner must be short in hearts. A 4♠ bid is a good gamble. As it happens, partner fits your hand extremely well. He holds

♠ Kxxxx ♡ None ◊ xxxx ♣ KQxx.

You don't need to find such a remarkable fit for 4♠ to pay off. Down one or two could be an excellent result.

You hold ♠ 1098xx ♡ AQxx ◊ K ♣ xxx.

WEST	NORTH	EAST	SOUTH
—	—	—	1♠
Pass	Pass	3♠	Double
?			

Partner asked you to bid 3NT with a spade stopper, and you have a spade stopper. Should you bid 3NT? I don't think so. Partner's solid suit has to be clubs. He is supposed to have eight top tricks. They almost have to be seven clubs and the ◊A. Since you and South have at least ten spades between you, who is likely to be short in spades? Obviously, it will be partner since he has length in clubs. His most likely distribution is 1–2–3–7, in which case only a heart finesse is needed through the opening bidder to make a club slam.

Suppose partner has 1–3–2–7 distribution. If his heart holding is as good as Jxx, you would almost certainly have a squeeze against South in the majors. So should you just bid 6♣? I've seen worse gambles, but since South made a foolish double you can find out more.

If you really trust your partner, you should pass. With two or three spades, partner will bid 3NT. He has already said he didn't have a spade stopper since he couldn't risk your bidding 4♣ without one (over 3♠). He could trust you not to pass his 3NT bid unless you had a stopper. With a singleton spade he would bid 4♣. With a void in spades he would redouble. Your pass asks partner to cooperate in finding the best contract, and surely these are the logical meanings for the various bids. As it happens, partner has

♠ None ♡ J10x ◊ Axx ♣ AKQxxxx

and you are cold for 7♣—not that you have to bid seven to get an excellent score.

You hold ♠ xx ♡ K10x ◊ 10 ♣ AQJxxxx.

WEST	NORTH	EAST	SOUTH
—	1♠	2♠*	?

* Michaels, showing hearts and a minor

When this hand was presented to a bidding panel, most of the panelists were worried about whether 3♣ would be forcing. If not, should they bid it anyway or double first and risk being preempted by a 3◊ bid? When I held this hand I bid 3NT! If you bid 3♣ West will know that his partner has diamonds. If you double and East runs to diamonds, West will know his partner has diamonds. But if you bid 3NT directly, he won't know which minor suit his partner has. He is just as likely to lead a club as a diamond. He might even lead the ♣K from a doubleton! However, rather than guess which minor his partner has, he will probably lead a heart. You may make 3NT with any lead. You may be defeated with any lead. I like your chances much better if West doesn't know which minor his partner has.

Up till now our objective has been to get to the best theoretical contract or obtain par results. Occasionally you have a chance to do better than par and steal from the opponents. There are various ways to do that. The most socially acceptable form of theft is to give out as little information as possible. A good example of that is to jump to game over a Drury response.

You hold ♠ AQxxxx ♡ KJxxx ◇ x ♣ x.

WEST	NORTH	EAST	SOUTH
—	Pass	Pass	1♠
Pass	2♣*	Pass	?

*Drury

Bid 4♠. Partner could hold

♠ Kxxx ♡ Ax ◇ Axx ♣ xxxx,

in which case you would belong in a slam, but you can't find out what you need to know without the risk of getting too high or disclosing your hand. Perhaps partner has

♠ Kxx ♡ xx ◇ KJxx ♣ Kxxx.

If you show a major two–suiter you won't be able to steal a diamond trick. Or if you lead up to the king of clubs and West wins the ace, he will shift to a diamond before you can discard your diamond on the king of clubs.

What does this have to do with competitive bidding? Many players tend to bid Blackwood on the way to a slam on the theory that it can't do any harm. But they are wrong! Suppose you hold

♠ AQ10xxx ♡ AKxx ◇ x ♣ Ax,

and partner makes a limit raise of your 1♠ bid. I am aware of the fact you could be cold for 7♠. Partner needs the ♠ K, a doubleton heart, the ◇ A, and a minor suit king. He might hold either

1. ♠ Kxxx ♡ xx ◇ AKxx ♣ xxx or
2. ♠ Kxxx ♡ xx ◇ Axx ♣ Kxxx.

But add another jack or change the doubleton heart to a singleton, and partner might consider his hand too strong for a limit raise. Finding partner with the perfect hand is a very remote. Suppose you bid Blackwood (Roman Key Card, of course). Partner responds 5♢ with

♠ Kxxx ♡ Jxx ♢ Qxx ♣ KQx,

RHO doubles for a lead, and your slam goes down. Without the double West would have led something else. This is much more likely than getting to the perfect grand slam. Suppose your hand is

♠ AQ10xxx ♡ AKxx ♢ Ax ♣ x.

Again you bid 4NT and partner responds 5♢. No one doubles, so you haven't lost anything, have you? Yes, because West has

♠ xx ♡ Qxx ♢ J109x ♣ J108x.

This time he has an important clue. His partner did not double 5♢ so he leads a club. The moral: If you are going to bid a small slam regardless of partner's response, don't bid Blackwood.

You hold ♠ AK10xxx ♡ None ♢ xx ♣ AJ109x.

WEST	NORTH	EAST	SOUTH
—	—	—	1♠
Pass	3♠	Pass	?

The scientific way to bid this hand is to bid 4♣. Hopefully partner will bid 4♢; you will bid 4♡; partner will bid 5♣; and once in a blue moon you may get to a cold grand slam. But RHO may double 4♢ for a lead. Suppose partner has

♠ Qxxx ♡ Kxxx ♢ Axx ♣ Qx.

Without a diamond lead you are cold for slam. With a diamond lead you have only a 50% play. Suppose partner holds

♠ Qxxx ♡ AKx ◇ Qxxx ♣ xx.

With a diamond lead you couldn't even make 5♠. Without a diamond lead you will make six.

The bid I like is 4◇, not 4♣. My second choice is 6♠. This example is extreme, and most of the bidding panel disagreed, but the general principle is valid. Don't try to be too scientific with freak hands with which you will seldom be able to find out what you want to know and don't adopt sequences in which an opponent's double or failure to double will help his partner choose the right lead.

East–West Vulnerable, IMPS.
Playing Flannery and a strong club.
You hold ♠ xx ♡ J10xxx ◇ Qx ♣ xxxx

WEST	NORTH	EAST	SOUTH
—	1♡	Pass	?

All of the conditions are just right for a psyche. Partner's failure to open 1♣ limits his hand. His failure to bid Flannery makes it very unlikely that he has four spades. The odds are at least 2 to 1 that the opponents can make 4♠. What can happen to you if you respond 1♠? I can imagine some far–fetched possibilities, but the worst thing at all likely to happen is that partner will raise to 2♠ with

♠ KQx ♡ Axxxx ◇ Axx ♣ Jx.

You would pass, of course, and the opponents would set you four tricks. That's –200 when the best the opponents could do without your help is score 140. –200 would be a disaster at matchpoints, but a trifling loss at IMPS. Suppose you respond 1♠ and the bidding continues 2♣

on your left, pass, pass to you. This is easy. Just pass. If you keep the bidding open the opponents will have another chance to find their spade fit. Suppose LHO passes your 1♠ response and partner bids 2♢. Now that partner has failed to raise spades the odds are at least 4 to 1 that the opponents could make 4♠, and it is certain they could outbid you. 2♡ would be a greedy bid. If your teammates are +620, there is only a 1 IMP difference between +110 and –100. You should pass 2♢. It will appear to West that you have a misfit for partner, and a reopening double with

1. ♠ KJxx ♡ x ♢ AJxx ♣ KQxx
2. ♠ Axxxx ♡ x ♢ Kxx ♣ AQJx

will not seem nearly as attractive over 2♢ as over 2♡. If West is a suspicious person he will distrust your 1♠ bid more if he discovers that you have a heart fit than if you conceal that fit. However, if you do bid hearts, 3♡ is a better bid than 2♡.

Do you remember this hand a few moments ago?

You held ♠ AK10xxx ♡ None ♢ xx ♣ AJ109x.

WEST	NORTH	EAST	SOUTH
—	—	—	1♠
Pass	3♠	Pass	?

My recommendation was to bid 4♢. But if you bid 4♢ and jump to 6♠ over partner's 4♠ bid, West will wonder why you bothered to bid 4♢. CONCEIVABLY you were hoping to get to a grand slam, but gave up and settled for six when partner failed to cue bid. But you would need a very unusual hand to be interested in a grand slam over a limit raise. If I were West, I would be suspicious of the 4♢ bid. Try to find a more credible sequence. Perhaps if you bid 5♡ partner will jump to 6♠, in which case you will probably get a club lead!

Quiz Eight

1. Matchpoints, North–South Vulnerable.
You hold ♠ 63 ♡ 73 ◇ J1096542 ♣ 84.

WEST	NORTH	EAST	SOUTH
—	2♣	2♠	Pass
3♠	Pass	4♠	?

What do you bid?

2. Matchpoints, None Vulnerable.
You hold ♠ AJ64 ♡ KQ7 ◇ A9865 ♣ J.

WEST	NORTH	EAST	SOUTH
2♡*	?		

*Octopus—a weak two spade bid, both minors, or a good club preempt.

What do you bid?

3. Matchpoints, None Vulnerable.
You hold ♠ 9 ♡ KJ107542 ◇ Q1076 ♣ 8.

WEST	NORTH	EAST	SOUTH
—	—	1♠	3♡
3♠	5◇	Pass	?

What do you bid?

4. IMPS, North–South Vulnerable.
You hold ♠ KQ7653 ♡ None ◇ KJ87 ♣ QJ9.

WEST	NORTH	EAST	SOUTH
—	—	3♡	3♠
5♡	Pass	Pass	?

What do you bid?

5. IMPS, Both Vulnerable.
You hold ♠ KQJ9832 ♡ 65 ◇ 7 ♣ Q109.

WEST	NORTH	EAST	SOUTH
—	—	1♡	3♠
4◇	4♠	5◇	?

What do you bid?

6. IMPS, East–West Vulnerable.
You hold ♠ A ♡ 97 ◇ 98 ♣ AKQ108752.

WEST	NORTH	EAST	SOUTH
—	—	3♠*	?

*Octopus—solid seven card minor, at most one side queen.
What do you bid?

7. Rubber bridge, None Vulnerable.
You hold ♠ A3 ♡ 8 ◇ AK92 ♣ AK9832.

WEST	NORTH	EAST	SOUTH
—	—	1♣	Pass
1♠	Pass	Pass*	2NT
3♡	Pass	4♡	?

*Roth–Stone psyche. 2–6 HCP with at least ♣ Qxxx
What do you bid?

8. IMPS, Both Vulnerable.

WEST	NORTH	EAST	SOUTH
—	Pass	Pass	1♠
Double	2◇	2NT	Pass
3NT	Pass	Pass	Pass

WEST	EAST
♠ A62	♠ KQ108
♡ KQ65	♡ A83
◇ None	◇ J8
♣ AKQJ43	♣ 10876

Apportion the blame for getting to this terrible contract.

Answers

1. **PASS**. Partner's "takeout pass" of 3♠, implies support for the unbid suits. Quite likely he has a singleton spade and 5♢can be made. But if you bid 5♢ immediately, partner may play you for a slightly better hand and bid 6♢. Pass, wait for partner to double, and then bid 5♢. Recall that pass and pull is WEAKER than an immediate bid when the hand that passes has never shown any values.

2. **PASS**. You should pass and let the opponents tell you what South has. If he has a weak two spade bid or both minors, you should stay out of the bidding. If he shows an opening 3♣ bid, you will double.

3. **FIVE HEARTS**. Partner must be directing a diamond lead. Whether he has diamond honors or shortness, with heart support, he fits your hand nicely, and you should do well. Passing 5♢might work out. If you pass, West must make a decision. If you bid 5♡, both opponents will have an opportunity to do something. On the other hand, 5♢ might be set eight or nine tricks, so the undoubled penalty could exceed the doubled penalty in hearts which should be no more than 300, and possibly only 100 in view of your fit. Since East passed in a non–forcing sequence the opponents are not likely to bid 5♠.

4. **FIVE SPADES**. 5♡ sounds more like an advanced sacrifice than a slam invitation. Partner should not allow himself to be stampeded into supporting you at the five level with

♠ Axx ♡ xxx ♢ Q10xx ♣ K10x,

but his pass shows a willingness for you to compete. Since you have an offensive hand you should bid 5♠.

5. **FIVE SPADES**. Since the 4♢ bid was forcing, partner's 4♠ bid allowed you to participate in the final decision. Your high cards are offensive rather than defensive.

6. **THREE NORUMP**. I am a gambler at heart. 3NT should make or be set 4–5 tricks. If someone doubles, the odds change, and it is best to make a cowardly retreat to 4♣.

7. **FIVE DIAMONDS**. Sidney Lazard had this South hand with me about 35 years ago when Roth–Stone psyches were the latest rage. Sidney figured West must have a pretty good hand, probably 5–5 or 6–5 in the majors, to keep bidding after his partner's psyche was exposed. East must have good heart support to raise despite having psyched. Conclusion: Neither opponent could have much length in diamonds. Sidney actually bid 6♢, but probably 5♢ is enough since he had to play it double dummy to make six. The four hands were:

NORTH
♠ Q10
♡ J54
♢ QJ8763
♣ J4

WEST
♠ KJ7642
♡ AKQ97
♢ 105
♣ None

EAST
♠ 985
♡ 10632
♢ 4
♣ Q10765

SOUTH
♠ A3
♡ 8
♢ AK92
♣ AK9832

8. **WEST 100%**. Obviously, East–West were not playing good–bad 2NT. If 2NT was natural, East's bidding was reasonable. Only a stopper in spades was needed since presumably West could take care of diamonds. West made a lazy bid. It couldn't hurt to bid 3♠, showing a spade stopper and implying a weakness in diamonds, in which case East would probably bid 4♠, and West would jump to 6♣. When South opened third hand with ♠ Jxxxx and ♢ KJxxx, he made it very difficult for you to reach 7♣, but there is no excuse for playing 3NT.